ENERGY RISK

Valuing and Managing Energy Derivatives

ENERGY RISK
Valuing and Managing Energy Derivatives

DRAGANA PILIPOVIĆ

SAVA Risk Management Corporation

McGraw-Hill

New York   Chicago   San Francisco   Washington, D.C.   Auckland   Bogotá
Caracas   Lisbon   London   Madrid   Mexico City   Milan
Montreal   New Delhi   San Juan   Singapore
Sydney   Tokyo   Toronto

Library of Congress Cataloging-in-Publication Data

Pilipović, Dragana.
    Energy risk : valuing and managing energy derivatives / by Dragana
Pilipovic.
      p.   cm.
    Includes index.
    ISBN 0-7863-1231-9
    1. Electric utilities.   2. Energy industries.   3. Commodity
futures.   4. Derivative securities.   I. Title.
    HG6047.E43P55 1997
    332.63'28—dc21   97-26541
                                                 CIP

McGraw-Hill

*A Division of The **McGraw·Hill** Companies*

7 8 9 10 11 12 DOC/DOC 0 9 8 7 6 5 4 3

ISBN 0-7863-1231-9

The sponsoring editor for this book was Stephen Isaacs, the managing editor was Kevin
Thornton, the editing supervisor was John M. Morriss, and the production supervisor was
Suzanne W. B. Rapcavage. It was set in Times Roman by Digitype (Broker—Editing,
Design, and Production).

Printed and bound by R. R. Donnelley & Sons Company.

McGraw-Hill books are available at special quantity discounts to use as premiums and sales
promotions, or for use in corporate training programs. For more information, please write to the
Director of Special Sales, McGraw-Hill, Professional Publishing, Two Penn Plaza, New York, NY
10121-2298. Or contact your local bookstore.

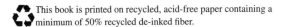 This book is printed on recycled, acid-free paper containing a
minimum of 50% recycled de-inked fiber.

To my children, Nevena and Saša

TABLE OF CONTENTS

Chapter 3

Essential Statistical Tools   39

Chapter 6

Volatilities 99

Chapter 7

Overview of Option Pricing for Energies   127

Chapter 8

Option Valuation   141

My lucky star has provided me with experiences in a wide variety of derivative markets: from equities and interest rates to natural gas and electricity. With every new market, I discovered further proof of something which I had only sensed at the very first: markets differ significantly from each other through differences in the types of fundamental price drivers and how they impact the market prices.

Each market follows its own unique price behavior: a summer event in the electricity markets is caused by an unexpected temperature spike which typically keeps the prices up for a week or so; a stock price jumps up on news of a take-over and remains at the newly reached levels unless there is further news that the take-over failed. Then why, I ask you, do the pricing experts insist on using the same set of models in markets that are so very different?

This question inspired this book. My motivation is to explain why energy markets are so different from the more traditional derivatives markets. My objective is to provide tools capable of handling these differences. Energy risk managers, particularly in the new power markets, need a comprehensive guide.

This book is a practitioner's book, not an academic one. *Energy Risk: Valuing and Managing Energy Derivatives* is the product of my ten years of being a "rocket scientist"—an ex-physicist working in financial markets. I faced all the questions in this book first-hand, "on the trading desk" as a quantitative analyst, trader and consultant. The problems always resembled a double-headed guard dog: first I had to determine a good analytical answer, then I faced the problem of implementation. I approached the problems by establishing benchmarks, setting standards of acceptability, and at the end of the day settled for ideas and technology that got the job done.

With the amazing growth of today's energy markets, particularly in electricity and power, I suspect there are many professionals who now find themselves in a position similar to mine in 1989 when I began trading, natural gas during its dawn of deregulation and again in 1995 when I began modeling electricity: they need practical answers to derivatives and risk management issues. This book is intended as a single-source, desk-top manual for getting reasonable answers to actual modeling and implementation problems surfacing in today's energy markets.

Dragana Pilipović

ACKNOWLEDGMENTS

I would like to thank many people for their help with this book. First I want to thank John Wengler, head of marketing for SAVA Risk Management Corporation, who first conceived of this book and then spent many sleepless nights helping me write and edit it.

I want to thank many professionals in chronological order for their help in developing the concepts and materials for this book: Harvard University's Deborah Hughes-Hallet for giving me my first job, teaching a course for people scared of math at the college and the wonderful cast of characters attending the Kennedy School of Government summer program; Brown University's graduate school of physics Professor Augustine Faliaros for the joy of applied mathematics and Professor Dave Cutts for giving me the chance to move to Chicago's Fermilab and understanding why I had to leave physics; Mike Parkinson of the former O'Connor & Associates for giving me my first job in finance and David Weinberger for supporting my research style; Continental Bank's Ken Cunningham and Philippe Comer for allowing me to form my ideas freely; Linda Rudnick of Harris Bank for providing a safe haven and one of my first consulting contracts; Kay Rigney of the First National Bank of Chicago's women's banking unit for invaluable support and advice; Southern Energy Marketing's Sean Murphy and Jeff Roark for inviting me into the world of electricity; Cinergy Corporation's Ken Leong and Paul Zhang for helping market-test my theories; the participants in the Chicago, Houston and Aspen seminars that served as the basis for this book; the forward thinking professionals at Dayton Power & Light, Sonat Marketing and NESI Power Marketing for their special participation in the seminars; Steven Isaacs of McGraw-Hill for agreeing that the market needed a book like this; Adrian O'Silva of the Federal Reserve Bank of Chicago and his bookshelf; Professor John Bilson of the Illinois Institute of Technology's Master's in Financial Markets and Trading for providing a teaching podium, and, last but not least, my colleague Aleksandar Pilipović, senior software engineer for SAVA Risk Management Corporation.

Finally, I would like to thank my family: My children, Saša and Nevena, for suffering and maintaining their happiness and lovingness while I wrote this book. My parents, Vera and Nikola, for their labors of love. My brother, Saša, for being a pillar of support. And my husband, John, for always believing in me.

Dragana Pilipović specializes in analytics for the electricity and energy derivative markets. Since founding SAVA Risk Management Corporation in 1993, she has developed the *PowerSuite*™ collection of valuation and portfolio analysis software. Ms. Pilipovic also actively consults and provides professional seminars throughout the country.

A true "rocket scientist," Ms. Pilipovic began her career as an experimental physicist. After performing graduate research at Fermilab near Chicago, she took the short drive to the city's financial district and served as a quantitative analyst for O'Connor & Associates. Before starting SAVA, Ms. Pilipovic was Head of Research for Continental Bank. She holds a bachelor's degree in physics from Harvard University, a master's in physics from Brown University, and an MBA from the University of Chicago.

Ms. Pilipović lives and works in Winnetka, Illinois, with her two children and her husband, John Wengler.

ENERGY RISK
Valuing and Managing Energy Derivatives

CHAPTER 1

What Makes Energies Different?

1.1. INTRODUCTION

The purpose of this book is to describe the valuation and management of energy derivatives. Our emphasis will be on the managerial and implementation aspects of "quantitative analysis." Quantitative analysis creates models that reflect market behavior in order to support trading in the actual market. If this book helps a novice build her first forward price curve, or inspires an expert to update a favorite model, then this book, *Energy Risk*, will have served its purpose.

The origin of quantitative analysis is rooted in the concept of "risk" itself. Since the days of the Romans, and perhaps even before then, people have "hedged their bets" against the unknowns of the future by entering into primitive futures and options contracts. Intuition, common sense, and experience probably served as the first quantitative tools for setting prices. (All three remain equally valid tools today!)

Today's energy markets follow the same impulses: energy producers and users alike wish to hedge their exposure to future uncertainty, or to obtain a particular risk-return strategy. Fortunately, in valuing these products our task will be easier than that of the Romans, thanks to modern mathematics and statistics, and the advent of computers.

1.1.1. Quantitative and Fundamental Analysis

In addition to quantitative analysis, a second discipline forms the basis of derivatives valuation and risk management: *fundamental* analysis. Fundamental analysis is an attempt to understand and describe market behavior in terms of the economics of supply and demand. Fundamental analysts attempt to identify, measure, and understand the relationship between the "fundamental price drivers" that cause markets to move up and down.[1] Quantitative analysis, on the other hand, attempts to replicate or model market behavior through mathematical models and statistical methodologies. In this book, quantitative analysis plays the leading role, while fundamental analysis contributes to the motivation and the intuition behind the models.

The interplay between fundamental and quantitative analysis is very much like the interplay between macroeconomics and microeconomics. Macroeconomics is the study of the forces and causes of economic fluctuations and their relationships. Microeconomics, on the other hand, is the study of the behavior of individual consumers and firms. The two are very much related, as assumptions about the economy depend on the assumptions about the individual players within the economy. A thorough understanding of macroeconomics requires a thorough understanding of microeconomics, and vice versa. Similarly, while fundamental analysts try to understand general price drivers, the quantitative analyst imposes the condition of rational market players who will not allow price arbitrage, resulting in an efficient marketplace. In this sense, fundamental analysis can be likened to macroeconomics, while quantitative analysis can be likened to microeconomics.

This book attempts to describe quantitative issues and techniques with very much of a fundamental flavor. Every quantitative approach and result is evaluated against the standard of consistency with the fundamental drivers of a marketplace. Therefore, understanding both the quantitative methodologies and the fundamentals of a marketplace is extremely important.

1.2. WHAT MAKES ENERGIES SO DIFFERENT?

Energies is only the most recent market to be transformed by derivatives and risk management. Compared to energies, the money markets stand as mature markets with relatively few modeling mysteries left to conquer. Bookstores already offer full shelves of excellent introductory and specialized books on fundamental and quantitative analysis based on the money markets.

Why, then, do we need another book? Because energies are very different from money markets (see Table 1–1). Fundamental analysis tells us that energy markets respond to underlying

TABLE 1-1

What Makes Energies Different?

Issue	In Money Markets	In Energy Markets
Maturity of market	Several decades	Relatively new
Fundamental price drivers	Few, simple	Many, complex
Impact of economic cycles	High	Low
Frequency of events	Low	High
Impact of storage and delivery; the convenience yield	None	Significant
Correlation between short- and long-term pricing	High	Low, "split personality"
Seasonality	None	Key to natural gas and electricity
Regulation	Little	Varies from little to very high
Market activity ("liquidity")	High	Low
Market centralization	Centralized	Decentralized
Complexity of derivative contracts	Majority of contracts are relatively simple	Majority of contracts are relatively complex

price drivers that differ dramatically from interest rates and other well-developed money markets. More importantly, quantitative analysis tells us that the differences in fundamental price drivers can exert a dramatic domino effect as they are applied to pricing and hedging models. The remainder of this chapter will introduce some of the energy market's fundamental price drivers and cite several examples of fundamental differences between the energy and money markets. While these examples skim the surface and the individual chapters provide the necessary details for true understanding, we offer these examples in the spirit of market-driven modeling that we hope permeates the entire book.

1.3. ENERGIES ARE HARDER TO MODEL

The interest rate and equity markets are "lucky." Their fundamental drivers number relatively few and easily translate into quantitative pricing models. For example, the deliverables in money markets consist of "a piece of paper" or its electronic equivalent, which are easily stored and transferred and are insensitive to weather conditions.[2] Energy markets paint a more complicated picture. Energies respond to the dynamic interplay between producing and using; transferring and storing; buying and selling—and ultimately "burning" actual physical products. Issues of storage, transport, weather, and technological advances play a major role here.

In the energy markets, the supply side concerns not only the storage and transfer of the actual commodity, but also how to get the actual commodity out of the ground. The end user truly consumes the asset. Residential users need energy for heating in the winter and cooling in the summer, and industrial users' own production continually depends on energy to keep the plants running and to avoid the high costs of stopping and restarting them. Each of these energy market participants—be they producers or end users—deals with a different set of fundamental drivers, which in turn affect the behavior of energy markets. These problems lead directly to the need for derivatives contracts; nothing even approaches these problems in money markets.

What makes energies so different is the excessive number of fundamental price drivers, which cause extremely complex price behavior. This complexity frustrates our ability to create simple quantitative models that capture the essence of the market. A hurricane in the Gulf of Mexico will send traders in Toronto into a tailspin. An anticipated technological advance in extracting natural gas could be influencing the forward price curve. How would you go about capturing these kinds of resulting price behaviors into a quantitative model that is also simple enough for quick and efficient everyday use on the trading desk?

1.4. MARKET RESPONSE TO CYCLES AND EVENTS

In the broadest sense, the traditional financial markets demonstrate almost a seamless transition from fundamental to quantitative analysis, while energies do not. The relative impact of economic cycles and frequency of events in the two markets demonstrates this difference.

Generally speaking, most economic markets appear to move "up" and "down" around some sort of equilibrium level. This equilibrium level could be a historical interest rate, return on equity, or commodity price. The equilibrium may also be called the "average" or "mean" level. The process of a market returning to its equilibrium level is termed "mean reversion."

Mean reversion will be a recurring theme in this book because it describes a critical difference between the energy and financial markets.

Interest rate markets exhibit relatively weak mean reversion. The actual rate of mean reversion in interest rates appears to be related to economic cycles, hence fundamental price drivers. The state of the economy as a fundamental driver can be directly translated into financial models through the inclusion of mean reversion.

In the case of energies, however, we see stronger mean reversion, and for dramatically different reasons than those that apply to interest rates. The mean reversion in energy commodities appears to be a function of either how quickly the supply side of the market can react to "events" or how quickly the events go away. Droughts, wars, and other news-making events create new and unexpected supply-and-demand imbalances. Mean reversion measures how quickly it takes for these events to dissipate or for supply and demand to return to a balanced state.

The Gulf War, for instance, greatly affected crude oil prices. The market forward prices of crude oil contained information on how long it would take the production side to respond to the sudden imbalance between supply and demand. Spot and short-term forward prices spiked, while longer-term futures remained relatively stable. In this case the mean reversion—as exhibited in forward prices—was tied to how quickly the production side could bring the system back in balance.

In another example, the summer heat wave of 1995 caused electricity prices to jump to a multiple of their average price levels. However, temperatures spiked only for several days and prices rapidly reverted to equilibrium. In this case the mean reversion had to do with the dissipation of an event.

1.5. IMPACT OF SUPPLY DRIVERS

Energies function with supply drivers that do not exist in money markets: production and storage. Consider the issue of longer-term effects, which have to do with expectations of market production capacity and cost in the long run. Effects of expectations of improvements in the technology of drawing natural gas from the ground will not be seen in the historical data but—if we are lucky—may be expressed by knowledgeable traders in determining forward prices. Their views would be captured through the levels or yields of long-term forward prices. Similarly, the effects of overcapacity in electricity markets, and how long the overcapacity will last, impact the price over a longer period of time.

This "storage limitation" problem creates volatile day-to-day behavior of varying degrees for electricity, natural gas, heating oil, and crude oil. Another consequence of limited storage is that while the spot prices exhibit extremely high volatility, the forward prices show volatilities that decrease significantly as the forward price expirations increase. The latter volatility characteristic has to do with the fact that in the long run we expect the supply and demand to be balanced, resulting in long-term forward prices that reflect this relatively stable equilibrium price level.

Ultimately, when discussing energy commodities, we are forced to confront the issue of storage capacity. Storage limitations cause energy markets to have much higher spot price volatility than is seen in money markets.

Electricity markets represent the extreme case of this storage limitation issue. In fact, electricity cannot be readily stored.[3] Once all the electric plants reach maximum allowable baseload and marginal capacity, there is no more "juice" to go around. While there is no more new electricity to sell, the same unit of electricity may be bought and sold, and hence you may still be able to obtain market price quotes. It should not come as a surprise that such extreme market conditions can cause electricity prices to easily reach levels in multiples of mean price levels.

1.6. ENERGIES HAVE A "SPLIT PERSONALITY"

From the big picture, the issue of storage accounts for energy prices exhibiting a "split personality." Energy prices are driven both by the short-term conditions of storage and by the long-term conditions of future potential energy supply. Energy forward prices reflect these two drivers, resulting in short-term forward prices with very different behavior from long-term forward prices. Figures 1–1 and 1–2 show the historical behavior of the one-month and the one-year forward price points off the West Texas Intermediate (WTI) and natural gas forward price curves, respectively. Furthermore, the storage problem gives energy markets "split personality." Short-term forward prices reflect the energy currently in storage, while long-term forward prices exhibit the behavior of future potential energy—i.e., energy "in the ground.[4]"

1.7. IMPACT OF DEMAND DRIVERS

If supply constraints can "shock" the system, demand exerts its own fundamental price drivers. In energies, demand drivers introduce the issues of convenience yield and seasonality that have no parallel in money markets.

FIGURE 1–1

NYMEX WTI Futures' Prices 1992–1996

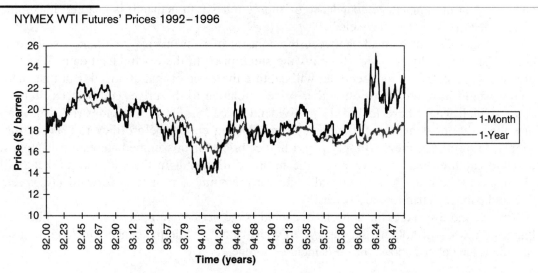

FIGURE 1-2

NYMEX Natural Gas Futures' Prices 1992–1996

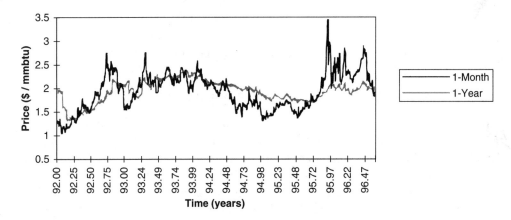

1.7.1. The Convenience Yield

On the industrial user side, the explicit purpose of derivative contracts is to keep plants running. These industrial users drive the market value of convenience yield. Factories seek to minimize their cost of production by avoiding the cost of shutting down and restarting the factory due to high prices or lack of available supply. (In a sense, minimizing price risk can be related to this function.) This urgency of production gives the industrial users an incentive to pay a premium to have the energy necessary to run their plants delivered *now, today*. This is not because they are being financially inefficient. Quite the contrary; they are factoring in the opportunity cost of having their production stopped while waiting around to get a better deal on energy or waiting for energy to become available. The premium they are willing to pay (or not, depending on the immediate abundance of supply relative to demand) is factored into something called the "convenience yield."

An analogy can be made between the concept of convenience yield and a stock dividend. Consider a shareholder who buys the stock prior to the ex-dividend date. When the dividend is paid, the new shareholder will capture the value of that dividend. But that shareholder would have had to pay a higher price—relative to the price paid post ex-dividend date—which would have included the dividend value. Similarly, the industrial users capture the value of their own production by purchasing energy before they run out of their supply. In doing so, they willingly pay a higher price for this immediate energy supply in order to capture their own, very specific in-house dividend. In the end, the markets will, given specific industrial user demand, reflect a premium of near-term forward prices relative to the longer-term forward prices.

To be more specific, the convenience yield is the net benefit minus the cost—other than financing costs—of holding the energy "in your hands." While the benefits include the user-specific value defined above, the costs include storage.

1.7.2. Seasonality

On the demand side we have to consider the significant seasonality effects of the residential users. Aggregate residential demand creates seasonality. For example, the United States consumes heating oil mostly during winter; hence heating oil prices tend to peak during winter and then drop to their annual lows in the summer months. Electricity, on the contrary, powers air conditioners in the summer months and is used less during winter for heating; its prices tend to reach highest peaks during the summer months, with semiannual humps during winter.[5] The relative highs of the summer and winter peaks—as clearly exhibited within the electricity forward price curves—are a function of the geographic regions within the United States. These seasonality effects can be seen and measured not only through historical spot price data, but also by observing the forward price markets.

1.8. REGULATION AND ILLIQUIDITY

When modeling energies, we must always remember their relative youth in terms of derivatives and risk management. Natural gas deregulated only in the past decade, and governments are deregulating electricity as this book is being written. Even the relatively older markets of heating oil and crude oil took root in the 1980s and continue to evolve in terms of theoretical sophistication and contract complexity and standardization. While the money markets took decades to evolve, energies might replicate this evolution in a shorter period. Clearly, lessons from deregulated markets should accelerate the trip up the learning curve.

Unfortunately, energy's relative youth presents a classic paradox: How can one price new products without having price histories and readily available market prices for benchmarks? In quantitative terms, energy markets suffer from lack of historical price information, as well as relatively small volumes of present-day market activity (this is referred to as an "illiquid" market). There is not enough spot and forward price information flowing through the market to establish a universally agreed-upon understanding of fundamental price drivers or the quantitative pricing methodologies. The lack of liquidity (i.e., "illiquidity") frustrates the process of "price discovery" through which market participants can view reasonable prices without necessarily having to trade them to see them. Since liquidity is the lifeblood of risk management, we can easily see how illiquidity sets energies dramatically apart from the more liquid markets. One of the objectives of this book is to get around this problem with quantitative tools that can plug the gaps in available price information.

1.9. DECENTRALIZATION OF MARKETS AND EXPERTISE

When one thinks of financial markets, Wall Street shines at the center. Companies throughout the nation list their stocks on the New York Stock Exchange, and New York also hosts most of the major U.S. banks. Of course, cities outside the Empire State play important roles, but major local and regional banks and financial institutions still turn to Wall Street, Chicago, and other major trading centers to hedge their portfolios. Thus, the financial markets are essentially centralized in terms of location, capital, and expertise.

Energy markets, on the other hand, are highly decentralized. To be sure, Houston serves as a mecca, as does Calgary. Energy producers and end users, however, spread from sea to shining sea. To whom does a Midwestern utility turn to hedge their price risk? If their risk is localized, chances are that their hedges will also be localized. While power marketing booms, there is no real outsourcing option like the banking network; these secondary markets and services are for the future. While many producers and end users may actively use futures contracts in New York and Kansas City, these contracts represent prices at specific delivery points that may behave very differently from the local market being hedged.

Decentralization introduces geographic "basis risk," which is unique to energies. In financial markets, today's dollar is worth a dollar anywhere in the country. In energy markets, price depends on location. A megawatt of electricity is priced according to delivery point; the same holds true for natural gas. Location is a fundamental driver of price.

At the most human level, even the jobs of energy risk managers are also more decentralized than in financial markets. Throughout North America, large end users and even moderate-sized utilities maintain energy purchasing officers and wholesale analysts at the least, and full trading and risk management staffs at the extreme.

Even the people working the energy desks are diverse. These professionals come from a wide variety of backgrounds, including trading, risk management, corporate treasury departments, and even engineering. Not surprisingly, their voices often conflict, sending mixed messages (and occasionally mispricing) to the market. These market inefficiencies will be resolved with time, of course, as growing market understanding (and knowledge transfer, as exemplified by this book) takes place. But until then, the market will reflect a wide degree of inconsistency further exacerbated by an unusually decentralized market.

1.10. ENERGIES REQUIRE MORE EXOTIC CONTRACTS

The final factor that makes energies so different can be found in the type of financial contracts required by the end users of derivatives. In interest rates, contracts tend to be standardized and relatively easy to model. For the most part, end users of financial derivatives find that relatively simple forwards, swaps, caps, floors, and swaptions suit the majority of their needs. (Not surprisingly, these contracts are made in highly liquid financial markets as compared to energies.) The market even uses the term "vanilla" for these simple contracts; traders immediately term nonvanilla contracts as "exotic."

What makes energy contracts so different is that energy's typical "vanilla" contract would be considered an "exotic" contract in mature money markets. Due largely to the needs of end users, energy contracts often exhibit a complexity of price averaging and customized characteristics of commodity delivery. The combination of a young derivatives market in development, supporting very sophisticated contracts, presents a terrific challenge to quantitative analysts and risk managers in the energy markets.

1.11. CONCLUSION AND ORGANIZATION OF THE BOOK

Energies differ from nonphysical markets for both fundamental and quantitative reasons. Compared to the traditional markets of interest rates and equities, energies react differently to such fundamental variables as macroeconomic cycles and events. The energy markets suffer from supply-and-demand constraints that dramatically influence both the valuation and management of energy risk. The differences even spread to the company level, where firms that would be considered small by financial market standards must still support trading and risk management operations never seen in like-sized banks.

In summary, this introductory chapter introduced energy derivatives and risk management by comparing the quantitative differences between energy and money markets. The markets share many characteristics as well. The main outcome of these parallel differences and similarities is that the energy markets demonstrate a "split personality." Energies act a little traditional money markets, but at the same time they have their own unique behavioral intricacies.

The balance of this book explores the specifics of modeling and managing the complex task of quantitative and fundamental analysis of the energy derivatives and risk management market. We will follow a progressive path:

- Chapters 2 and 3 cover the type of modeling principles and skills demanded by the complexities of the energy markets.
- Chapters 4 and 5 describe how to model the underlying price behavior of the spot and forward markets. These prices act both as an end to themselves and as valuable inputs for the quantitative analysis covered in the remaining chapters.
- Chapter 6 explains volatility and introduces a new comprehensive method for its modeling.
- Chapters 7 and 8 cover energy option pricing modeling and implementation.
- Finally Chapters 9, 10, and 11 pull together the fundamental and quantitative analysis of market behavior into the context of risk management and portfolio analysis.

ENDNOTES

1. Hall & Taylor, pp. 3, 4. *Macroeconomics: Theory, Performance, and Policy* (New York: W.W. Norton & Company, 1988).
2. However, this was not always so. Remember the gold standard? In the gold standard days, the interest rate markets acted much more like today's energy markets than like today's interest rate markets.
3. Water reserves do represent a form of potential electricity storage for hydro plants; several utilities employ off-peak power to pump water up to a reservoir, only to reverse the flow to capture the potential energy during peak periods.
4. "In the ground" is used here as an expression of speech. In the case of electricity, it is not that simplistic.
5. Ironically, most of the residential demand remains in the regulated portion of electricity generation although this is currently changing.

CHAPTER 2

Modeling Principles and Market Behavior

2.1. THE MODELING PROCESS

Modeling market behavior should be approached like any business: with a good amount of common sense. It should not be some mysterious process that Ph.D.'s perform in isolation, with no view of the overall trading business goals. The full energy team of managers, traders, quantitative analysts, and engineers should be able to understand the basics of modeling principles and market behavior. This way, modeling can become a well-defined process, with goals and procedures that are discussed, set up, and agreed upon by several key players in a company structure, just like any other business branch of a company.

The first step in getting the full energy team to communicate is to define the modeling process, which should include both trader insights about the markets and expert insights about quantifying and valuing the products in that marketplace. In the spirit of developing a standardized language that both traders and valuation experts can use to better define the modeling business goals, this chapter will define the basics of modeling and some commonsense requirements that the modeling process ought to satisfy.

2.2. THE VALUE OF BENCHMARKS

Modeling is often left to itself in its struggle to arrive at pricing models that traders can use. There is usually no real beginning, middle, or end to the process. By this I mean that the beginning ought to consist of an analysis of the available models and their appropriateness for the particular product. Hence, the beginning should be the benchmarking between active market behavior and the modeling choices, resulting in a final choice of a model, given possible implementation constraints. The middle ought to be the actual development of the chosen model, and the end ought to be the actual implementation of the chosen model.

The most difficult and also the most important part of this process is the first, the beginning. If the model chosen is not appropriate for the product, given the market in which the product is traded, then the last part of the process, the implementation, is likely to drag on—sometimes for months and even years.

Quite often the critical first step of the process, the model benchmarking, is not performed. This can be a very costly mistake. While the company is paying its valuation experts a good deal of money to finish the long-awaited implementation of the choice model, it is also paying a price for not being able to participate in the trading of the product because the traders cannot yet price it. It is often such poor modeling management (and poor management in general) that results in the traders coming up with their own—however simplistic and maybe even inappropriate—spreadsheets for pricing products.

What we are really talking about here is the cost a trading business has to pay for not benchmarking and testing between the models in the laboratory before bringing them out onto the trading desk. If you were to buy a new suit, and you decided to spend a good amount of money on it, wouldn't you shop around and try on different suits for fit and look? Then why wouldn't a company that wants to invest a good amount of money in a modeling methodology not do the same?

2.2.1. Diffusing Personalized Attachments to Models

I would like to discuss an important issue, which I like to refer to as the "my model, your model" problem. This problem often arises in trading companies that have invested money in research development and there is more than one modeling expert, but each is driven by a separate system of beliefs about modeling. Hence, it would not be surprising to find these valuation experts in what might appear as lethal warfare with no real means of concluding it.

Unfortunately, the valuation experts, just like most of us when it comes to something that we know a great deal about and have been working on for years, tend to take the modeling issues very personally. (As hard as I try to be objective, I remain aware of this weakness in myself as well.) The problem is not that the experts might have different opinions; in fact, this is rather a good thing, as they could probably learn quite a bit from each other. The problem is that they have not agreed on modeling benchmarks and have had no help from the trading or management sides in deciding what benchmarks really ought to be used, given the trading strategies and business goals of the company.

Even worse than the "my model, your model" problem is the problem of having a single expert who has a favorite model that the company decides to implement without any benchmarking and testing. The typical story goes as follows: The expert's favorite model is implemented, but since it might not be appropriate for the market in question, any implementation and new product problems are dealt with "modeling Band-Aids." The resulting valuation system very quickly becomes cumbersome if not impossible to use, not to mention that the cost of maintaining it can become quite high.

Besides introducing modeling benchmarks, the trading organization must also approach the modeling side with the spirit of always searching for a better understanding of the marketplace and its products. This means that managers, traders, and valuation experts should form a team, which would provide a framework for sharing knowledge, and set the team's valuation goals, including determining the benchmarks for deciding on methodology routes.

With all the above said, I recognize that this book in fact introduces you to one particular view on modeling. However, if the book achieves its purpose, you will not walk away from it thinking about *the author's* modeling views. Instead, you will walk away empowered to form your own views and you will encourage others around you to do the same.

2.3. THE IDEAL MODELING PROCESS

The recipe for efficient modeling as applied to a trading operation includes five steps:

* Establish corporate goals that are within the context of the risk/return framework and are expressed through the risk management policy. (See chapters 9 and 11.)
* Prioritize the market characteristics, which should be captured by the model. Define the benchmarks that describe the market against which any model will be judged.
* Select the models to be tested and evaluated against the benchmarks. Perform time series analysis and distribution analysis for comparison. The models should be selected in the order of the evaluation results.
* Estimate the implementation constraints and costs for each model.
* Finally, identify the model that best satisfies both the market benchmarks and the implementation requirements.

This process would require the participation of at least the producers (the valuation experts and implementers) and the users (the traders). Ideally, the management also has a representative who adds the necessary degree of management support, understanding, and guidance from a higher level of the trading business goals.

2.4. THE ROLE OF ASSUMPTIONS: MARKET BEFORE THEORY

The goal of quantitative analysis is to develop and implement models that reflect market behavior. The process forces us to make some fundamental assumptions about the marketplace and the products we are trying to model. For example, the famous Black-Scholes differential equation for option prices is based on the fundamental assumption that a hedged portfolio consisting of an option, a stock, and a bond must earn the risk-free rate of return because we have eliminated all the stock price risk by hedging the option with the stock. Expressed in terms of partial differential equations, this fundamental assumption forms the basis of quantitative analysis of option prices.[1] One nice feature of making unrealistic assumptions is that we can enforce them to simplify a problem, and then later relax the assumption for a more general, realistic solution.

Similarly, if we make the fundamental assumption that electricity prices are related to coal and natural gas prices, we can arrive at a solution for electricity prices by assuming that we can create a risk-free portfolio consisting of electricity, coal, and natural gas. On the other hand, we may assume that electricity prices tend to revert to equilibrium price levels, which are determined by supply-and-demand conditions. In these cases, our different fundamental assumptions would possibly lead us to very different solutions.

Fundamental assumptions about the marketplace dramatically influence quantitative models developed and implemented for pricing and risk management purposes. Every quantitative result ought to be consistent with the characteristics the fundamental drivers ultimately give to the behavior of the marketplace. Therefore, understanding the fundamental drivers of the marketplace as well as how these drivers are captured in the behavior of the market is extremely important in arriving at models that reflect market reality.

Furthermore, in order to arrive at such models we need not only to understand the fundamental drivers of the marketplace but also to translate these fundamental drivers into pricing models that are both arbitrage free and practical for implementation onto a trading desk. This is by no means an easy task.

2.4.1. Typical Assumptions

Some typical assumptions are that the markets are efficient and arbitrage free. In money markets, prices are often assumed to be lognormal. Through such assumptions, we define our version of reality. One person may assume that volatilities are constant, while another may assume the volatilities vary along different points of the forward price curve (i.e., have "term structure"). Another common assumption is hedging continuously.

Everyone has probably heard of the Black-Scholes option pricing model.[2] While valuing European options on stocks, Black and Scholes assumed that the stock prices are lognormal and have constant volatilities. Hence, the randomness that the stock prices exhibit is assumed to always be of the same magnitude.

Although most people agree that the stock prices are indeed lognormal, most disagree that the volatilities remain constant. In reality, the randomness of the stock price behavior is not constant and volatilities do possess term structure. Black and Scholes were forced to make this unrealistic assumption because allowing the volatility to also exhibit a nonconstant behavior made solving for the option price far too difficult. After all, one of the best features of the resulting model is its ease of use. This is a terrific example of how unrealistic assumptions might help to create practical solutions.

An important consideration in making assumptions is that they be correctly implemented within models. For example, consider the assumption that price mean reversion exists in interest rates. While most people believe this to be true, when this assumption is implemented within a single-factor model, the result is a volatility term structure that goes to zero over time. Since most interest rate models are in fact single-factor, and since the volatility's term structure does not in fact go to zero over time, we see a potential conflict.[3]

The lesson that can be learned from Black-Scholes and similar modeling experiences is that some assumptions that reflect market reality should be relaxed in order to arrive at a workable valuation model. However, when we relax assumptions but recognize them to be true in the real world, we should make sure that the valuation methodology's implementation captures the assumption—even though the valuation methodology itself does not.

So, in the case of Black-Scholes, we can correct for the constant volatility assumption by allowing each option price of different maturity to have a different volatility value. Thus we somewhat capture market reality of the marketplace (at least allowing for marked-to-market option prices)—not in the valuation model but rather in its implementation.

If we had just ignored the fact that in reality energy volatilities are not constant, we could be making a grave mistake, perhaps costing the trading operation a great deal of money. Hence, here is an excellent example of why it is very important to have traders communicating with the valuation experts, particularly when the implementation is very informal: If they do not understand the model assumptions they may end up using the models blindly and without the appropriate checks on implementation assumptions.

2.4.2. Market Variable vs. Modeling Parameter

The above section on the fundamental assumptions and the modeling process leads us directly to the issue of distinguishing between "market variables" and "modeling parameters." (See Table 2–1.) A market variable is defined by the marketplace, which exhibits randomness and has a certain set of characteristics associated with its behavior. A modeling parameter is assumed to be either fixed or deterministic—we always know (or hope to know) its value. These distinctions have important implications for the modeling process and risk management. Problems might creep in when we treat a market variable as a modeling parameter for the sake of simplifying the modeling process.

During product valuation we are often forced to treat what we know are market variables as modeling parameters for the sake of simplicity or cost reduction in model development and maintenance. Remember the problem of volatility that is treated as a modeling parameter by the Black-Scholes option pricing model, but which is in reality a market variable. The give and take between the cost of model development, which would reflect the true behavior of volatilities and the benefit of having a more realistic valuation model, should determine how volatilities should be treated for valuation purposes.

A risk manager wants to ensure that such simplifications or at least their side effects are minimized. In the analysis of portfolio risks, in the derivation of optimal hedges, and in the calculations of trading book value-at-risk (VAR) numbers, we want to make sure that we capture all the market variables that are out there, regardless of the types of simplifications we might

TABLE 2–1

A Sample Choice of Market Variables and
Model Parameters

Market Variables	Model Parameters
Spot prices	Time
Forward prices	Mean-reversion rate
Volatilities	Equilibrium prices
Correlations	Seasonality factors
Discount rates	

have made during the valuation process. A lack of understanding of the full market risks can be costly. If a market risk remains unrecognized, then the trading book's true exposure cannot be discussed, and no attempts can be made to manage the risk. In the event that unknown risks appear, you would truly find yourself caught off guard.

2.4.3. Testing Assumptions Through Benchmarks

Fundamental assumptions can be tested against modeling benchmarks. If we assume that a market is mean-reverting, we could use the implied market characteristic of the forward price volatilities as modeling benchmarks. In other words, we can ask if a particular model implies the same forward price behavior as that seen in the market.

For example, if we assume that a market mean-reverts, decreasing volatilities of forward prices as we allow their time to expiration to increase, we would expect forward price points that are far out on the forward price curve to be much more stable (i.e., less volatile) than those forward prices in the near-term portion of the forward price curve. The consequence of a mean-reverting assumption can be tested against the market forward price behavior.

Figures 2–1 and 2–2 show the historical volatilities of the NYMEX futures prices (adjusted for rollovers) for WTI and natural gas. In modeling these two markets we might require that our models imply the same types of volatility term structures across the forward prices as seen in Figures 2–1 and 2–2.

Modeling benchmarks should be prioritized based on their impact on product valuation. For example, in electricity the spot prices tend to exhibit extremely volatile day-to-day price returns. Yet over a period of time, the values of the spot prices tend to be mostly within a rather narrow range (see Figure 2–3). This is an important benchmark which, if not captured by the consequences of our assumptions, might cause electricity options to be priced unrealisti-

FIGURE 2–1

NYMEX WTI Rolling Futures' Historical Volatility

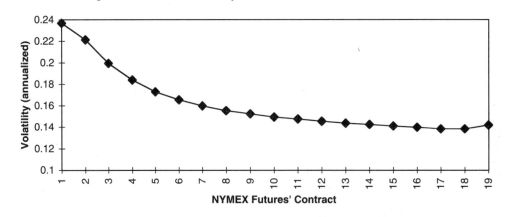

F I G U R E   2-2

F I G U R E   2-2

NYMEX Natural Gas Rolling Futures' Historical Volatility

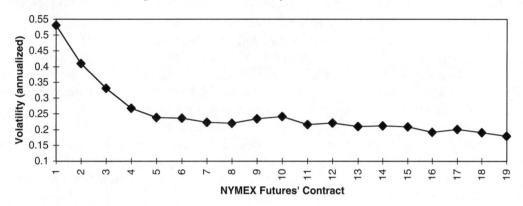

cally high. If a trading operation indeed trades a lot of options, then this is an extremely important market characteristic, which needs to be used as a benchmark when deciding between models.

2.4.4. Assumptions and Implementation

In the previous sections I have argued that some fundamental assumptions about market behavior ought to be relaxed in order to provide us with a working valuation model—as long as these market characteristics can later be captured through implementation. However, which assumptions should be made and which should be relaxed is a very "personal" decision to be made only upon a detailed analysis of the costs involved and the benefits to be

F I G U R E   2-3

SPP On-Peak Electricity Price Distribution (11/94 through 07/96; Spot Price Volatility = 224.69%)

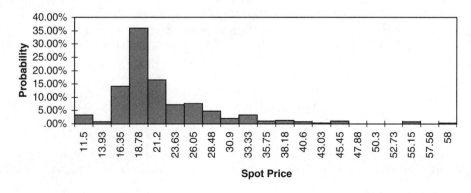

gained by constraining the model to some fundamental assumptions or relaxing those assumptions.

To what extent a model should capture the market realities has to do with how sensitive
the particular trading business is to the particular imperfections resulting from relaxing assumptions. For example, a market maker that provides risk management services and primarily
makes money off the bid-ask spreads might be wise to invest time and money in a sophisticated
portfolio analysis methodology that provides minimum-variance hedges. An arbitraging operation, on the other hand, would want to ensure that their valuation models are extremely sophisticated: How could they expect to capture market arbitrage if they are at the same level of sophistication as the general marketplace?

Regardless of what the ultimate valuation/implementation strategy is in capturing the fundamentals of the marketplace, it is always the best practice to capture as much of the market reality as possible. This will ensure that as little money as possible is lost on valuation errors and
that as little money as necessary is paid for hedging.

2.5. CONTRACT TERMS AND ISSUES

Derivatives are contracts, so we must define the terms of such contracts as they relate to modeling principles.

2.5.1. Underlying Price or Market

The *underlying price* (or underlying market) refers to the spot prices (or market) in the case of
an energy market where there is no seasonality. When we are indeed talking about an energy
market with seasonality, the underlying price refers to the spot price with the seasonality factors taken away:

$$S_t = S_t^{Und} + seasonality\ factors \tag{2-1}$$

where: S_t = the spot price at time t
S_t^{Und} = the underlying spot price at time t

The seasonality effects can sometimes obscure the underlying price processes, i.e., the
processes of the spot prices stripped of seasonality. We need to strip the effect of seasonality
out of price data in order to analyze the underlying price behavior. This nomenclature allows us
to talk about modeling seasonality separately from talking about modeling the underlying price
processes. (Note: Ultimately, seasonality should be modeled as a stochastic process.)

2.5.2. Derivative Contract

A *derivative* is a contract whose value is a function of a spot price. A forward price is a derivative product in the sense that it is a function of the spot price behavior at some future point in
time. Similarly, an option on either the spot price or the forward price is a derivative contract.

2.5.3. Option Settlement Price

The price the option settles on is referred to as the *settlement price.* If the option is on the spot price, then the settlement price is the spot price. On the other hand, if the option is on a forward price, then the settlement price is the forward price. If the option is an average spot price option, then the settlement price is the average of spot prices over a period of time. I make the above distinctions because in the energy markets the spot price is not often also the option settlement prices.

2.5.4. Delivery

Delivery is the contractually agreed-upon location and timing of the exchange of the commodity or cash. The actual commodity could be delivered and paid for, or only cash could be exchanged resulting in cash-settled contracts.

2.5.5. Complexity of Contracts for Delivery

As stated in this book's introduction, energy markets differ from money markets in part due to the complexity of the common contracts. Due to the nature of delivery, "vanilla" energy contracts would be considered "exotic" in financial markets. Let us consider the following three modeling issues for energy contracts:

- ◆ Modeling when the underlying market price is a physical commodity
- ◆ Valuing contracts for physical delivery
- ◆ Valuing cash-settled energy contracts

2.5.5.1. Underlying Market Price Is a Physical Commodity

In energy markets the derivative contracts are typically for delivery of energy: one side pays cash, and the counterparty delivers the energy commodity. This contract requires the specification of location of delivery. Every place of delivery will have its own underlying price, and there are many such locations. While this problem is great in the magnitude of information, it is really no different from the problem many equity players have to deal with: that of dealing with a huge set of underlying commodities.

The large number of underlying price processes in the energy markets offers both good news and bad news. On the good side, the greater the number of different underlying price exposures in a trader's book, the greater is the effect of diversification. The trader can use the risk diversification to her benefit, as long as there is some means of hedging off the systematic (or market) risks,[4] very much the way an equity trader would use the S&P 500 index to hedge off the systematic risk of her book, which contains a large number of different kinds of stock exposure. The bad news is that the energy trading organizations have to become sophisticated enough to handle such problems and appropriately calculate the minimum-variance hedges.

It is often very tempting to dump two different commodity markets into the same commodity bucket without doing the analysis of the correlation in their behavior. This can be dangerous to the extent that it is the easiest path and also one that is easy for traders to get used to. It allows the traders to sleep at night believing that their books are perfectly hedged purely based on the assumption that because they defined two different market price risks to be perfectly correlated they are off the hook. If this is the case, then it is the management that should spend sleepless nights until they sort out the issue of just how reasonable is the particular assumption of high correlations between the commodities in question. But we will devote a good deal more discussion to this issue in the chapters on Risk Management and Portfolio Analysis.

2.5.5.2. Valuing Contracts for Physical Delivery

When modeling derivative products that are functions of spot prices of energies for delivery, we have to incorporate all the characteristics of the particular delivery location into the modeling process. In other words, the modeling of the derivative product will be a function of the particular underlying price model for the particular delivery point.

A good example here is electricity. The electricity market is extremely local, due to the constraints of production, transmission lines, and even regulation. Hence, even if the same general underlying price model applies to most electricity delivery nodes, we can be sure that the parameters of such a general model would be very different across the delivery nodes. Winter effects are much stronger in the North than the South, hence winter seasonality will be much more pronounced in the North. Similarly, the Texas region tends to use quite a bit of natural gas in the generation of electricity, while the Northwest region of the United States has a good amount of hydroelectric generation. These different generation methodologies will have an impact on how the two markets tend to react to temperature events.

2.5.5.3. Valuing Cash-Settled Energy Contracts

Even when the derivative products are cash-settled, and there is no delivery of energy, as long as the product is linked to the underlying prices of energies that are intended for delivery, the derivative product will have to be modeled as a function of the behavior of the underlying prices of energies for delivery. Even the OTC cash-settled energy derivatives are not able to get away from the fundamental drivers of energies markets.

2.6. MODELING TERMS AND ISSUES

Before we get into the details of modeling that will be presented throughout this book, we need to define some modeling terms that will be used.

2.6.1. Price Returns

The *daily price change* is simply the difference between today's price and yesterday's price, while the *daily price return* is the daily price change divided by yesterday's price. In general, a price return over some time period is the percentage price change over that time period. Equation 2–2 and Equation 2–3 show these definitions in mathematical terms:

$$dS_t = S_{t+dt} - S_t \tag{2-2}$$

$$\frac{dS_t}{S_t} = \frac{S_{t+dt}}{S_t} - 1 \tag{2-3}$$

where: dS_t = the price change

$\dfrac{dS_t}{S_t}$ = the price return

Here dt is the time period between price observations S_{t+dt} and S_t. In the case of daily price returns, dt would equal *1/365*. In case of weekly observations, dt would be *1/52*. Similarly, in the case of monthly price return calculations, dt would be set to *1/12*.

2.6.2. Elements of a Price Model

Every financial model, regardless if it is for an interest rate, a price, a log of a price, etc., starts with the basic assumption of how the market variable being analyzed behaves over a short period of time. The change in the market variable, *x*, consists of the *deterministic* (or "drift") and the *stochastic* (or "random") terms:

$$d\tilde{x} = \text{deterministic term} + \text{stochastic term} \tag{2-4}$$

where: $d\tilde{x}$ = the change in the market variable $\tilde{x}$ over time period dt

The deterministic term represents the portion of the movement in the market variable $\tilde{x}$, which we expect to see with certainty. The stochastic term represents the portion of the market variable change that is random, and cannot be predicted. The deterministic term is also referred to as the drift term, and it is proportional to the time period over which the change in the variable is measured:

$$\text{deterministic term} \propto dt \tag{2-5}$$

2.6.2.1. Random Variables
The stochastic term is proportional to a normally distributed variable, $d\tilde{z}_t$. (The little hat above the $\tilde{z}$ denotes that it is a random variable.) This normally distributed variable has a mean of zero, and a variance of dt:

$$\text{stochastic term} \propto d\tilde{z}_t \tag{2-6}$$

$$d\tilde{z}_t \sim \aleph(0, dt) \tag{2-7}$$

The randomly distributed variable (aka "random variable") is a key concept that is used throughout this book. The random variable allows us to capture market movement in our models, and our understanding from mathematics and statistics of random variable properties provides us with many shortcuts to be used in valuation and risk management.

We can generalize the definition of the random variable, $\tilde{z}$, from time period t_1 to t_2, $\tilde{z}_{t1,t2}$, to be normally distributed with a mean of zero and a variance of $(t_2 - t_1)$:

$$\tilde{z}_{t1,t2} \sim \aleph(0, t_2 - t_1) \qquad (2-8)$$

One property of a random variable is that its value is cumulative over time. (We will use this property when solving for forward prices and during portfolio analysis.) Figure 2–4 demonstrates how a random variable "walks" through time.

Specifically, the normally distributed variable $\tilde{z}$ has the following characteristic: it is additive. A random variable representing the randomness from time period t_1 to t_3, let us call it $\tilde{z}_{t1,t3}$, would be equivalent to two random variables, one representing the randomness from time period t_1 to t_2, $\tilde{z}_{t1,t2}$, and the other representing the randomness from time period t_2 to t_3, $\tilde{z}_{t2,t3}$:

$$\tilde{z}_{t1,t3} = \tilde{z}_{t1,t2} + \tilde{z}_{t2,t3} \qquad (2-9)$$

The mean of zero is preserved, as is the variance being proportional to the time period. Because these are normally distributed variables, the correlations between the random variables during periods that do not overlap is zero:

$$E\left[\tilde{z}_{t1,t2}, \tilde{z}_{t2,t3}\right] = 0 \qquad (2-10)$$

It follows that the correlation between two random variables with the periods overlapping is not zero. For example, we would have:

$$E\left[\tilde{z}_{t1,t3}\tilde{z}_{t1,t2}\right] = E\left[(\tilde{z}_{t1,t2} + \tilde{z}_{t2,t3})\tilde{z}_{t1,t2}\right] = E\left[(\tilde{z}_{t1,t2})^2\right] + E\left[\tilde{z}_{t1,t2}\tilde{z}_{t2,t3}\right] = t_2 - t_1 \qquad (2-11)$$

For very small changes in time, we have the following:

$$\tilde{z}_{0,t+dt} = \tilde{z}_{0,t} + \tilde{z}_{t,t+dt} \qquad (2-12)$$

We define $d\tilde{z}_t$ to represent the normally distributed randomness of the process over the time period dt, from time t to time $t + dt$:

$$d\tilde{z}_t \equiv \tilde{z}_{t,t+dt} = \tilde{z}_{0,t+dt} - \tilde{z}_{0,t} \qquad (2-13)$$

FIGURE 2-4

Random Walk

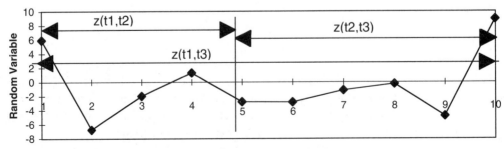

Time (measured in steps)

2.6.2.2. Factors

In a model, a *factor* represents a market variable that exhibits some form of random behavior. The Pilipovic Model for the Forward Price Curve is a two-factor model because it assumes that the spot price and the long-term price are both market factors, with their own random behaviors. (See Sections 2.9.3 and 2.9.4 for continued discussion.)

2.6.3. Convenience Yield

The convenience yield represents the overall benefit minus the cost—with the exception of the financing cost—that a holder of a commodity receives by holding the commodity. The holder of a commodity would reap benefits by using the commodity to generate value that is dependent on the use of the commodity as a fuel, such as for example a factory that needs the fuel to keep running. Since the convenience yield represents the net value of holding the commodity, excluding the financing cost, it can be either positive or negative. It is positive when the benefit of having the fuel on hand outweighs the cost, and it is negative when just the opposite is true.

The convenience yield, Cy, while driven by the user's needs, is in general a measure of the balance between the available supply and the existing demand. If we introduce L_t as the equilibrium price—i.e., the price of the commodity when the supply and the demand are in balance—and S_t as the spot price, both at time t, then the difference between the two represents the measure of the market imbalance. Since the convenience yield is a function of this imbalance, we can make a general statement:

$$Cy \propto (S_t - L_t) + K \qquad (2-14)$$

where K is some constant. (As you will see in Chapter 5, the constant K can be related to the equilibrium price growth rate adjusted for the cost of production and storage as well as the cost of risk.)

The contribution to the convenience yield of the market supply and demand imbalance, as captured by the difference between the values of the spot price and equilibrium price, ought to go to zero over a long period of time, as in the long run we could assume that the prices approach the equilibrium levels:

$$Cy \rightarrow K \text{ as } t \rightarrow \infty \qquad (2-15)$$

The difficulty in modeling the commodity prices is in specifically defining the convenience yield. The measure of the value that the commodity generates for the user by having it on hand as the user needs it—or rather, on the flip side, the value lost to the user in not having the fuel on hand as needed—is user specific. As there is no standardized formulation of convenience yield in the marketplace, there are huge degrees of freedom in defining it. Typically, it is expressed in terms of a continuously compounded rate. An example of a convenience yield function and how it impacts the derivation of differential equations for commodity derivatives is provided in chapter 5.

The convenience yield helps with understanding the differences between short- and long-term price behavior in energy markets. Short-term markets reflect the fundamentals of the readily available and stored energy; long-term markets reflect the fundamentals of the energy yet to be "dug out of ground" and put into storage. It is really not that surprising that the short-term and the long-term products would concentrate on different fundamentals. Convenience yield provides us with a bridge between the short-term and long-term price fundamentals.

Some of the short-term fundamental drivers would include supply-side events such as storms, strikes, wars, or other events that might disrupt immediate delivery of the energy. On the demand side, unexpected temperature spikes in the summer and temperature drops in the winter would cause a short-term imbalance between the demand and the immediately available supply. The convenience yield reflects these short-term supply and demand imbalances, as the users are willing to pay a premium for near-term delivery in response to the supply shortage.

Another set of fundamentals tends to influence the long-term supply-and-demand sides. Here we are dealing with the expectations of future potential supply and costs of production/storage, and the expectations of future potential demand. New discoveries of energy in the ground and new technologies affect the long-term outlook for energy prices. However, these fundamentals tend to be much more stable and less susceptible to frequent events as compared to the short-term fundamental drivers.

It is this divergence between the short-term and the long-term market fundamentals that also gives the short-term and the long-term energy products a different set of behavioral characteristics. Recall from chapter 1 how energies exhibit a "split personality": one that we see in the short-term and another that we expect to observe in the long-run. Just how "short" the short-term is can be measured by how quickly the market tends to revert to the equilibrium levels after an event hits.

In the case of crude oil the short-term markets driven by the short-term behavior fundamentals go out about three to six months relative to today. Typically, event corrections and supply/demand imbalances tend not to vary beyond this time period. For the heating oil and natural gas markets, short term is even shorter: the short-term fundamentals tend to affect the market out to about three months. Finally, in the electricity markets the short term is truly short-term, with the short-term fundamentals driving the market within only a couple of weeks out.

Given the split personality of energy markets, the difficulty in quantitative modeling is in coming up with valuation and risk management models that can capture both the short-term and long-term behavior. The spot prices are driven primarily by the fundamentals of the short-term market factors; however, they still get influenced by the longer-term expectations of equilibrium price levels, as slight as this influence might be.

Similarly, the longer-term energy products are primarily driven by the effects of the long-term market fundamentals. And yet, they might still feel some small effects of the near-term fundamentals. Most importantly, there is that gray transitional market area where the energy products feel both the short-term and the long-term fundamentals, but with different weightings.

Any model that we want to test out for consistency with the spot price behavior on a day-to-day basis must also be tested with the spot price behavior over a longer period of time. Similarly, we can use the longer-term energy products, such as the full strip of forward prices, to ensure the consistency between the model and the market reality.

2.6.4. Cost of Risk

We define the *cost of risk,* λ, as the differential between the actual return that an asset pays vs. the risk-free rate, normalized by the asset's volatility:

$$\lambda = \frac{(\mu - r)}{\sigma} \tag{2-16}$$

where: λ = cost of risk
μ = rate of return on the asset
r = risk-free rate
σ = volatility

It turns out, in the simple case of a stock price paying no dividends, that the cost of risk is given by:

$$\lambda = \frac{\ln\left(\dfrac{E_t\left[\widetilde{S}_T\right]}{F_{t,T}}\right)}{\sigma(T - t)} \tag{2-17}$$

where: λ = cost of risk
S = spot price
F = forward price
t = time of observation
T = time of forward price expiration
$T - t$ = time to forward price expiration
σ = volatility

or to put it another way:

$$\frac{E_t\left[\widetilde{S}_T\right]}{F_{t,T}} = e^{\lambda\sigma(T - t)} \tag{2-18}$$

The cost of risk is equal to the log of the ratio of the forward price to the expected spot price, $E_t[S_T]$, normalized by the volatility and the forward price time to expiration, $T - t$.

2.7. QUANTITATIVE FINANCIAL MODELS ACROSS MARKETS

We will use this section to introduce some of the quantitative financial models descriptively rather than mathematically. The next chapter will take you through the details of the models as well as how to quantify them.

2.7.1. Lognormal Market

The *lognormal* model was the first well-developed quantitative financial model. It has proven to be the most versatile and also the simplest model to be applied in describing price behavior

F I G U R E   2–5

Sample Path of a Lognormal Price

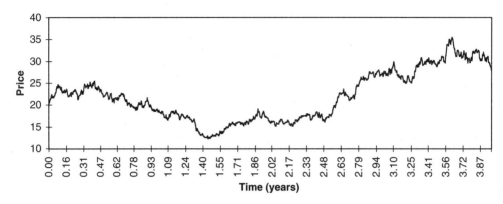

in various markets. We will see, however, that this model does not work well for energy markets (especially when compared to the mean-reverting models described in the following section).

A lognormal price is one that behaves so that the price return—which is the percentage change in the price—is normally distributed. This means that the percentage change in price over some time period is centered on some value—the drift, or the price yield—and its distribution around this drift is symmetric. The price return has as much of a chance of being positive as it does of being negative when the drift is zero. The drift represents the expected price return.

Normally distributed price returns translate into lognormally distributed prices. When the price return is normally distributed, the actual prices are guaranteed never to be negative. Figure 2–5 shows the path that the S&P 500 price made from 1992 through 1996. This is an ex-

F I G U R E   2–6

Sample Path Lognormal Price Distribution (Drift Rate = 13%; Spot Price Volatility = 30%)

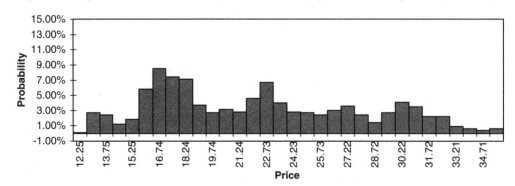

FIGURE 2-7

Path 1 Time Series

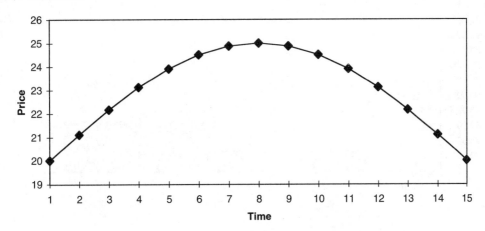

ample of a lognormal price path. Because of its simplicity, this model is favored across money markets in general. (Again, its popularity in money markets should not be taken as reason enough for applying it to energy markets.) A graph of the lognormal price distribution (see Figure 2–6) shows that a lognormal price process exhibits a positive skew (i.e., a distribution skewed to the right).

In the case when events occur in the marketplace but do not leave lasting effects, the distribution of price returns may be rather wide, which reflects the effect of events, and yet the distribution of the prices may not be that wide, which reflects the fact that the events do not have a long-lasting effect. In this case, if we took a stock and an energy that have very similar looking price return distributions, and then compared their price distributions, what we might find is that their price distributions look very different.

FIGURE 2-8

Path 1 Return Distribution

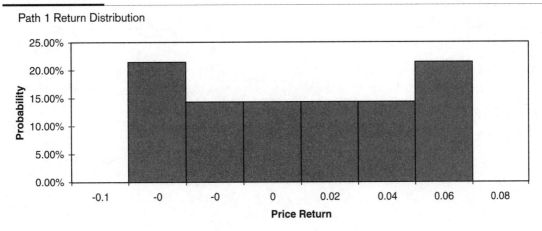

F I G U R E 2-9

Path 1 Price Distribution

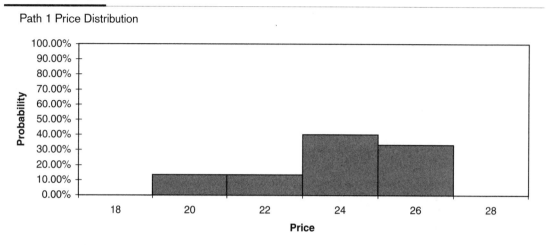

Figures 2–7 through 2–12 show two paths, Path 1 and Path 2, which have exactly the same price return distributions, but their price distributions look very different. Path 1 is representative of markets where events do not happen often, but when they do happen they tend to have long-lasting effects, such as long-term growth or decline. Path 2 is representative of markets where events happen often, but they do not tend to have long-lasting effects.

Path 2 shows the type of behavior that is mean reverting in nature. When the price move-up tends to be followed by a price move-down and vice versa, the short-term price moves might be very large, but the end result is a price range that is fairly narrow. This type of behav-

F I G U R E 2-10

Path 2 Time Series

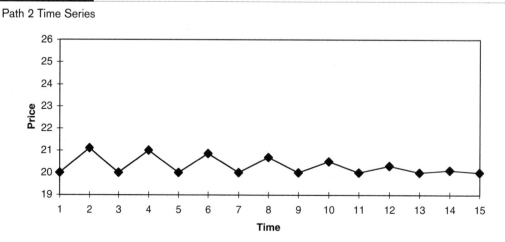

Path 2 Return Distribution

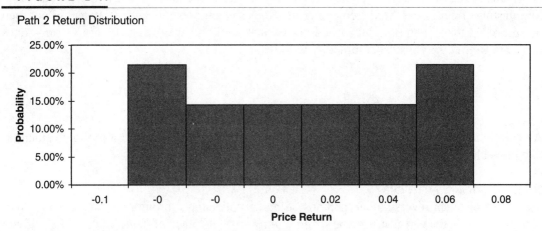

ior tends to be seen in energy markets: Events tend to be corrected, either through the dissipation of what caused them or through the response of the supply side. Either way, events tend
not to have long-lasting effects the way they do in the equity markets.

Path 2 behavior has a mean-reverting character, which a simple lognormal model would
not capture. Instead, a lognormal model that exhibits similar magnitude of short-term price
moves, as in our example above (Path 1), would result in a price range that is much wider compared to the price range in the example. Hence, while the lognormal model and a mean-reverting model might show very similar magnitudes of daily price moves, when looked at over a period of time, the range of actual price levels covered during that time period would be wider for
a lognormal model.

Path 2 Price Distribution

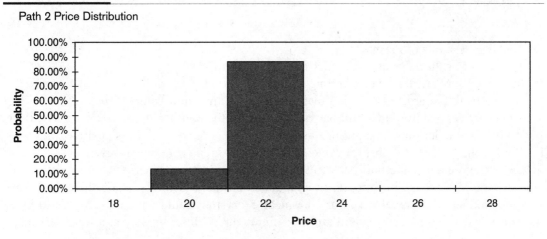

This is one of the key differences between energies and equities. An event generally has a long-lasting effect on the S&P (remember the stock market crash of 1987?). It should not then be surprising that a lognormal distribution—which works so well in the equity world—does not work well in the physical commodity world.

2.7.2. Mean-Reverting Market

As will be suggested in chapters 4 and 5, price mean reversion is the most appropriate quantitative model for energy markets.

2.7.2.1. Violin Analogy
The effect of mean reversion can perhaps be better understood through the violin string analogy: if we pluck the violin string, the string will revert to its place of equilibrium. We could not possibly measure just how quickly this reversion back to the equilibrium location would happen unless we actually plucked the string. Similarly, the only way to measure mean reversion is when the prices get plucked away from their nonevent levels and we observe them go back to more or less the levels they started from. If the prices consistently stay at their equilibrium level, we have no real means of measuring or deciding on how strong the mean reversion is. We might have to observe a great amount of data, over a long period of time, in order to capture the true behavior.

2.7.2.2. The Mean-Reversion Process
A *mean-reversion process* has a drift term that brings the variable being modeled back to some *equilibrium level*. The end result is that the variable tends to oscillate around this equilibrium. Every time the stochastic term gives the variable a push away from the equilibrium, the deterministic term will act in such a way that the variable will start heading back to the equilibrium. The stronger the mean reversion the quicker will be the trip of the variable from some extreme point away from the equilibrium back to it.

When a variable, $\widetilde{x}$, is mean reverting, it will have a deterministic term defined as follows:

$$E_t\left[d\widetilde{x}_t\right] = \alpha(\bar{x}_t - \widetilde{x}_t)dt \qquad (2-19)$$

where: α = rate of mean reversion
  $\bar{x}$ = the value around which x tends to oscillate

In the above equation, the mean-reverting parameter, α, must be positive.

If the variable at time t, $\widetilde{x}_t$, is greater than its equilibrium value at time t, $\bar{x}_t$, the drift term is negative, resulting in a pull back down toward the equilibrium level. Similarly, if the variable $\widetilde{x}_t$ is smaller than its equilibrium value at time t, the drift term is positive, pulling $\widetilde{x}_t$ back up to the higher equilibrium value. Note that the greater the mean-reverting parameter value, α, the greater is the pull back to the equilibrium level. Furthermore, for a daily variable change, the change in time, dt, in annualized terms is given by 1/365. If the mean-reverting parameter had a value of 365, the mean reversion would act so quickly as to bring the variable back to its equilibrium within a single day. While this is just a rough estimate, the value of $365/\alpha$ gives you an idea of how quickly the variable takes to get back to the equilibrium—in days.

Mean reversion can be either in the prices, or the log of prices, or in the yields (or rates). If the mean reversion is in the rates, x_t would represent the short-term rate. On the other hand, if mean reversion is in the price, x_t would be the price at time t. Finally, if mean reversion is in the log of the price, then x_t would be the natural log of the price at time t.

2.7.2.3. Mean Reversion Expressed as the Inverse of Time

When physicists measure the rate of decay of a particular substance, they often use the notion of half-life: the time it would take a given amount of the substance to decay to half its mass. Similarly, we can talk of measuring mean reversion in terms of the expected time it would take the variable to revert to some mean value, given that it is starting at an extreme point away from the mean value.

For example, the mean reversion measured from short-term interest rate historical data translates to a period of roughly three years. Hence, on average, it takes roughly three years for interest rates to decline to near their average values, given that they are starting from a point of high extreme, and similarly it takes roughly three years for interest rates to revert to the higher mean levels, given that they are starting from a point of low extreme.

Since the state of the economy changes relatively slowly, the effect of mean reversion has to be looked at on a time scale of years and even decades. The reversion force remains fairly weak from day to day, week to week, and even month to month. However, it is there nonetheless, and ignoring it would result in being at odds with the market reality. The valuation of long-term products ought to take this mean-reverting behavior into account.

Fundamental economic cycles do not appear to influence energy markets as much as they do interest rates. Instead, the mean reversion in energies appears to be directly related to their event behavior. Either a correction on the supply side, to match the demand side, or the actual dissipation of the event, such as the temperatures reverting to their more average seasonal levels, tends to cause the energy market prices to come back to their typical levels fairly quickly. Mean reversion in the energy markets is extremely strong, particularly when compared to the mean reversion measured in the interest rate markets.

In interest rate markets the mean reversion is assumed to directly affect interest rates rather than bond prices. These models are thus referred to as the *yield-mean-reverting* models. A rate- or yield-mean-reverting model allows the yields or the rates to mean-revert toward some mean level. By comparison, a *price-mean-reverting* model allows the prices to revert to some sort of a mean or equilibrium price level. Hence, the basic difference is that a price-mean-reverting model assumes that the mean reversion has a direct affect on the price, whereas a yield-mean-reverting model would have a secondary effect on the actual prices of bonds or assets driven by the underlying rate or yield model. Finally, the *log of the price-mean-reverting* model assumes that mean reversion affects the log of price directly, and the price itself only indirectly.

While we will be performing benchmarking and quantifying a few models in the next chapter, we will not spend a great deal of time in this book on the actual theoretical derivations of yield- or rate-mean-reverting models, as these have been described in quite a bit of detail in many books, articles, and publications.[5] Instead we will spend much more time on the model derivations of the other mean-reverting models.

2.8. THE TAYLOR SERIES AND ITO'S LEMMA

"Taylor series" and "Ito's Lemma" are mathematical relationships that we will use when building differential equations, pricing options and, perhaps most importantly, performing portfolio analysis. While the phrase "Ito's Lemma" may be justifiably scary to even those of us lucky enough to have technical degrees, I still feel that a passing knowledge of these concepts is a prerequisite for any risk manager.

2.8.1. The Taylor Series

Taylor series expansion helps model energy risk and portfolio returns in terms of the market's discrete building blocks. All of the differential equations that we solve in this book begin with the building of a Taylor series for portfolio returns. The Taylor series allows us to express the change in the value of a function, f, in terms of the changes in the variables determining the value of the function f. Specifically, if f is a function of variable $\tilde{x}$, the Taylor series expansion is expressed as follows:

$$df = \frac{\partial f}{\partial x}\,dx + \frac{\partial f}{\partial t}\,dt + \frac{1}{2}\frac{\partial^2 f}{\partial x^2}\,d\tilde{x}^2 + O(dt) \qquad (2-20)$$

where: f = function
            $\tilde{x}$ = variable
      $O(dt)$ = higher order terms in dt

The variable $\tilde{x}$ follows its own process. If it is normally distributed, the process for $\tilde{x}$ is defined by the following:

$$d\tilde{x} = a\,dt + b\tilde{\varepsilon}\sqrt{dt} \qquad (2-21)$$

where: a = the mean value of $\tilde{x}$

        b = the annualized standard deviation of $\tilde{x}$

        $\tilde{\varepsilon}$ = a normally distributed variable

Note that $d\tilde{x}$ has terms of order dt and $\sqrt{dt}$, while $(d\tilde{x})^2$ would have terms of order dt, dt^2, and $dt^{3/2}$.

The first important assumption in the above equation is that the stochastic term in the change in the variable $\tilde{x}$ is proportional to the square root of time. The second important assumption is that the change in time, dt, is assumed to be small. In the Taylor series expansion (Equation 2–20), these two assumptions allow us to retain the terms of order $\sqrt{dt}$ and dt, and let all higher order terms in dt go to zero. In the expansion, all the higher order terms in dt are denoted as $O(dt)$. Thus, the assumption is that $O(dt)$ goes to zero. However, we can also relax this assumption, resulting in the inclusion of higher order terms in dt, which we do not assume away as insignificant.

2.8.2. Ito's Lemma

Ito's Lemma represents a specific treatment of the stochastic variable in the Taylor expansion. We assume that as the increment of time dt goes to zero, we can ignore all terms of order higher than dt (such as dt^2 or $dt^{3/2}$). In the derivation of differential equations this assumption is consistent with the assumption of continuous hedging.

Given the assumption that dt goes to zero, and given the character of the normally distributed stochastic variable, $\widetilde{\varepsilon}$, with a mean of zero and a standard deviation of one, the following must hold:

$$E\left[\widetilde{\varepsilon}\sqrt{dt}\right] = 0 \tag{2-22}$$

$$E\left[\widetilde{\varepsilon}^{2}dt\right] = dt \tag{2-23}$$

$$E\left[\widetilde{\varepsilon}^{4}dt^{2}\right] = O(dt^{2}) \rightarrow 0 \tag{2-24}$$

Since the expected value of the stochastic term in $d\widetilde{x}$ raised to the fourth power—is of order dt^2, this term must go to zero, requiring that the stochastic term squared must be a constant, specifically dt:

$$\widetilde{\varepsilon}^{2}dt = constant \tag{2-25}$$
$$\widetilde{\varepsilon}^{2}dt \rightarrow dt \tag{2-26}$$

We can now plug the above results into the Taylor series for the function, f, to obtain the following:

$$df = \frac{\partial f}{\partial x}dx + \frac{\partial f}{\partial t}dt + \frac{1}{2}\frac{\partial^{2}f}{\partial x^{2}}b^{2}dt = \left(\frac{\partial f}{\partial x}a + \frac{\partial f}{\partial t} + \frac{1}{2}\frac{\partial^{2}f}{\partial x^{2}}b^{2}\right)dt + \frac{\partial f}{\partial x}bd\widetilde{z} \tag{2-27}$$

where: $d\widetilde{z} = \widetilde{\varepsilon}\sqrt{dt}$

We will be using Ito's Lemma, and thus the assumption of continuous hedging, in deriving the differential equations for forward prices and option prices. We will be using the Taylor series, without the additional constraints of Ito's Lemma, in performing portfolio analysis.

2.9. LESSONS FROM MONEY MARKETS

The equity markets were the first markets to develop and mature. The interest rate markets followed with the deregulation of the banking industry in the United States. The interest rate markets are now the largest derivative markets in the country, and the crude oil, heating oil, and natural gas markets—while nothing to sneeze at—are still relatively small when compared with the interest rate markets. The electricity markets are currently going through deregulation, and they may prove to be truly a rival in size to the interest rate markets.

The electricity markets, as well as other energy markets that have a long way to go toward maturing in terms of trading liquidity and market sophistication, can learn a number of lessons from the growth in the interest rate markets.

2.9.1. Modeling Price vs. Rate: Defining the Market Drivers

One of the most difficult tasks of financial modeling is to define what exactly ultimately to model in order to provide a basis for all other valuation and risk management calculations. In the example of interest rate markets, do we start by modeling the fundamental market drivers such as inflation and the Federal Reserve moves and then translate these drivers into bond-price models, or do we start by modeling the bond-price behavior? The general market has answered this question by modeling the interest rates; interest rates capture all the fundamental market driver effects and yet directly relate to bond prices.

In the interest rate markets, most of the models are applied to short-term interest rates. These interest rate models are then applied to arrive at arbitrage-free pricing of bonds or other derivative products. The underlying process, then, is for the interest rates rather than for the bond prices.

In the commodity markets we are faced with the same problem. Do we model the energy generation process or the economics of supply and demand, or do we model the prices for each month of the year, to ultimately value all the energy products? Or maybe we can cut down the number of explanatory variables to just a few, and perhaps model only the spot price, the equilibrium price under no events, and the seasonality factors? Another choice is to model the underlying price yields, very much the same way that in the interest rate markets the rates are modeled and then the prices are modeled as a function of the underlying rate models. This would be consistent with some of the convenience yield models, where instead of modeling the actual prices, forward price yields are used to capture some of the supply-and-demand and storage effects unique to physical commodities.

While in the interest rate markets the trading world truly is driven by the behavior of the interest rates—the Fed moves the discount rates directly—in the physical commodity world the price yields are, from an intuitive trader view, of secondary importance. Instead, the prices tend to be the direct media within which market factors tend to portray themselves. Of course, this could be very much a discussion of a personal nature unless we have a set of quantitative benchmarks against which we can judge what came first: the chicken or the egg, i.e., the commodity prices or their yields.

However, if we are indeed to learn from the experience of the interest rate markets, which during their own development of many years had to come up with a set of models that were interest-rate-market specific, we should be looking at new ideas for the physical commodity markets if we are truly to capture all the specifics of the physical commodity behavior—rather than trying to "Band-Aid" the existing models from interest rates and equities to conform to the commodity price behavior. Ultimately, it should be the modeling benchmarks that should help us decide on what model is most appropriate.

2.9.2. Yield vs. Forward Rate Curves

A topic that has received a good amount of analysis by the interest rate trading houses is not necessarily one that you would see much of in the academic literature on interest rate behavior. Rather it is more of an issue of implementation and has to do with constructing forward rate or yield curves. A forward rate curve is a curve of short-term rates—such as 3-month LIBOR rates—as seen at different points in time in the future. A yield curve, on the other hand, is a discount rate curve, with each point on the curve representing the discount rate from today to the point of discounting.

The yield curve represents average rates from today to points along the time axis, whereas the forward rate curve represents the short-term rates at different points in time. The interest rate relationships, required by no-arbitrage conditions, allow the translation of the yield curve to the forward rate curve and vice versa. Since the yield curve is in fact an average-rate curve, it tends to look much smoother and is generally much easier to build. Even when using linear interpolation between the yields, we can obtain a fairly smooth-looking yield curve.

So it was that most trading places did exactly this: they built nice, smooth yield curves, typically using linear interpolation between the points, and everybody appeared pretty happy. That is, everybody but the forward rate traders, who often noticed that the forward rates resulting from these generally smooth yield curves tended to take rather nonintuitive jumps into very large or very small (even negative) values at what appeared to be almost random points in the future. The problem was that even the smallest-looking kink in the yield curve, which is an average-rate curve, translated into huge jumps in the forward rate terms. Hence, while linear interpolation might have been a quick and dirty implementation that worked just fine for yield curve building, it tended to be too crude for implementation in building forward rate curves.

We have a similar problem in energies regarding the building of price and volatility curves, particularly in the case of electricity. There is really nothing wrong with building average price and average volatility curves as long as all the settlement prices of derivative products and all the hedges are also defined as averages. However, this is generally not the case, and all of a sudden the average price and average volatility curves become problematic.

Instead, developing a methodology for the building of discrete price curves and volatility matrices—while requiring a bit more thought in the implementation process than just using linear interpolation—will provide a basis for an extremely flexible and versatile framework for pricing the full spectrum of energy derivative products.

2.9.3. Drawbacks of Single-Factor Mean-Reverting Models

Most players in the interest rate markets will agree that the interest rates do exhibit some amount of mean reversion. They might also acknowledge that such a mean-reverting model ought to have at least two drivers, a short-term rate and a long-term mean, or equilibrium rate. The long-term mean rate tends to affect the behavior of the forward rates far out into the future, while the short-term rate defines the behavior of the interest rates in the near future. All the rates in between reflect a mix of the two behaviors, with various weightings on the short vs. the long-term mean rate.

While most players will agree that this framework might reflect the market reality fairly well, very few have actually implemented a two-factor mean-reverting interest rate model. The reason is typically that the costs tend generally to outweigh the benefits. Even a sophisticated trading operation that has made a large investment in the pricing methodologies might shy away from implementing a two-factor option pricing model if that model takes a long time to run for each deal being priced. Instead, a good number of interest rate trading houses have implemented a single-factor interest rate mean-reverting model that assumes that the long-term mean rate remains fixed over time. Of course, this is not representative of reality, and hence the long-term mean rate needs to be recalibrated on a continuous basis in order to ensure that the resulting curves are marked to market.

However, the biggest drawback of installing a single-factor mean-reverting model is in the case of options pricing: the fact that the long-term rate is fixed results in a model-implied volatility term structure that has the volatilities going to zero as expiration time increases. Hence, in order to get around this point another model "Band-Aid" needs to be put on: Spot volatilities have to be increased to nonintuitive levels so that the long-term options do not lose all the volatility value—as in the marketplace they certainly do not.

It is in such cases that a simpler model, such as Black-Scholes or Black, might have been a better choice, because the model inputs would have retained the flexibility and the intuitiveness that ends up being lost by implementing a half-baked model. Or rather, if you want to be sophisticated in modeling, getting only halfway there may put you in a worse position than not attempting it at all. Quite a few banks had to discover this the hard way, and after they had already spent quite a bit of money on the implementation. With this said, let me also say that a good, sophisticated model can be quite valuable, not only for product valuation but also for hedging and risk management precision. And there are also a number of banks that have proven that this approach can be a successful strategy.

2.9.4. Drawbacks of Single-Factor Non-Mean-Reverting Models

The above section dealt with the downfalls of a single-factor mean-reverting model. This section, on the other hand, will deal with the downfalls of not using a mean-reverting model when the market is indeed mean-reverting. Assuming a simple lognormal model for the underlying distribution when the underlying distribution is in fact not lognormal will impact valuation and hedging. The differences between the distributions are particularly obvious when pricing out-of-the-money options, where the tails of the distribution play a very important role. It is no surprise then that if a lognormal model is used to price a far out-of-the-money option, the price can be very different from a mean-reverting model's price.

A general problem that has occurred in the interest rate markets is that a simple Black, and hence lognormal, model was used to price an at-the-money option, and was sufficient when the deal was struck. However, as time went by and the market moved, the option found itself out-of-the-money and therefore extremely sensitive to the lognormal distribution assumption. Most of such tail-effects did generally get treated by the trading groups through the inclusion of volatility strike-structures (which also include other effects, such as that of illiquidity or the smallest price ticks allowed on the exchanges). However, unless the market exists for such out-of-the-money options, it is very difficult to "guesstimate" the effect on volatility without an actual two-factor model implementation.

2.9.5. Volatility Market Discovery

Finally, for those energy market participants who are waiting for the development of certain options markets in order to be participating in and/or performing option mark-to-market valuations, a word of caution learned from the—by comparison—well-developed interest rate markets: Chances are that the options markets will take a while to develop, and chances are that certain option products will never achieve the level of liquidity a mark-to-market valuation always craves.

The swaptions interest rate market never reached the liquidity levels of interest rate caps and floors. There is enough trading to allow a certain amount of market discovery, but not necessarily the full picture. In such situations it is up to the market players to fill in the picture in order to do the valuation and the hedging. Hence, the lesson to be learned here is that as options markets develop in the energy markets, a market maker would be wise to consider volatility estimation methodologies that will allow for proper valuation of options in the absence of liquid options markets, and that will allow for easy integration once the options markets do become active.

ENDNOTES

1. Jarrow & Rudd, "Approximate Option Valuation," p. 104.
2. When the Black-Scholes model first emerged from the academic world, it provided a new paradigm of pricing arbitrage-free options. Once accepted by the marketplace, the model was here to stay.
3. The end result of a single-factor mean-reverting model is that the volatilities of such a process tend to go to zero over a long period of time. Most market players would agree that this is not reflective of the market reality. And yet, some people still use the model by making certain adjustments during implementation.
4. For more information, see Brealy, Myers, and Marcus, *Principles of Corporate Finance,* chapter 7 (New York: McGraw-Hill, 1995.
5. For a good introduction to yield-based models, see Hull, *Options, Futures and Other Derivative Securities,* chapter 15.

CHAPTER 3

Essential Statistical Tools

3.1. INTRODUCTION

To value and manage energy risk, we need to be equipped with the essential quantitative and statistical tools. These tools capture the reality of the market and express its characteristics. In addition, statistics provides the essential benchmarks for testing models and judging between them.[1] This chapter will introduce these statistical tools and demonstrate how they can be used.

Many books have been written about statistical analysis of various sorts. Here we will go into the details of statistical analysis only to the extent that it is useful in energy modeling.[2] Hence, we will view statistical analysis as one particular toolbox with a particular set of tools. We will leave the detailed description of how these statistical tools were made and the description of their various uses to other books.

The necessity of using statistics offers good news and bad news for energy managers. The good news is that statistics provide terrific valuation tools. The bad news is that even managers need to understand some basic statistics. During the writing of this book, serious thought was given to relegating these methods to an appendix, out of the way so as not to scare the readers who hated *Statistics 101* in college. Instead, I decided to confront statistical analysis up front, out in the open, because valuing and managing energy derivatives absolutely depends on time series and distribution analysis. Quantitative experts should be able to explain and defend their models in terms of these tools; managers should possess at least a passing knowledge of the terms and their benefits.

3.2. TIME SERIES AND DISTRIBUTION ANALYSIS

Time series analysis and *distribution analysis* are two important data analysis methods used throughout this book. They represent two approaches to analyzing data (see Table 3–1). In time series analysis changes in the price from day to day are examined. In distribution analysis price levels over a period of time are evaluated. In businesses today, time series analysis occurs much more commonly than distribution analysis but, with luck, distribution analysis will

T A B L E 3–1

Comparison of Time Series and Distribution Analysis

	Time Series Analysis	Distribution Analysis
Purpose	Analyzes price change from day to day	Analyzes price behavior over period of time
Good for	• Parameter calibration • Event and seasonal calibration	• Testing, benchmarking, and selecting models • Getting insights about option pricing
Use in business	Relatively common	Uncommon but should be used more

become more common since, as shall be seen, each method offers its own unique value. Time series and distribution analysis each tells a "different part of the story." Both should be used for proper valuation and risk management.

3.2.1. Time Series Analysis

Time series analysis is the process of analyzing daily price returns. A very simple type of time series analysis involves taking a data set of prices and calculating the price drift and annualized volatility.

The most common application of time series analysis is in the calibration of model parameters. The process involves using statistical "fitting" procedures to best match a data set with a model. The object is to estimate model parameter values for the model that "best fit" or explain the data. For complex models, nonlinear statistical estimation may be required. Additionally, the estimated parameters typically will not precisely "match" the data set. The difference between the model predictions and the actual data set results in model *residuals*:

$$Actual\ data = Model\ predictions + residuals \qquad (3-1)$$

If the model does a good job, these residuals should essentially be "noise," the random by-products of a nonbiased difference between the actual data and model predictions. These residuals need to be tested to ensure that they are normally distributed. (See later sections of this chapter for testing model appropriateness.)

Price return analysis is performed either through linear or nonlinear regression analysis. Model parameters from a simple model, such as the lognormal model, can be estimated through a linear regression, while more complicated models, such as price mean reversion, might require nonlinear regression analysis. The decision of using linear vs. nonlinear analysis has to do with how the model processes can be translated so that when the regression is performed the residuals can correctly be assumed to be normally distributed.

A historical time series of prices will give us some first clues as to the price behavior. When the seasonality factors are very strong—as in the case of electricity markets—they can be identified simply by a quick look at the price time series. By comparison, looking at price returns instead of prices may obscure the effects of seasonality due to the typically very large randomness in the daily price returns of energy markets. By looking at the price time series we might be able to identify the historical seasonality effects. Figure 3–1 shows the time series of spot prices for Southwest Power Pool (SPP) electricity. You might be able to see both winter and summer seasonality peaks within the historical data. Figure 3–2 shows the same data fitted for the seasonality factors.

Similarly, if the market tends to experience a good number of events, followed by a strong reversion toward what might be considered the equilibrium price level, then even this may be observed from the time series of price. The general market trend—up, down, or flat—and the general market behavior around some equilibrium level is what typically can be observed through the historical time series of prices.

3.2.2. Distribution Analysis

Distribution analysis focuses on price behavior over time. It provides meaningful insights into market behavior. The technique helps with:

- Creating benchmarks for actual market behavior
- Testing models against such benchmarks
- Comparing models

A price distribution defines the probabilities of prices taking on various values. If we are analyzing actual data, the distribution is defined by the "path" of prices observed over the time period. If we are simulating a model, the distribution shows all the possible values that the spot price might take on over some time period with associated probabilities. We represent distributions visually as histograms or probability graphs.

F I G U R E   3 – 1

SPP on Peak Electricity Spot Prices

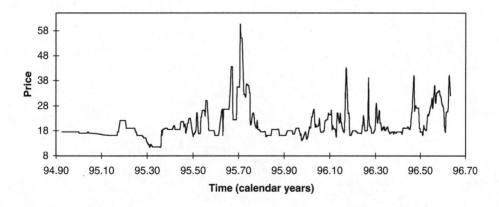

SPP on Peak Spot Prices and Fitted Seasonality

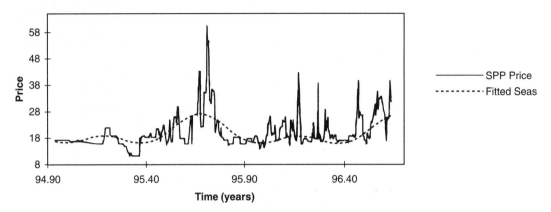

3.2.2.1. Characteristics of a Distribution

One nice feature about distributions is that they demonstrate unique characteristics, which can be used in describing them. Figure 3–3 demonstrates the most important statistical characteristics:

- The "mean" represents the value around which the distribution is centered.
- The "standard deviation" suggests the width of the distribution. One standard deviation roughly equals the width of the distribution in which a price will fall 66% of the time the percentage is exact in case of a normal distribution; two standard deviations roughly represents the price range in which a price would fall 95% of the time; three standard deviations roughly represents the price range for 99% of the time.

Variable X Distribution

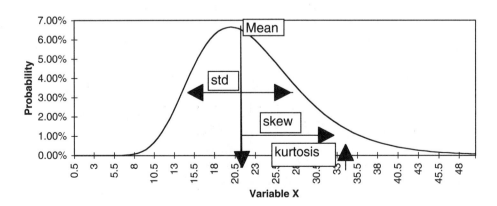

◆ The "skew" reflects whether the prices distribute symmetrically around the mean or are skewed to the left or to the right of the mean.

◆ Finally, "kurtosis" describes the "fatness" of the tails of the distribution. Kurtosis helps us understand the likelihood of extreme events; fat tails suggest higher chances of prices being very high or very low.

The concepts of mean, standard deviation, skew, and kurtosis will be used throughout this book, particularly because they represent characteristics that we can visualize. We will not, however, usually employ the concepts in our equations. A related and preferred method is the concept of mathematical "moments," which are described in the following section.

3.2.2.2. The "Moments" of Truth

A distribution can be characterized through mathematical concepts called "moments." These moments directly relate to mean, standard deviation, skew, and kurtosis of a distribution (see Table 3–2). The energy risk manager should understand and employ moments for three important reasons:

◆ Moments are relatively easy to calculate.

◆ Moments can be used for correcting modeling errors.

◆ Moments can be very important during option valuation.

The *n-th* moment of a distribution for variable $\tilde{x}$ is the expected value of the variable raised to the *n-th* power. Mathews and Walker[3] express this as:

$$E[\tilde{x}^n] = \int p(x)x^n dx \qquad (3-2)$$

where: $E[...]$ = represents the taking of an expected value
   $\tilde{x}$ = variable
   $p(x)$ = the probability that the variable takes on the value x

While one can calculate as many moments as one wishes, the most important moments used in characterizing a distribution are the first four moments.

The first moment is the expected value of the variable raised to the first power, or simply

---

TABLE 3–2

Moments

Moment	Related to
First, M_1	Mean
Second, M_2	Standard deviation
Third, M_3	Skew
Fourth, M_4	Kurtosis

put, the mean or average of a distribution. Using spot prices as our variable, we calculate the first moment as:

$$M_1 = E[\widetilde{S}_t] = S_t \tag{3-3}$$

where: M_1 = the first moment of the distribution

$\widetilde{S}_t$ = spot price at time t

S_t = mean of the distribution of $\widetilde{S}_t$

The second moment is a measurement of the distribution's width:

$$M_2 = E[(\widetilde{S}_t)^2] \tag{3-4}$$

We can derive the variance of spot price levels by using the first and second moments as follows:

$$Var(\widetilde{S}_t) = E[(\widetilde{S}_t - S_t)^2] = M_2 - M_1^2 \tag{3-5}$$

The standard deviation is then given by:

$$STD(\widetilde{S}_t) = \sqrt{Var(S_t)} = \sqrt{M_2 - M_1^2} \tag{3-6}$$

The third moment is the expected value of the variable raised to the power of three:

$$M_3 = E[(\widetilde{S}_t)^3] \tag{3-7}$$

where: M_3 = the third moment

The skew of the distribution is the third moment adjusted for the distribution center. Skew can be expressed as follows:

$$Skew = E[(\widetilde{S}_t - S_t)^3] = M_3 - 3M_2M_1 + 2M_1^3 \tag{3-8}$$

And finally, the fourth moment is given by

$$M_4 = E[(\widetilde{S}_t)^4] \tag{3-9}$$

where: M_4 = the fourth moment

The fourth moment relates to the kurtosis of the distribution as follows:

$$Kurtosis = E[(\widetilde{S}_t - S_t)^4] = M_4 - 4M_3M_1 + 6M_2M_1^2 - 3M_1^4 \tag{3-10}$$

Note: In the case where the distribution is centered around the mean of zero, the first moment would equal zero. Thus, in this special case, the second moment, M_2, equals the variance; the third moment, M_3, equals the skew; and the fourth moment, M_4, equals the kurtosis.

3.2.2.3. Relating Actual and Model Distributions

As suggested, distribution analysis plays a key role in judging the appropriateness of models. We use the distribution moments to relate the actual to the model-generated distributions.

Given a spot price model, the model defines what the distribution of the spot prices should look like at some point in time. This model-generated distribution shows all the possible values that the spot price might take at a single instant in time, with associated probabilities. However, the actual historical data that we have to work with represent not a distribution of prices at a single point in time, but rather a path of prices over a period of time. Thus, the actual historical prices reflect a price distribution of a path of prices over time.

In order to be able to relate our model-implied distributions to the historical price distributions, we need to define a set of moments that represent time averages over a period of time t:

$$M_n^{AV} = \frac{1}{T} \int_t^T dt\, M_n(t) \qquad (3-11)$$

where: $M_n(t)$ = the n-th moment as observed at time t

3.2.2.4. Useful Common Distributions
Another nice thing about distributions is that we understand very well certain general types of useful and common distributions. When we recognize a type of a distribution, we can then apply what we know about that type of a distribution. Two types of distributions are commonly used in valuation and risk management of derivative products:

- Normal distributions (see Figure 3–4) are commonly used throughout science and business. A normal distribution is perfectly symmetric. The skew is equal to zero, with a kurtosis given by three times the variance squared. If the mean is zero, this can be written as:

$$M_4^{Normal} = 3\left(M_2^{Normal}\right)^2 \qquad (3-12)$$

- Lognormal distributions (see Figure 3–5) are often used in financial models. The lognormal distribution is skewed to the right and its values are always positive.

FIGURE 3-4

Normal Distribution

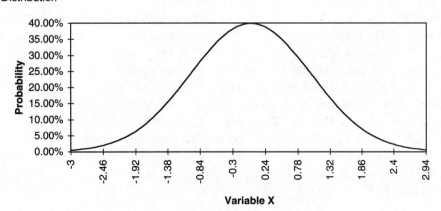

FIGURE 3-5

Lognormal Distribution

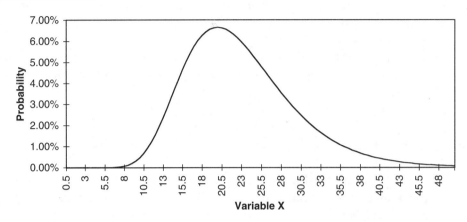

3.3. OTHER STATISTICAL TESTS

In addition to time series and distribution analysis, we need to add several statistical tests to our modeling toolbox.

3.3.1. The Q-Q Plot

A common modeling process includes determining if a data set is normally distributed. For example, consider residuals (between actual and model estimated values) that are assumed to be normally distributed. We need a test to check that they are indeed normally distributed and include no bias. One test for normality is the quantile-to-quantile (Q-Q) test or plot. It also provides a quick visual test.

The Q-Q test compares the actual probabilities of the random variable to the expected probabilities if this variable were normally distributed. If the variable is indeed normally distributed, the Q-Q plot looks like a nice diagonal line, indicating that the actual variable probability distribution matches the expected probability distribution for a normally distributed variable. Figure 3–6 shows a Q-Q plot for a normally distributed variable.

Figure 3–7, on the other hand, shows the Q-Q plot for the case where the random variable is not normally distributed. The actual probability distribution does not match the expected distribution for a normally distributed variable, and we do not get a one-for-one fit from the Q-Q plot. In fact, this kind of "S"-shaped Q-Q plot tells us the following: The rather flat and wide middle section implies that the variable has too many occurrences of values in the middle range, more than it should given that it is supposed to be normally distributed. Similarly, the flat ends of the S-shaped graph tell us that the tails of the variable distribution are not what they would be if they indeed were normally distributed.

FIGURE 3-6

Q-Q Plot for a Simulated Normal Variable

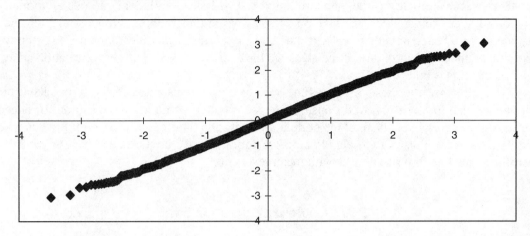

Mathematically, the basic idea is that a normally distributed random variable, $\tilde{x}$, with a standard deviation of one, will have the probability of having some value k defined as follows:

$$p(\tilde{x} = k) = \left(\frac{e^{-(k^2/2)}}{\sqrt{2\pi}} \right) \qquad (3-13)$$

Every type of distribution has a specific probability function, which we can use when taking expected values, a process that is very important in valuation and portfolio analysis.

FIGURE 3-7

Q-Q Plot for a Simulated Nonnormal Variable

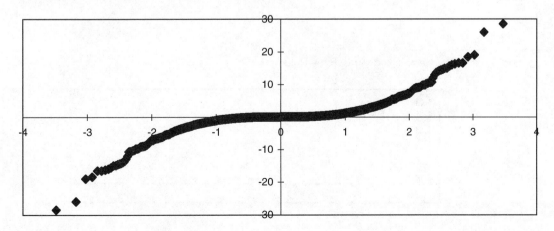

3.3.2. The Autocorrelation Test

Another test for normality is the autocorrelation test. If indeed a random variable is normally distributed, then the variables will take on values that are uncorrelated. For example, let's say that we go on a ten-step random walk. If our steps are normally distributed, then every step we take will be independent of any of the steps we have already taken. The autocorrelation analysis tests that this is indeed true.

The autocorrelation test calculates the various correlations between the steps taken: for adjoining steps, for once-removed steps, for the steps two steps removed, and so on. If indeed the steps are uncorrelated, then all the correlations between the steps will be zero. Figures 3–8 and 3–9 show the plots of two sets of autocorrelations, one for price returns that are normally distributed and one for price returns with mean reversion.

3.3.3. Measures of Fit

As described above, the primary application of time series analysis is in the calibration of model parameters using statistical iterations applied to a distribution of actual prices. The optimum parameters are often judged by measures of fit, including the R^2 statistic. The "square root of mean squared error" is another measure of fit directly related to the R^2 statistic.

3.3.3.1. Mean-Squared Error
The mean-squared error is the standard deviation of model residuals. Since we would like our model to predict as much of the actual market data as possible, we would therefore like the mean-squared error to be as small as possible.

3.3.3.2. R-Squared
The R^2 statistic is a measure that tells us how much of the actual uncertainty in the actual data is captured (or explained) by the model being tested. R^2 is measured in percentage terms. If R^2

FIGURE 3–8

Autocorrelations for Sample Lognormal Price Returns

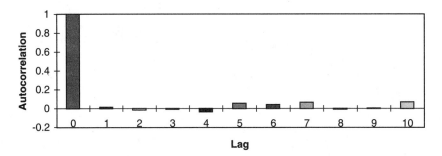

FIGURE 3-9

Autocorrelations for Sample PMR Price Returns

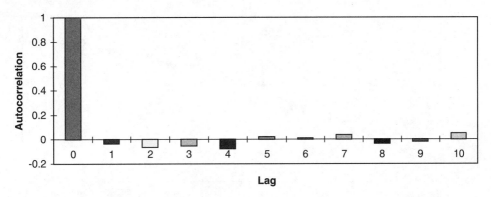

equals 1.0, the model has 100% predictive power. On the other hand, if R^2 equals zero, then the model has no predictive value. Specifically, the statistic is given by the following:

$$R^2 = 1 - \left(\frac{\text{Mean Squared Error}}{\text{Var(actual data)}} \right) \qquad (3-14)$$

And in the case where the mean of the residuals is zero, we have:

$$R^2 = 1 - \left(\frac{\text{Var(model residuals)}}{\text{Var(actual data)}} \right) \qquad (3-15)$$

3.4. HOW STATISTICS HELPS TO UNDERSTAND REALITY

Now that we have laid some ground rules, let's start with a simple example of how our statistical methods can be used to understand market reality. Then we will proceed to more complex, realistic examples.

3.4.1. A Simple Case

Consider an oversimplified example of extreme price mean reversion: Suppose, in a particular market, the price of electricity jumps between $10 and $12 from day to day for a year.[4] Using time series analysis of price returns, we calculate a huge annualized daily volatility of over 300%. Does such a large volatility tell us everything we need to know about this price behavior? Definitely not.

If we simply assumed that this was a lognormal price process, we would expect prices to range roughly between $0 and $40 roughly 66% of the time, and to be outside this range roughly 34% of the time. But if we also perform distribution analysis, we find that the price distribution over the year remains very narrow. By combining time series and distribution analysis,

F I G U R E   3–10

Path 1 Time Series

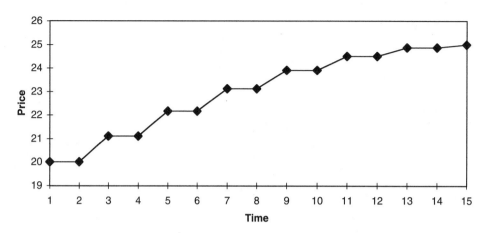

we can tell the full story of this particular market price behavior. The end result is that a simple lognormal model would not be appropriate for this price behavior.

3.4.2. The Difference Between Price and Return

Additional examples are provided in chapter 2 where, for example, we present two price paths that have the same resulting price-return distributions but very different price distributions (see Figures 2–7 through 2–12). Figures 3–10 through 3–15 show yet another set of two paths.

F I G U R E   3–11

Path 1 Return Distribution

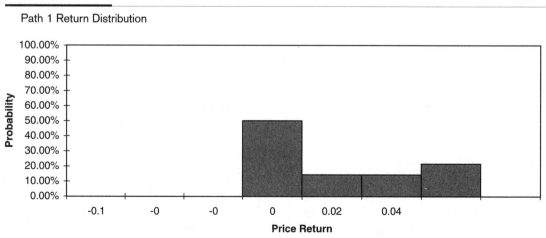

F I G U R E 3–12

Path 1 Price Distribution

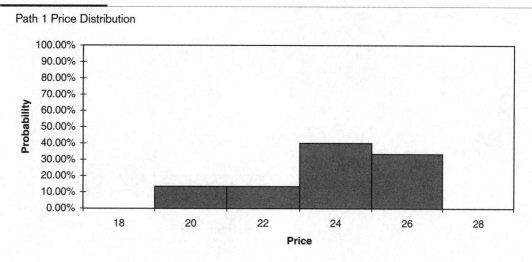

While Paths 1 and 2 share identical price distributions, their price return distributions vary significantly. In the above examples, by neglecting to analyze either the price returns or the price distribution, we exclude key information from our analysis.

3.4.3. Distinguishing Drift Terms

From a modeling point of view, perhaps the biggest reason for using both time series and distribution analysis relates to the need for the use of both methods in order to fully capture the effects of the drift and stochastic elements of a price model.

F I G U R E 3–13

Path 2 Time Series

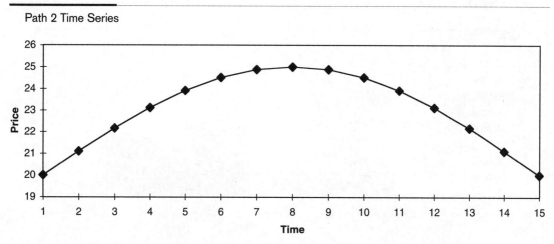

F I G U R E   3–14

Path 2 Return Distribution

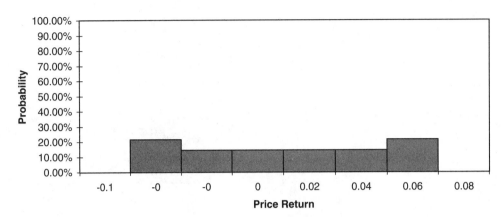

Both drift (deterministic) and stochastic (random) elements contribute to price levels and their returns. The problem is that the stochastic behavior captured by the price return is generally much greater in magnitude than the deterministic behavior. We perform time series analysis of actual market data to estimate model parameters. But we also need to perform distribution analysis to visibly identify the deterministic behavior over time. This phenomenon also represents one of the most important reasons why using time series analysis cannot enable us to judge between competing models and why distribution analysis is absolutely required.

F I G U R E   3–15

Path 2 Price Distribution

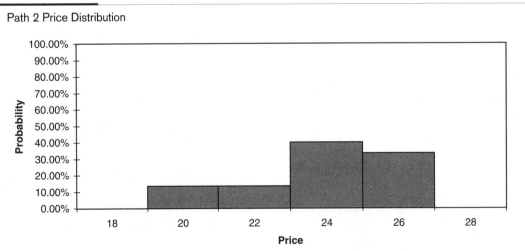

3.5. THE SIX-STEP MODEL SELECTION PROCESS

Our essential statistical tools provide the benchmarks to test the effectiveness of individual models and to compare alternatives. In order to get the "full story," we will apply different types of reality tests to capture the various behavior characteristics:

- ◆ Time series analysis of price returns
- ◆ Distribution analysis of price levels
- ◆ Other statistical tests

Remember: A good model should be able to capture most of the market characteristics defined by the different types of analysis.

Selecting the most appropriate model involves the following six-step model selection process:

Step 1: Informally look at the actual market data.

Step 2: Create a short list of possible models.

Step 3: Calibrate parameters through time series analysis.

Step 4: Generate distributions from models.

Step 5: Perform distribution analysis.

Step 6: Compare results and select the most appropriate model.

3.5.1. Step 1: An Informal Look

The very best way to compare models is to begin by analyzing the market data. The first look at the data should involve a descriptive, nonquantitative analysis of the price time series. Ask an experienced staff member to comment on the price spikes or the market turbulence in the data and how these can be related to any fundamental drivers. Such comments can be extremely helpful in getting a first feeling for the price behavior.

3.5.2. Step 2: A Short List of Possible Models

The second step involves creating a short list of models that should be considered. The models selected should offer characteristics that fit with what one would expect are the market characteristics based on an informal review of the data or experience in the market. In this book, our short list will include lognormal price model and mean reversion models.

3.5.3. Step 3: Time Series Analysis

The third step of the analysis includes a close look at the historical time series of daily price returns. Analyzing the price returns provides us with estimates for model parameters and seasonality parameters.

The analysis of daily price returns yields the model parameter values, which are important in defining the day-to-day behavior of spot prices. Specifically, the expected daily drift in the spot price returns—while generally insignificant compared to the magnitude of the stochastic portion of the daily price return—can still be calibrated from the time series of price returns.

The autocorrelation of price returns might point at whether a mean-reverting model might be more appropriate than a non-mean-reverting model. Negative autocorrelation is a sign of strong mean reversion in the spot prices. However, performing a rough autocorrelation measurement that assumes a constant drift term will carry a good amount of noise in its estimate. This noise may be overpowered in the case where the mean reversion is very strong.

The daily price returns are also valuable sources of information on market volatility, both in noneventful times and during events. Furthermore, they show the effects of events on the marketplace in terms of how long the events tend to stick around and affect the prices.

Because the stochastic term is generally so much greater than the deterministic term in the daily spot price returns, chances are that any model fitted to the daily price returns will yield roughly the same R^2 values, and they will typically be small. This is all the more true in energies, which have generally much greater daily spot volatility than can be seen in interest rate markets or even equity markets, resulting in a stochastic term that therefore has a greater power over the deterministic term. Using R^2 values as a means of benchmarking in the analysis of daily price returns is of no real value when the R^2 values are roughly the same across various models.

To conclude this third step, the means of testing the spot price model for performance when applied to the daily price returns is not through the model's forecasting power, but rather through its giving us residuals that are normally distributed. The normality tests, such as the Q-Q plots or the autocorrelation analysis of the residuals, are an indicator of how appropriate the model is to the actual spot price behavior.

3.5.4. Step 4: From Underlying Price Models to Distributions

The next step is to generate distributions based on the model(s) that are being tested. Every spot price model implies a particular price distribution. Given a model, we can formulate the spot prices as functions of time, the model parameters, and random variables that are normally distributed. From this formulation we can either mathematically calculate what the model-implied moments ought to be, or we can simulate the prices and from these simulations estimate the moments. Either way, a model will give us a set of price distribution moments for each point in time. We can integrate these moments over time to obtain the model-implied price distribution moments over a period of time.

While the spot price models specifically provide us with a means of defining the spot price behavior from day to day, their implied distributions provide us with a means of looking at what the models tell us about price behavior over a longer period of time. A good model, which truly captures market reality, will do so both in the short term and in the long run. A good model will capture the day-to-day market behavior characteristics as well as the long-term market price distribution characteristics.

When we perform time series analysis and extract the normally distributed residual terms, we should check that these normally distributed residuals are indeed what the model claims they are: normally distributed. As stated earlier, a normally distributed variable will have a well-defined distribution, with well-defined probabilities of the variable reaching certain values. The Q-Q plot and auto-correlation tests are ideal for checking for normality.

3.5.5. Step 5: Distribution Analysis

Distribution analysis gives us the means of understanding how the fundamental drivers of the marketplace and the financial models ultimately converge to reflect the characteristics of the price behavior. The financial models, through a bit of mathematics or simulations, can be used to tell us how the price distributions ought to look over time, given the particular model assumptions. The fundamentals of the actual market give us the historical price distributions. The comparison of the two tells us how well the models capture the reality.

Figure 3–16 shows us two types of price distributions: one is the distribution resulting from a lognormal spot price model, and the other is the distribution resulting from a price mean-reverting spot price model. In the simulations of these models, both models were given the same daily price return volatility, or randomness, and yet the price mean-reverting distribution has a much narrower width as compared to the lognormal.

The above example follows in the footsteps of the 2-path examples provided in chapter 2 (Figures 2–7 through 2–12) and earlier in this chapter (Figures 3–10 through 3–15) to show us the value of distribution analysis. Distribution analysis is the necessary tool in deciding how well the pricing model fits the market reality. It provides us with an almost immediate visual test, and also with a means of translating what might appear as very theoretical and nonintuitive modeling concepts into the concrete reality of price behavior. It is the ultimate benchmarking tool between models.

FIGURE 3–16

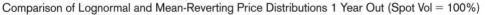

Comparison of Lognormal and Mean-Reverting Price Distributions 1 Year Out (Spot Vol = 100%)

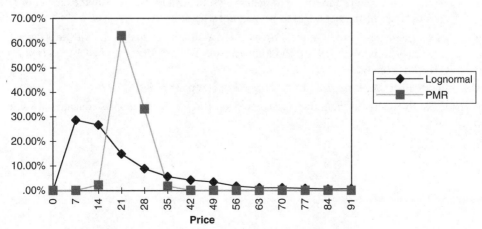

3.5.6. Step 6: Select the Most Appropriate Model

Once all the work is done in the first five steps, the energy risk manager must weigh all the evidence and select the most appropriate model. One should employ the kinds of intuition, statistical tests, and business judgment described through the first three chapters of this book.

3.6. RELEVANCE TO OPTION PRICING

In addition to benchmarking, the distribution analysis helps us gain an intuitive understanding of the option pricing issues in a particular market. For example, if the historical price distribution has very fat tails, then an option pricing model that does not capture this market reality and instead implies much thinner tails would end up underpricing the out-of-the-money options. We can use the distribution characteristics to help us determine the pricing issues key in properly valuing options.

For example, a lognormal price distribution and a mean-reverting price distribution, which give the same standard deviation of prices, will have different distribution tails. In fact, the price mean-reverting process results in slightly fatter tails compared to those of a lognormal process — with the price distribution's standard deviation held equal. If we insisted on using a lognormal model for pricing options, such as Black or Black-Scholes, in the case where the markets are actually mean reverting, we will be forced to introduce the "volatility smile" in the pricing of options across different strikes. Using a lognormal model to price an option where the distribution tails are fatter than the tails implied by the lognormal model would force us to increase the volatilities of the out-of-the-money options in order to mark-to-market these options. This results in volatility curves as a function of option strike price, which is referred to as the volatility smile.

E N D N O T E S

1. Ideally, these statistical tools should always remain simply that: tools. Our objective is to let the market lead us to the appropriate model. In practice, however, the problem of the "mad scientist" often arises: the tools become a means unto themselves. In such a case, we run the danger of having the model tell us what the market ought to be, and not what it is.

2. Useful books on statistics include Anderson, Sweeney, Williams, *Statistics for Business and Economics* (Minneapolis: West, 1970), and Mathews and Walker, *Mathematical Methods of Physics* (Glenview, IL: Addison-Wesley, 1996).

3. Mathews and Walker, *Mathematical Methods of Physics*, pp. 381–82.

4. This would hardly qualify as "random" price behavior. But for the sake of its educational value, let's treat it as such.

CHAPTER 4

Spot Price Behavior

4.1. INTRODUCTION

All fundamental and quantitative modeling starts with spot price behavior. Supply and demand effects converge in the spot market prices, and all derivative contracts anticipate this convergence. If we can fully understand the market behavior of spot prices, we will possess the means for valuing and managing energy derivatives.

In this chapter we will follow the six-step model selection process introduced in chapter 3 in order to identify the most appropriate model for energy spot prices:

Step 1: Informally look at the actual market data.

Step 2: Create a short list of possible models.

Step 3: Calibrate parameters through time series analysis.

Step 4: Generate distributions from models.

Step 5: Perform distribution analysis.

Step 6: Compare results and select the most appropriate model.

As will be seen, the mean-reversion models are the most appropriate for energy spot prices and will serve as the basis for much of the valuation and risk management methodologies in this book.

4.2. LOOKING AT THE ACTUAL MARKET DATA

We will take a look at a cross section of energy markets with increasing seasonal complexity. We will also look at an equity index for the sake of comparison. All markets other than electricity will be analyzed for the years between 1992 and 1996. For the WTI crude oil, heating oil, and natural gas prices, we will analyze the first-nearby NYMEX future's prices as proxies for the spot price values. In doing so, we have to account for rollovers and averaging effects.[1]

Electricity market data were available for shorter periods. Since the electricity markets are just now in the process of deregulation, there is not a great deal of electricity price data available to work with. Still, we will take what we can get, and as limited as this data set is, it

Time Series of S&P 500 Prices (1992–1996)

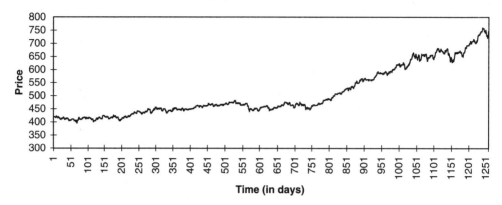

is still a valuable source of information about how the electricity markets have acted in 1995 and 1996. Of course, we have to keep in mind that any parameters calibrated from this data may not be the parameters we will be seeing in the future. The deregulation of the electricity markets is bound to cause changes in the way the prices act.

The markets to be analyzed include:

♦ As the example of stock market behavior, we will take a look at the Standard & Poor's 500 (S&P 500) stock index. Figure 4–1 plots the time series for the index over the years 1992 through 1996.

♦ West Texas Intermediate (WTI) crude oil first nearby future from the New York Mercantile Exchange (NYMEX). Figure 4–2 plots the time series for the first nearby WTI future over the years 1992 through 1996.

♦ Heating Oil #2 (HO) first nearby from NYMEX. Figure 4–3 plots the time for the first nearby HO future over the years 1992 through 1996.

Time Series of WTI First-Nearby Future Prices (1992–1996)

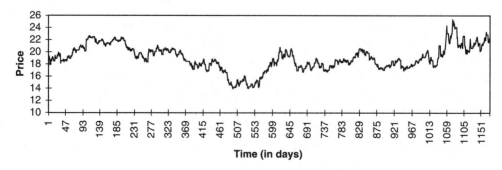

FIGURE 4-3

Time Series of Heating Oil First-Nearby FuturePrices (1992-1994)

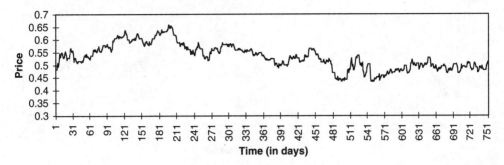

- Natural Gas (NG) futures from NYMEX. Under the NYMEX futures contract, natural gas is delivered over the next calendar month past contract expiration at the Henry Hub delivery node near the Gulf of Mexico. Figure 4–4 plots the time series for the first nearby NG future between 1992 and 1996. These futures are based on delivery of natural gas over the whole contract month. Hence, these futures are not ideal proxies for the spot price behavior. We will still go ahead and analyze the data, but keep in mind that we are analyzing an average rather than a discrete spot price.
- California-Oregon Border (COB) on-peak and off-peak spot prices from the Dow Jones index. Figures 4–5 and 4–6 plot the time series for COB's on-peak and off-peak spot prices for the years 1995–1996.
- The Mid-Columbia (MC) over-the-counter electricity spot price. We are using the Dow Jones daily price index during the years 1995-1996. Figures 4–7 and 4–8 plot the time series for the MC's on-peak and off-peak spot prices for that period.

FIGURE 4-4

Time Series of Natural Gas First-Nearby Future Prices (1992-1996)

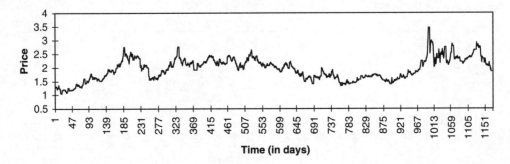

F I G U R E 4-5

Time Series of COB On-Peak Spot Prices (05/95–07/96)

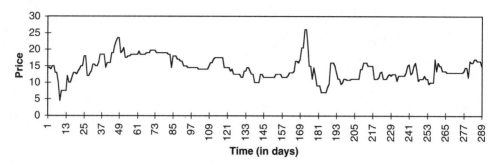

F I G U R E 4-6

Time Series of COB Off-Peak Spot Prices (05/95–07/96)

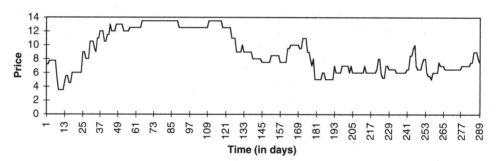

F I G U R E 4-7

Time Series of Mid Columbia On-Peak Spot Prices (07/95–07/96)

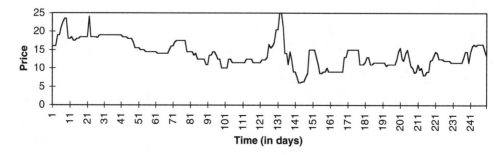

◆ The Southwest Power Pool (SPP) on-peak and off-peak prices. We will be using the Dow Jones daily price index during the years 1995–1996. Figures 4–9 and 4–10 plot the time series for the SPP's on-peak and off-peak spot prices for that period.

Based purely on the graphs, we can observe some differences across the markets. S&P 500 prices appear to have a drift term, which is significant in determining the S&P price behav-

F I G U R E   4-8

Time Series of Mid Columbia Off-Peak Spot Prices (07/95–07/96)

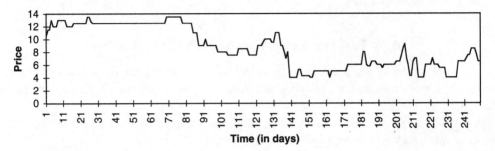

F I G U R E   4-9

Time Series of SPP On-Peak Spot Prices (11/94–07/96)

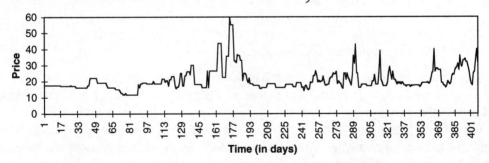

F I G U R E   4-10

Time Series of SPP Off-Peak Spot Prices (11/94–07/96)

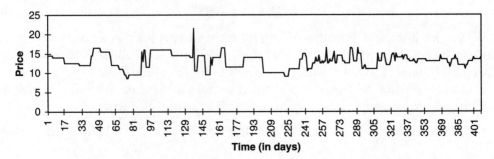

ior as compared to the stochastic term. This appears not to be the case across the energy markets, where the prices appear to exhibit a much greater uncertainty, with the drift term being hard to observe. It is hard to see the seasonality effects, but they are indeed there in the seasonal markets, particularly electricity. The electricity prices show both summer and winter peaking prices, with the summer being the more dominant.

4.3. A SHORT LIST OF POSSIBLE MODELS

The set of models we will discuss are the basic lognormal model and two mean-reverting models seen in the energy markets.

4.3.1. The Lognormal Price Model

The lognormal model is the most famous model of all, particularly in nonenergy markets. It is extremely simple to use, and as such, provides a good amount of flexibility in its implementation.

In a single-factor lognormal model, the change in the price from time t to time $t + dt$, dS_t, where dt is very small ($dt \ll 1$), is given by Equation 4–1:

$$d\widetilde{S}_t = \mu S_t dt + \sigma S_t d\widetilde{z}_t \qquad (4-1)$$

where: S = spot price
        t = time of observation
        μ = the drift rate
        σ = volatility
    $d\widetilde{z}$ = random stochastic variable

This change in the price over time dt has two components, the first being the drift, or deterministic term of $\mu S_t dt$. The second component is the stochastic, or random, contribution to the change in the spot price, $\sigma S_t d\widetilde{z}_t$.

Both the drift and the stochastic terms are proportional to the spot price level at time t. The greater the price, the greater is both the expected change in the price and the randomness about it. The stochastic term contains the variable $d\widetilde{z}_t$, which is a normally distributed random variable with a mean of zero, and a standard deviation that grows as the square root of time dt:

$$d\widetilde{z} \sim N(0,dt) \qquad (4-2)$$

$$STD(d\widetilde{z}_t) = \sqrt{dt} \qquad (4-3)$$

We use the differential Equation 4–1 to solve for the spot price as a function of its model parameters, including the stochastic variable $d\widetilde{z}_t$, and also to learn about the characteristics of the spot price behavior under the assumption that the spot prices are lognormal.

In order to solve for the spot price, we use some tricks of the trade. We start by performing a variable transformation where we define a new variable, x_t, to be the natural log of the price:

$$x_t \equiv \ln(S_t) \qquad (4-4)$$

By applying Ito's Lemma to the new variable, we find out that it is normally distributed:

$$d\tilde{x}_t = \left(\frac{\mu - \sigma^2}{2}\right)dt + \sigma d\tilde{z}_t \tag{4-5}$$

This allows us to first solve for the new variable $\tilde{x}_t$, and from this solution to derive the solution for the spot price at time T contingent on the spot price at time t:

$$\tilde{S}_T|_t = S_t e^{\left(\mu - \frac{\sigma^2}{2}\right)(T-t) + \sigma\tilde{z}_{t,T}} \tag{4-6}$$

where: $\tilde{S}_{T|t}$ = spot price at time T contingent on spot price at time t

By taking the expected value of both sides of the above equation, we obtain Equation 4–7, the solution to the expected spot price at time T as observed from time t:

$$E_t[\tilde{S}_T] = S_t e^{\mu(T-t)} \tag{4-7}$$

As you can see from the above derivation, in a lognormal model, the expected spot prices grow exponentially over time, with an expected rate of return given by the Greek character, μ. Note that the randomness in the price over time is always in the exponential, guaranteeing that the prices will always be positive. If the random variable, $\tilde{z}$, takes on very large negative values, the spot prices approach zero, but are never negative.

One of the reasons why the lognormal model is so popular and why so many academics like it is the latter fact: It guarantees that the prices will never be negative.

4.3.2. Mean-Reverting Models

As will be seen from our analysis results, energy markets require mean-reverting models. In fact, the price mean-reverting model turns out to do the best job of capturing the distribution of energy prices. The log of price mean-reverting model performs not too badly in capturing the distribution width (i.e., the second distribution moment and standard deviation), but does a poor job of capturing the distribution's tails (i.e., the fourth distribution moment and kurtosis).

Both energy models presented here have the characteristic of giving the changes in the spot prices a negative autocorrelation, a characteristic that is very much a part of the energy markets, particularly electricity. In fact, autocorrelation is a characteristic of a mean-reverting model. Both models presented here are mean-reverting models, one with mean reversion in the log of the price, and the other with mean reversion in the price.

4.3.2.1. Mean Reversion in Log of Price

Mean reversion in the natural log of the spot price is a model that has been used in the energy markets, particularly in electricity. It has the spot price behavioral characteristics which are very much like the characteristics of prices derived from interest rate models. However, it is a bit simpler to use. The nonnegative nature of spot prices is preserved through the modeling of the log of the price rather than the price itself. The mean reversion is therefore applied to the log of the price rather than to the price itself:

$$\widetilde{x}_t = \ln(\widetilde{S}_t) \tag{4-8}$$

$$d\widetilde{x}_t = \alpha(b - x_t)dt + \sigma d\widetilde{z}_t \tag{4-9}$$

where: S = spot price
$\quad\quad t$ = time of observation
$\quad\quad \alpha$ = rate of mean reversion
$\quad\quad \sigma$ = volatility
$\quad\quad b$ = long-term equilibrium of x
$\quad\quad d\widetilde{z}$ = random stochastic variable

From the above differential equation, we can solve for the log of the price, x_T, conditional on time t:

$$\widetilde{x}_T\big|_t = \left\{ \begin{array}{l} x_t e^{-\alpha(T-t)} + b(1 - e^{-\alpha(T-t)}) + \\ \sigma e^{-\alpha(T-t)} \displaystyle\int_t^T d\widetilde{z}_x e^{\alpha x} \end{array} \right\} \tag{4-10}$$

and therefore also for the spot price itself:

$$\widetilde{S}_T\big|_t = \{S_1 e^{-\alpha(T-t)}\overline{S}^{(1-e^{-\alpha(T-t)})}\exp(\sigma e^{-\alpha T|_t^T dz, e^{\alpha x}}\} \tag{4-11}$$

where: $\overline{S} \equiv e^b$
$\quad\quad \widetilde{S}_T\big|_t$ = the spot price at time T contingent on the spot price at time t

From this we can obtain the expected spot price at time T as observed from time t:

$$E_t\left[\widetilde{S}_T\right] = S_t^{e^{(-\alpha(T-t))}}\overline{S}^{\{1-e^{(-\alpha(T-t))}\}}\exp(\sigma^2/4a)\{1-e^{(-2\alpha(T-t))}\} \tag{4-12}$$

In the case where T is very close to t, i.e., $T \equiv t + dt$, and $dt \ll 1$, the above solution for the spot price and its expected value reduce to the following approximations:

$$\widetilde{S}_{t+dt}\big|_t \cong S_t^{(1-\alpha dt)}\overline{S}^{(\alpha dt)}e^{\sigma d\widetilde{z}_t} \tag{4-13}$$

$$E_t\left[\widetilde{S}_{t+dt}\right] \cong S_t^{(1-\alpha dt)}\overline{S}^{(\alpha dt)}e^{0.5\sigma^2 dt} \tag{4-14}$$

Similarly, when T is very large, $T \gg t$, the expected spot price approaches the value:

$$E_t\left[\widetilde{S}_T\right] \cong \overline{S}e^{(\sigma^2/4\alpha)} \tag{4-15}$$

4.3.2.2. Mean Reversion in Price

Another model that has been used in the energy marketplace is a two-factor model, where the first factor is the spot price, and the second factor is a long-term equilibrium price (the Pilipovic Model). The spot price is assumed to mean-revert toward the equilibrium price level, while the equilibrium price level is assumed to be lognormally distributed:

$$d\widetilde{S}_t = \alpha(L_t - S_t)dt + S_t\sigma d\widetilde{z}_t \tag{4-16}$$

$$d\widetilde{L}_t = \mu L_t dt + L_t \xi d\widetilde{w}_t \qquad\qquad (4-17)$$

where: S = the spot price
L = the equilibrium price
t = time of observation
α = rate of price mean reversion
σ = volatility
μ = drift of the long-term equilibrium price
ξ = volatility in the long-term equilibrium price
$d\widetilde{z}$ = random stochastic variable defining the randomness in the spot price
$d\widetilde{w}$ = random stochastic variable defining the randomness in the equilibrium price

We can solve these differential equations to obtain the spot price solution and its expected value:

$$E_t\left[\widetilde{S}_T\right] = S_t e^{-\alpha(T-t)} + {}^k L_t (e^{\mu(T-t)} - e^{-\alpha(T-t)}) \qquad\qquad (4-18)$$

where T = some future point in time, i.e., $T > t$.

$$k \equiv \frac{\alpha}{\alpha + \mu} \qquad\qquad (4-19)$$

We can approximate k with the value of one in the case where the mean reversion, α, is much greater than the equilibrium price rate of return, μ.

Note that setting the long-term equilibrium price volatility, ξ, to zero, has the effect of reducing the two-factor model to a single-factor model for the energy commodity spot price.

4.3.3. Cost-Based Models for Electric Utilities

Historically, electric utilities have used cost-based or structural models to arrive at expected costs in regulated markets. These fundamental cost distribution models for electricity tend to tie in the integrated production cycle for electricity generation in order to arrive at future expected spot price for electricity, as well as their distributions.

Such models are excellent for understanding the characteristics of electricity cost behavior unique to a particular utility. However, they do not tell the full market price story. First, the cost is not also the market price of electricity. Second, such distribution models cannot satisfy the arbitrage-free requirements of forward prices. Third, and most important, these models do not allow for mark-to-market valuation. The end result of using a cost-based model to value the products in a book is that it gives the energy producers their internal mark-to-cost valuation, and not the mark-to-market valuation. Ideally, a producer has both a cost-based model and a mark-to-market financial model. The different book values resulting from the two approaches define the producer-specific arbitrage opportunities.

4.3.4. Interest Rate Models

Note: Appendix B contains several interest rate and bond models provided for comparison and reference.

4.4. CALIBRATING PARAMETERS THROUGH TIME SERIES ANALYSIS

Next, we will perform the time series analysis of prices and their daily returns. The first step will be for us to perform the time series analysis of price returns in order to obtain seasonality parameters and model-specific parameters for all three models, the lognormal model and the two mean-reverting models. After we perform the time series analysis, we will also calibrate the seasonality factors. Ultimately, this will allow us to perform distribution analysis on the underlying spot prices stripped of seasonality effects.

In the case of the lognormal model:

$$d\widetilde{S}_t^{Und} = \mu S_t^{Und} dt + \sigma S_t^{Und} d\widetilde{z}_t \qquad (4-20)$$

the time series analysis will result in estimated values for the price rate of return and the price volatility: μ, and σ.

In the case of the model with mean reversion in the log of the price, we have:

$$x_t = \ln(S_t^{Und}) \qquad (4-21)$$

$$d\widetilde{x}_t = \alpha(b - x_t)dt + \sigma d\widetilde{z}_t \qquad (4-22)$$

This translates to a differential equation in the underlying spot price:

$$d\widetilde{S}_t^{Und} = S_t^{Und}\left[\left(\alpha \ln\left(\frac{\overline{S}}{S_t^{Und}}\right) + \frac{\sigma^2}{2}\right)dt + \sigma d\widetilde{z}_t\right] \qquad (4-23)$$

In this case time series analysis will provide us with estimates for the rate of mean reversion, α, the log of the price around which mean reversion occurs, $\overline{S} = e^b$, and the price volatility, σ.

Finally, in the third case where mean reversion is in the price:

$$d\widetilde{S}_t^{Und} = \alpha(L_t - S_t^{Und})dt + S_t^{Und} \sigma d\widetilde{z}_t \qquad (4-24)$$

$$d\widetilde{L}_t = \mu L_t dt + L_t \xi d\widetilde{w}_t \qquad (4-25)$$

Time series analysis of spot price will result in the rate of mean reversion, the value of the equilibrium price at the start of the historical data set, the rate of return on the equilibrium price, and the spot price volatility: α, L_0, μ, and σ.

Unfortunately, if we are trying to fit a two-factor price mean-reverting process, ideally we have the forward prices to help us in estimating the long-term equilibrium price on a day-by-day basis. For the sake of simplicity we will assume that the only data we have to work with are the market spot prices or the first nearby future used as a proxy for the spot price. In this case we are forced to reduce the two-factor price mean-reverting model to a single factor. This means that during this analysis we will assume that the equilibrium

prices in the price mean-reverting model do have a rate of return but have zero volatility—
i.e., they are perfectly stable.

4.4.1. Incorporating Seasonality with Underlying Models

For all three models we will assume that the spot price is a function of an underlying spot
price, S_t^{Und}, plus seasonality effects:

$$S_t = S_t^{Und} + \text{seasonality effects} \tag{4-26}$$

$$S_t = S_t^{Und} + \beta_A \cos(2\pi(t - t_A)) + \beta_{SA} \cos(4\pi(t - t_{SA})) \tag{4-27}$$

where: S_t = spot price at time t
  S_t^{Und} = underlying spot price value
  b_A = annual seasonality parameter
  t_A = annual seasonality centering parameter (time of annual peak)
  b_{SA} = semiannual seasonality parameter
  t_{SA} = semiannual seasonality centering parameter (time of semiannual peak)

From the above, we can derive the change in the price over time dt as:

$$d\widetilde{S}_t = d\widetilde{S}_t^{Und} - \left\{ \begin{array}{l} 2\pi\beta_A \sin(2\pi(t - t_A)) \\ + 4\pi\beta_{SA} \sin(4\pi(t - t_{SA})) \end{array} \right\} dt \tag{4-28}$$

Thus, the seasonality terms will be defined the same way for all three models. However,
the change in the underlying spot price, i.e., the spot price stripped of the seasonality effects,
will be defined uniquely by each model being tested. The calibration of the model-specific parameters and the seasonality parameters will be performed simultaneously. For each model we
will end up calibrating the model-specific parameters, the seasonality parameters β_A and β_{SA},
as well as the centering parameters for seasonality, t_A and t_{SA}.

4.4.2. Results from Time Series Analysis

The time series analysis calibrations for the lognormal, mean-reverting in the log of the price,
and price mean-reverting models are provided in Tables 4–1 through 4–3, respectively.
    Note that the seasonality parameter estimates also change as a function of the model be-
ing analyzed, although the differences are not that significant. In the case of the S&P 500 and
WTI data, we "turned off" the seasonality factors and only estimated the model-specific parameters. In the case of HO, we only estimated the annual seasonality, corresponding to the winter peaking prices. For all the other markets we estimated both the annual and the semiannual
seasonality. Note that the electricity markets have very strong seasonality factors—in the
rough range of 25% of their price levels. By comparison, the NG results show the seasonality
factor to be only in the rough range of 10% of the price levels.
    This result for NG is dampened by the fact that NYMEX NG contracts are average-price
rather than discrete-price contracts. Had we analyzed the corresponding NYMEX discrete spot

TABLE 4–1

Parameters from Lognormal Model

Market	β_A	β_{SA}	μ	σ	R^2
S&P 500	0	0	8.57%	10.32%	0.31%
WTI Crude	0	0	23.12%	23.61%	0.52%
Htg Oil #2	0	0	6.13%	23.43%	0.04%
Nat Gas	0	0.1606	11.55%	43.47%	2.73%
COB On	5.20	2.52	0.00%	163.43%	28.92%
COB Off	6.10	2.59	7.01%	110.48%	45.74%
Mid C On	6.12	0	15.00%	145.00%	21.57%
Mid C Off	7.13	0	0.00%	121.42%	46.52%
SPP On	4.08	4.00	25.00%	212.21%	10.80%
SPP Off	2.77	1.53	25.00%	137.98%	8.10%

prices, we would have found greater seasonality magnitudes. In other words, averaging dampens seasonality.

    This is probably a good place to consider the intuition behind the seasonality factor values. In the case where the annual seasonality factor is estimated to be significant and positive, while the semiannual factor is roughly zero, the market exhibits primarily single annual peaks—either in the winter or the summer. In the case where the semiannual seasonality factor is estimated to be significant and positive, while the annual factor is roughly zero, the market exhibits both annual peaks—in the winter and the summer—and with equal magnitudes. Where both seasonality factors are positive, there are both summer and winter peaks, but one is

TABLE 4–2

Parameters from Mean Reversion in Log of Price Model

Market	β_A	β_{SA}	σ_{DRIFT}	α	$\bar{S}$	σ	R^2
S&P 500	0	0	41.71%	0	439.97	10.32%	0.31%
WTI Crude	0	0	100%	0.5364	29.42	23.88%	0%
Htg Oil #2	0	0	5.05%	2.92	0.5394	23.36%	0.65%
Nat Gas	0	0.161	0%	1.14	2.2138	43.43%	2.89%
COB On	4.75	2.21	236.2%	19.41	11.79	158.7%	32.94%
COB Off	5.22	0	4.01%	15.43	9.08	115.0%	41.19%
Mid C On	5.86	0	0%	12.86	13.70	143.6%	23.32%
Mid C Off	6.96	0	0.11%	4.90	5.97	120.4%	47.43%
SPP On	4.08	3.66	99.37%	15.67	19.37	204.1%	15.26%
SPP Off	2.35	0.95	0%	16.25	13.46	135.4%	11.48%

TABLE 4-3

Parameters from Mean Reversion in Price Model

Market	β_A	β_{SA}	μ	α	L_0	σ	R^2
S&P 500	0	0	25%	1.18	367.68	10.30%	0.73%
WTI Crude	0	0	15%	1.07	11.66	23.43%	2.11%
Htg Oil #2	0	0	0%	2.94	0.5371	23.35%	0.69%
Nat Gas	0	0.1611	0%	1.00	2.0951	43.43%	2.88%
COB On	4.80	2.16	25%	20.16	11.36	158.43%	33.20%
COB Off	5.92	2.17	25%	10.01	7.73	108.80%	47.38%
Mid C On	5.77	0	3.20%	14.14	13.17	143.63%	23.25%
Mid C Off	6.96	0	0%	6.97	6.10	120.32%	47.48%
SPP On	3.97	3.45	16.10%	12.11	17.33	206.15%	13.50%
SPP Off	2.43	1.07	11.64%	12.19	12.23	135.73%	11.07%

greater than the other. In the case of electricity, the summer peak tends to be generally greater than the winter peak, as the use of electricity for cooling in the summer tends to be greater than the use of electricity for heat generation in the winter.

The model-specific parameters vary significantly from market to market. However, we can see some general behaviors here. In the case of all the markets, the spot price volatility across models is roughly the same regardless of the model being calibrated. This indicates that the drift terms indeed are not nearly as significant as the stochastic terms, resulting in spot price volatilities that are generally indifferent of the type of the drift term being calibrated.

Note how the volatility values across markets grow with the complexity of the market-place. The S&P 500 has the smallest volatility of all, followed by WTI and HO. The natural gas and particularly the electricity markets show much higher volatilities. (In fact, since the natural gas contract is based on an average price over a month, its discrete price volatility would be even higher, and quite close to electricity volatility levels.) The weather-dependent nature of these markets and the storage limitations result in such high volatilities. This makes the modeling of these markets all the more difficult.

Finally, the mean reversion calibrated for both mean-reverting models also grows with the complexity of the marketplace, just like the spot price volatilities. This tells us that, while events happen quite a lot in these markets, they are relatively localized in time—i.e., they do not have long-lasting effects. The pull back of the spot price toward the equilibrium price is extremely quick in electricity markets.

The R^2 values for all three models are given in Table 4-4.[2] Note by how much these values grow for seasonal markets. Also note that for these seasonal markets the model R^2 values are not that different across models. These facts tell us that the seasonality factors explain a great deal of the price movement in the seasonal markets, and that the underlying price models really do not add that much to that explanatory power, i.e. to predicting the next day price changes. These facts should convince us that the seasonality factors have to be included in the

TABLE 4-4

R^2 Summary for "Next Day" Price Change Forecasting

Market	Lognormal	Log Mean Reversion	Price Mean Reversion
S&P 500	0.31%	0.31%	0.73%
WTI Crude	0.52%	0%	2.11%
Htg Oil #2	0.04%	0.65%	0.69%
Nat Gas	2.73%	2.89%	2.88%
COB On	28.92%	32.94%	33.20%
COB Off	45.74%	41.19%	47.38%
Mid C On	21.57%	23.32%	23.25%
Mid C Off	46.52%	47.43%	47.48%
SPP On	10.80%	15.26%	13.50%
SPP Off	8.10%	11.48%	11.07%

modeling of spot prices for seasonal markets. However, these facts also tell us that purely based on time series analysis, we cannot decide between what are the most appropriate models across the markets. We need distribution analysis for this.

Finally, we will conclude this section with a brief look at the model residuals, which we expect to be normally distributed. Figures 4–11 through 4–14 and 4–15 through 4–18 show the quantile-to-quantile plots for the S&P 500 and for COB on-peak, respectively. Note how much more normal the S&P 500 residuals look. The analysis we have performed for the price mean-reverting model did not include the second factor. Instead, we assumed that the equilibrium prices were deterministic. If we had included the historical equilibrium prices—which can be estimated from the forward price curves—we would have found the energy market residuals for the price mean-reverting model to look normally distributed.

FIGURE 4-11

S&P 500 Price Returns

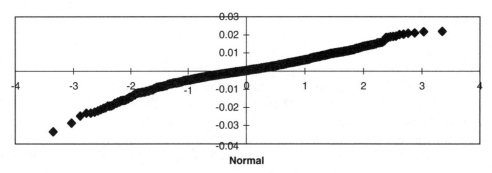

FIGURE 4–12

S&P 500 Lognormal Model Residuals

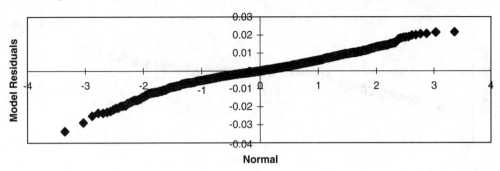

FIGURE 4–13

S&P 500 Log of Price Mean-Reverting Residuals

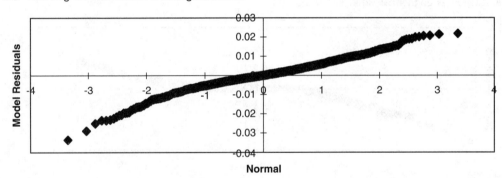

FIGURE 4–14

S&P 500 Price Mean-Reverting Residuals

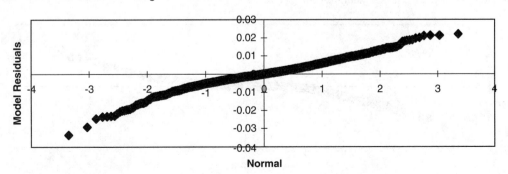

F I G U R E   4–15

COB On-Peak Price Returns

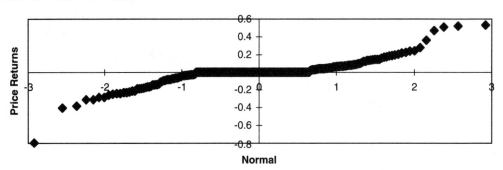

F I G U R E   4–16

COB On-Peak Lognormal Model Residuals

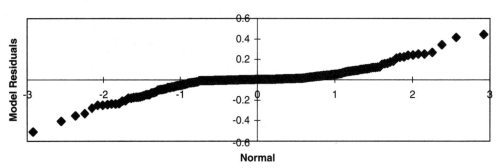

F I G U R E   4–17

COB On-Peak Log of Price Mean-Reverting Residuals

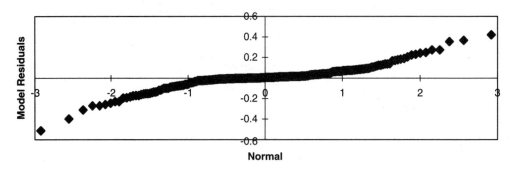

FIGURE 4-18

COB On-Peak Price Mean-Reverting Residuals

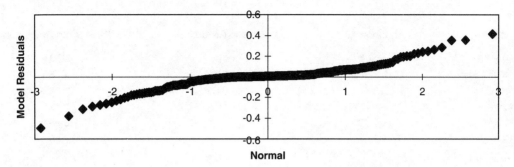

Table 4–5 shows the fourth moment of the model residuals divided by the second moment squared. As discussed in chapter 2, this ratio ought to equal exactly 3 in the case of a normally distributed variable. Table 4–5 shows that the ratio is almost 3 in the case of the S&P 500 residuals, but this is not so true with the energy markets. Again, this has to do with the fact that we really need to incorporate the second factor in the analysis.

Similarly, Table 4–6 shows the autocorrelations of price returns with just a single time lag (roughly one business day). Note that for energy markets, particularly electricity markets, we see some very strong negative correlations. To bring these down even further, we need the second factor again.

TABLE 4-5

The "3" Test of Moment Residuals

Market	Lognormal	Log Mean Reversion	Price Mean Reversion
S&P 500	4.93	4.93	4.98
WTI Crude	7.46	6.75	6.96
Htg Oil #2	5.94	6.05	6.06
Nat Gas	6.08	6.08	6.08
COB On	8.61	8.38	7.95
COB Off	8.78	8.71	8.96
Mid C On	6.99	6.68	6.67
Mid C Off	12.22	11.70	11.66
SPP On	8.29	7.75	7.98
SPP Off	16.80	17.11	17.06

TABLE 4-6

Autocorrelations

Market	Lognormal	Log Mean Reversion	Price Mean Reversion
S&P 500	−1.99%	−1.98%	−1.90%
WTI Crude	5.11%	5.21%	4.85%
Htg Oil #2	10.81%	11.34%	11.28%
Nat Gas	−1.42%	−1.14%	−1.12%
COB On	−8.57%	−4.09%	−3.98%
COB Off	−5.13%	2.47%	−3.85%
Mid C On	0.95%	3.12%	3.25%
Mid C Off	−1.03%	−0.9%	−0.86%
SPP On	−13.57%	−0.25%	−10.67%
SPP Off	−17.18%	−14.38%	−14.81%

4.5. PERFORMING DISTRIBUTION ANALYSIS

During the time series analysis steps we capture all the necessary model parameter values. In the distribution analysis we will be testing the models for how well they act over a longer period of time as compared with the actual market. It is this data analysis step that will ultimately give us the answer as to which model is consistent with both short-term and long-term price behavior.

Specifically, we will be comparing the historical market spot price distributions to the distributions implied by each of the models we are testing. While the width of the distribution will be of primary importance, we will also want to look at how well the models capture the skew and the kurtosis—or tails—of the historical price distributions.

4.5.1. Implementation of Distribution Analysis

We will be performing Monte Carlo simulations in order to obtain our model-implied distributions. The advantage of such simulations is that we get to see what the distributions look like visually, as well as estimate the first four distribution moments.

However, there is another way to obtain the distribution characteristics, and it does not involve simulations. Instead, we can use mathematics and the probability distributions of random variables to obtain the distribution moments implied by a model. While this procedure does not give you the visual satisfaction of a distribution plotted, it does give you the moments calculations, which are more precise and a lot quicker to calculate on a computer than are the simulations. The drawback is that the procedure requires quite a bit of up-front math work and the results may be complicated. In the case of the lognormal model, the results are actually pretty simple. The first four moments of a lognormal distribution of spot prices over time are given in the following equations:

$$M_2\Big|_t^T = \frac{(e^{\sigma^2(T-t)} - 1)}{(\sigma^2(T - t))} \tag{4-29}$$

$$M_3\Big|_t^T = \frac{(e^{3\sigma^2(T-t)} - 1)}{(3\sigma^2(T - t))} \tag{4-30}$$

$$M_4\Big|_t^{T,} = \frac{(e^{6\sigma^2(T-t)} - 1)}{(6\sigma^2(T - t))} \tag{4-31}$$

Calculating these moments for the log of price and price mean-reverting models requires quite a bit of time and math muscle, and the results are much more complicated than what you see for the lognormal model.

We are now ready to benchmark between models by performing distribution analysis. We do so through simulations of the underlying spot price models. This means that in order to compare these model-implied price distributions with the actual historical data, we need to strip out the seasonality effects from the historical data:

$$S_t^{Und} = S_t - \begin{Bmatrix} \beta_A \cos(2\pi(t - t_A) \\ + \beta_{SA} \cos(4\pi(t - t_{SA}) \end{Bmatrix} \tag{4-32}$$

Hence, from here on we work purely with the underlying spot prices, which exhibit no seasonality.

4.5.2. Results of Distribution Analysis

Figures 4–19, 4–20, and 4–21 show the graphs of what the actual and sample model simulated distributions look like for the S&P 500, and COB on-peak markets. (These graphs show just a small number of sample paths for both markets.) To get convergence we need to run simulations to the point where the moments of distributions stabilize. Tables 4–7 and 4–8 show the second and fourth distribution moments—normalized by the first moment—across mar-

FIGURE 4–19

Sample S&P 500 Probability Distribution

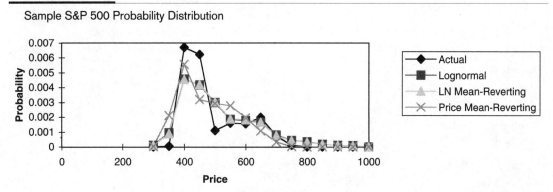

FIGURE 4-20

Sample COB On-Peak Probability Distribution: With Lognormal Model

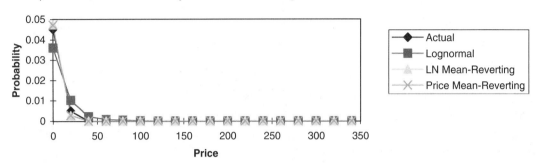

kets and models, based on simulations of over 100,000 random variables per market and per model.

The model-generated distributions' characteristics can now be compared to the actual data distributions. As Tables 4–7 and 4–8 show, the lognormal model does indeed capture the behavior of the S&P 500 best, while the price mean-reverting model best captures the behavior of most of the energy markets with seasonality components. The WTI market appears best defined by the mean reversion in the log of the price. These results are summarized in Table 4–9.

For the S&P 500 market the lognormal model outperforms both mean-reverting models. There are some people in the equity markets who believe that there is mean reversion in the equity prices. Based on the distribution analysis of five years' worth of S&P 500 data, the lognormal model still outperforms both the log-of-price mean-reverting and the price mean-reverting model.

The WTI energy market shows that mean reversion effects are better put in the log of the price rather than in the price directly. This is interesting, as the remaining energy markets ana-

FIGURE 4-21

Sample COB On-Peak Probability Distribution: Without Lognormal Model

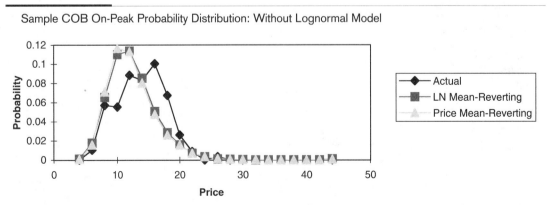

TABLE 4–7

Actual and Model Simulated Second Moments

Market	Actual Market	Lognormal	Log Mean Reversion	Price Mean Reversion
S&P 500	1.034684	1.046965	1.094674	1.052993
WTI Crude	1.011416	1.309480	1.097284	1.196067
Htg Oil #2	1.008763	1.089186	1.017804	1.009211
Nat Gas	1.041688	1.703756	1.198176	1.100271
COB On	1.077774	3.698361	1.118830	1.076969
COB Off	1.085743	1.926589	1.080757	1.067829
Mid C On	1.064172	4.944871	1.348947	1.083054
Mid C Off	1.101369	2.865343	1.556297	1.121842
SPP On	1.172609	46.544616	1.248151	1.218094
SPP Off	1.058771	3.911982	1.105536	1.087383

lyzed all show a clear preference for the price mean-reverting model and also share the presence of at least one seasonality component.

The remaining seasonal markets, HO, NG, COB on- and off-peak, MC on- and off-peak, and SPP on- and off-peak all appear to show a preference for the price mean-reverting model, particularly when it comes to the tails of the distributions (see Table 4–8).[3] The price mean-reverting model also outperforms the mean reversion in the log of the price model across all the seasonal energies, with the exception of the COB off-peak market. There the log of price mean-reverting model appears to do a little better in capturing the distribution width.

TABLE 4–8

Actual and Model-Simulated Fourth Moments

Market	Actual Market	Lognormal	Log Mean Reversion	Price Mean Reversion
S&P 500	1.235772	1.344655	1.739988	1.501494
WTI Crude	1.068398	5.556455	1.734861	3.262117
Htg Oil #2	1.053628	1.721548	1.123074	1.056888
Nat Gas	1.267883	39.630070	7.194671	1.832976
COB On	1.487009	1,113.5308	6.227328	1.583931
COB Off	1.528925	53.895197	2.709431	1.497315
Mid C On	1.481214	11,799.479	1,010.58450	1.653454
Mid C Off	1.675225	2,225.5578	185.224593	2.054546
SPP On	2.551227	3,281,746.0	53.712150	3.623448
SPP Off	1.353443	915.2752	5.805491	1.678291

TABLE 4-9

TABLE 4-9

Best Model by Market

Market	Best Model Implied Distribution
S&P 500	Lognormal
WTI	Log of Price Mean-Reverting
HO	Price Mean-Reverting
NG	Price Mean-Reverting
COB On	Price Mean-Reverting
COB Off	Log of Price Mean-Reverting (STD) and Price Mean-Reverting (Kurtosis)
MC On	Price Mean-Reverting
MC Off	Price Mean-Reverting
SPP On	Price Mean-Reverting
SPP Off	Price Mean-Reverting

4.6. CONCLUSION

Hopefully, this chapter has presented you with some case studies of market analysis, and maybe even with some useful measures and insights about the energy markets. The progression from the lognormal model through the mean reversion in the log of the price to the price mean-reverting model, as the complexity of the markets in question increases, is fascinating.

More research is needed for a true understanding of why the seasonal markets tend to be better explained by one as opposed to the other mean-reverting model. Also, ideally, we would run this comparison by allowing both mean-reverting models to have a second random variable, and then performing the analysis, with the equilibrium prices also being given a stochastic nature. In order to do this we need to use the histories of full strips of forward prices so that we can back out the equilibrium price behavior from the behavior of these forward prices — yet another research topic for future work.

ENDNOTES

1. Rollovers occur when the first nearby future expires and what used to be the second nearby future becomes the first nearby future. The price returns calculated on the rollover dates include the effect of the price shift from one futures contract to the next. Thus, the price returns calculated on the rollover days must be excluded from the analysis, as they add noise to the true market volatility.

2. Keep in mind that the R^2 values here measure how well we can predict the day-to-day price-changes and not the price levels. Since the price changes are comprised primarily of the random term, with the deterministic term being relatively insignificant, the R^2 values in Table 4–4 are predictably small.

3. Capturing this tail behavior is particularly important when pricing out-of-the-money options. If we used the log-of-price mean-reverting model to price our options, we would end up assuming fatter tails in the process, giving us option prices biased upward.

CHAPTER 5

The Forward Price Curve

5.1. INTRODUCTION

Forward prices are key inputs to any derivatives pricing and risk management calculation. No matter how sophisticated an option pricing model is, if the forward price curve used as an input to the option pricing calculations is not appropriate, the forward price errors will overshadow any additional value the sophistication of the option pricing model has to offer.

A trading operation that invests a good deal of money into product valuation and risk management should budget between valuation projects the same way that the company budgets between businesses and/or investments. One of the projects that should always be on the list of possible valuation projects is forward price curve building methodology development and upgrade. The most common valuation management mistake is to put all the efforts into pricing exotic products, while the forward price curves that affect the valuation of the whole portfolio remain tainted by poor building methodology and/or implementation. The building of forward price curves truly deserves a chapter all to itself.

5.1.1. The Difference Between Forwards and Futures

Before we begin the study of forward prices, we need to distinguish between the futures and the forwards. A *forward price* contract is an agreement between two parties for an exchange at some future point in time of a commodity and its cash value. The cash value is fixed at the time of the contract signing.

A *futures* contract is a specific type of forward. It is traded at an exchange, and the cash value is marked-to-market on a day-by-day basis. (The largest energy trading center is the New York Mercantile Exchange, which is commonly known as NYMEX.) For example, if I have bought a NYMEX futures contract on WTI and have agreed on a price of $20 per barrel of crude oil, and the price settled at $19 at the time of the business day's close, then I would have to pay one dollar into what is known as "margin account" at the futures exchange. The next day, if the price closed at $21, I would receive $2 in my margin account from the exchange.

This margin account also earns an interest rate. Hence, if the futures prices show a nonzero correlation with the interest rates the margin account earns, then there would be a bias in the futures prices relative to forward prices, which carry no such correlation sensitivity.

This futures vs. forward price bias exists in the bond and IMM markets, where the futures prices are directly related to interest rates and hence show a good amount of negative correlation to the short-term rates that the futures margin account earns or pays. In these cases a long futures position results in a margin account that earns a smaller interest rate on the profit than it pays on the loss. In these markets the futures prices are smaller than the corresponding forward prices.

However, in the energy commodity markets, the correlations of the energy futures prices to the interest rates are typically null. In the energy markets the futures and the forward prices are valued in the same manner, even though the actual cash collection is different. Energy future price and forward price can be used interchangeably, as both reflect the same value.[1]

5.2. READING THE CURVE

Forward prices are directly tied to the spot price models: forward prices are risk-adjusted and net cost-adjusted expectations of the spot prices at forward points in time. Therefore we can use spot price behavior to tell us about forward price behavior, and vice versa. Just as when modeling spot price behavior we want to ensure that the model we choose captures the characteristics of the spot price market both on a day-by-day basis and over a longer period of time, so we want to ensure that the model that describes the forward price behavior is consistent with the spot price behavior.

In order to get an understanding of what the forward price model ought to look like in energy markets, we need to start with the forward price market. Figures 5–1 and 5–2 show two sample WTI crude oil forward price curves. The first is the case of a *contango*, a market in

F I G U R E   5-1

WTI Forward Price Curve on Dec. 23, 1993

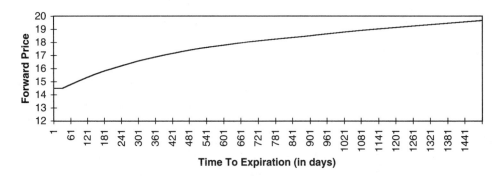

F I G U R E 5–2

WTI Forward Price Curve on Sep. 25, 1992

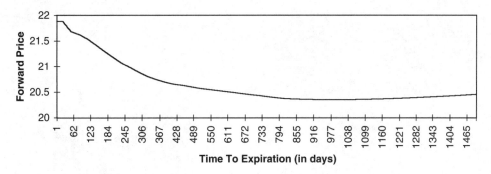

which the forward prices increase with the expiration times. The second case is called *back-wardation*, to reflect that the forward prices actually decrease as the expiration time increases. The energies that have price seasonality can exhibit both of these states, although it may be hard to see this with the seasonality factors laid on top.

The contango and backwardation markets are the simplest market states we can find out there. More typical are more complicated market states, which allow for the short-term and the long-term portions of the forward price curve to independently take on the contango or backwardation states. For example, the forward price curve might exhibit backwardation in the short term, i.e., for short-term forward price expirations, and contango in the long term portion of the forward price curve. Figure 5–3 shows one such case for the WTI market. Finally, Figure 5–4 shows an even more complicated state, where the contango is in

F I G U R E 5–3

WTI Forward Price Curve on Feb. 29, 1996

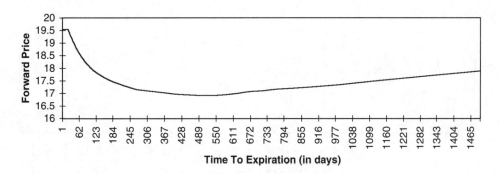

FIGURE 5–4

WTI Forward Price Curve on Dec. 11, 1992

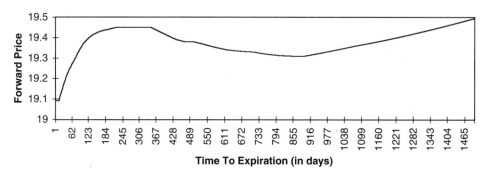

the near term, followed by backwardation and then contango in the long-term portion of the forward price curve. The latter is a case of an event hump, and like all of the previously de-scribed market states, it has to do with the expectations of the supply-and-demand imbal-ances going forward in time.

In the case of WTI, it is easy to see contango and backwardation states in the forward prices as there are no seasonality effects. Heating oil forward prices, an example given in Fig-ure 5–5, exhibit annual seasonality, with the peaks in the winter and the lows in the summer. Heating oil is used primarily for heating in the winter, and this winter demand peak is reflected in the forward prices. Here we see an example of a market where we need to extract the sea-sonality in order to clearly see the state of the underlying price. Figure 5–5 shows the heating oil market in contango, while Figure 5–6 shows natural gas market in backwardation followed by contango in the long term.

FIGURE 5–5

Heating Oil Forward Price Curve on Jul. 27, 1995

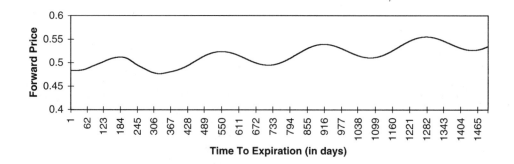

FIGURE 5-6

Natural Gas Forward Price Curve on Feb. 19, 1996

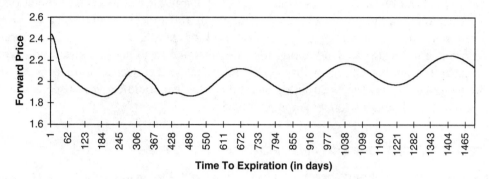

5.3. SEASONALITY IN THE FORWARD CURVE

Seasonality complicates the forward price curve. The job of detecting the forward price behavior underlying the seasonality factors gets even tougher when we look at energies that exhibit two seasonality factors during a single year, thus having two price peaks and two low price periods within a single year. Figures 5–6 and 5–7 show two such cases. The graph of natural gas forward prices shows the evident appearance of a winter peak, while the summer peak can only sometimes be seen, and is typically of very small magnitude. The electricity prices, however, clearly reflect the summer and the winter peaks, followed by the lows in the spring and the fall. Electricity's summer peak tends to be dominant, although the magnitude of this dominance over the winter peak varies depending on the region of North America in question. Typically, the use of electricity in the summer for cooling is much greater than the use of electricity in the winter for heating, although this is very much a function of the geographic location.

FIGURE 5-7

ECAR Electricity Forward Price Curve on Nov. 21, 1996

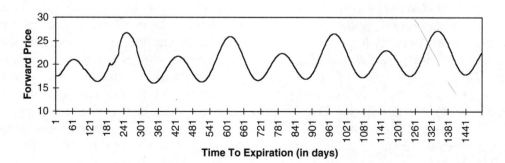

Natural gas, on the other hand, is used like heating oil primarily for heating in the winter. However, when electric utilities reach a maximum allowed capacity generating electricity using their first generation fuel, such as coal, the utilities might kick into second-generation production, using the currently more expensive natural gas for greater supply capability. Hence, during very hot summers, natural gas may be also used for cooling purposes, giving natural gas prices a rise due to greater demand during the summers, and resulting in forward price curves that recognize this additional seasonality behavior. In fact, if the electric utilities switched entirely to using natural gas for electricity generation, what we could expect to see is a natural gas curve that would have a stronger summer behavior.

5.4. THE EVOLUTION OF THE FORWARD CURVE

To the extent that the spot price behavior tells us about how the forward prices act, so does the forward price curve tell us about how the spot prices act. In this section we will build up our understanding of forward price behavior by looking at progressively complicated forward price processes. By following this "evolution," we will be able to read even the most complex curves for markets like electricity.

5.4.1. S&P 500

The S&P 500 forward price curves tend to show smooth growth. This is an exponentially increasing curve. Historical correlations between the S&P 500 forward prices and the spot price for the S&P 500 are very high (close to 100%), indicating that a single-factor model would be sufficient for this market. Furthermore, the exponential shape of the curve indicates that a simple single-factor lognormal model would be consistent with this forward price curve.

5.4.2. WTI Crude Oil

The WTI forward price curves, unlike the S&P 500 forward price curves, can take on a whole variety of different shapes: contango, backwardation, backwardation in the near-term portion of the curve with contango in the back, or event humps followed by contango in the back section of the curve (Figures 5–1 through 5–4). A single-factor lognormal model cannot cover all these possible market states.

The small correlations between the forward prices far out on the curve with the forward prices in the near-term portion of the curve indicate that at least two factors are necessary to explain the behavior of the forward prices. One factor should capture the behavior of the short-term forward prices; another factor should capture the behavior of the long-term forward prices. The long-term section of the forward price curve appears to enter a simple contango state, similar to S&P 500 forwards, implying that the long-term forward prices approach a lognormal long-term price behavior. The short-term forward prices, on the other hand, appear to mean-revert towards the long-term contango state with increasing expiration times. Only a two-factor mean-reverting model is capable of capturing the types of forward price curves seen in WTI markets.

5.4.3. Seasonal Markets

Heating oil is an extension of the type of behavior seen in WTI (Figure 5–5). We still need an underlying price model that tends to exhibit both backwardation and contango in the near-term and a contango in the long-term portion of the forward price curves. We still have long-term forward prices that are not highly correlated with the short-term forward prices. However, we also have the additional complication of seasonality effects. In the case of heating oil, only a two-factor mean-reverting model with an annual seasonality component added could attempt to capture the different heating oil market states. With natural gas (Figure 5–6) and electricity (Figure 5–7) we have to add one more seasonality factor: the semiannual seasonality factor, which captures the additional summer seasonality.

5.5. INTUITION BEHIND FORWARD PRICE MODELING

By observing the forward prices of the markets we need to model, we can decide on what we want the forward price model and its implementation to capture. The forward price model has to tie back to the spot price model through an arbitrage-free relationship between the two. The spot price model has yet one more test to pass in addition to all the tests we have already discussed in the previous chapters: the test of consistency with the market forward price curves.

It is not necessarily an easy step, going from the spot price model to the forward price model. For example, while we may define the forward prices to be proportional to the expected spot prices, they are not—as a rule—equal to the expected spot prices. However, we do have something to lean on in the process of transforming what we know about the spot price behavior into information we can use to define the forward price behavior, and that is the no-arbitrage condition.

5.5.1. The Arbitrage-Free Condition

Here's how it goes: Under the simplest scenario, I should be indifferent between entering into a forward price contract for delivery of the commodity at some time in the future and purchasing the actual commodity now and holding it until that same time in the future. Now, to make the comparison a valid one where we do indeed compare oranges to oranges—rather than oranges to lemons—we do need to go through the actual cash-flow analysis in present-value terms. In Section 5.6.1 we will take you through the details of this process.

Our forward price model should be "arbitrage-free." One way to describe the arbitrage-free concept is to assume that we can construct a portfolio of the forward price, the spot price, bonds, and whatever other market products we need to make this portfolio risk-free. A risk-free portfolio must earn the risk-free rate of return. This argument also gives us a mathematical means that we can use to derive the forward price model based on the underlying spot price model assumptions. In this process we end up with a differential equation for forward prices. This differential equation can then be used to derive the forward prices.

5.5.2. Identifying Characteristics

Early on in the process we have to decide on which of the spot and forward price market characteristics we want to treat within the model and which we want to treat within model implementation. As in any other modeling and implementation project, there is a give-and-take between the modeling and the implementation sophistication. If the model captures all the market realities, then the model implementation should be a fairly well-defined process. However, if the model captures the primary market realities, but leaves some to be dealt with during the implementation stage, then the implementation process is more involved and needs close involvement of the valuation and risk management experts.

How much is left to the implementation versus what is captured within the model has to do with the costs and benefits of choosing model sophistication. Capturing all the market realities within the model generally results in solving differential equations for forward prices, which do not have closed-form solutions. The cost of arriving at approximations may outweigh the benefits. Similarly, letting the implementation take the burden of capturing some of the market realities might benefit from a very practical and quick methodology development.

5.5.3. Influence of the Convenience Yield

The difficulty in the modeling of energy commodity forward prices and solving the forward price differential equation comes in defining the value of convenience yield. The convenience yield is unique to every user of an energy commodity, as it reflects the value it brings to the user of having the energy on hand, as needed, minus the cost that the user would have to pay for storing and maintaining the fuel. If a factory's production depends on a consistent delivery of an energy, and if there is a cost of stopping and restarting the factory due to lack of energy, as well as a cost to the share price due to the factory appearing dysfunctional in the marketplace, then the factory owners may be willing to pay a premium for prompt and consistent delivery of the energy as needed. In other words, the value of having the energy on hand might be very large. The convenience yield, as measured within the market forward price curve, reflects an overall market user's perception of this convenience yield value.

The convenience yield does not directly appear in the modeling of spot prices, although during supply shortages, the spot prices in effect ride up the convenience yield curve—as the spot prices capture the premiums the users are willing to pay to have the commodity on hand. Similarly, the spot prices in effect ride down the convenience yield curve as the events dissipate, resulting in the users being willing to pay less and less of the premium as the supply and demand go back to a balanced state.

While the spot prices will exhibit effects of convenience yield during events, the convenience yield is ever present in the market forward prices, and hence it must appear in the modeling of forward prices. It must be incorporated in the differential equation for the forward prices, and hence in the assumptions we make about what a perfectly hedged forward price commodity portfolio ought to have as its risk-free rate of return.

As discussed in previous chapters, in a financial sense, being a commodity holder is just like being a holder of a stock. If the stock pays dividends, then the holder captures this value.

On the other hand, a holder of a forward on a stock would not capture this dividend value until the stock is actually delivered. Similarly, the user of an energy commodity who is an owner of a forward on this commodity does not capture its value until the energy is actually delivered. Therefore, just like the risk-free rate is adjusted for the value of the dividend yield in the case of a stock, the risk-free rate must be adjusted for the value of the convenience yield in the case of the energy commodity.

The huge ambiguity about just how exactly the convenience yield can be quantified is what makes the modeling of energy forward prices difficult. However, there are a couple of pointers we can use. The convenience yield is the value the energy commodity brings to the holder beyond the storage and maintenance costs of holding the commodity. This value is a function of the spot price relative to the equilibrium price and can be positive as well as negative. There may be times that the value that the holder obtains from having the commodity on hand may be less than the cost of storage, hence the cost outweighs the benefit of holding the energy.

This negative convenience yield rate occurs when there is a large abundance of the energy in the spot market. In this case the user might not see any value in having the energy on hand, and would be better off not having to pay the cost of storage and maintenance; the user would rather buy than store the energy. But on the flip side, the greater the spot price relative to the equilibrium price of the moment, the smaller is the supply relative to the demand, and the greater is the convenience yield. We can use these intuitions to guide us in ultimately defining the convenience yield in a mathematical form.

5.6. FORWARD PRICE MODELING

We will start with discussing why it is that the forward prices, as a rule, are not the expected spot prices. This will naturally lead us to the no-arbitrage assumption and how to apply this assumption to forward price curve creation.

5.6.1. Why Spot and Forward Prices Are Different

In order to show that the forward prices are not—as a rule—equal to the expected spot prices, we need to go through a cash-flow analysis of two portfolio scenarios. To make this simple, instead of considering energy commodities we will work with a simple stock that pays no dividends and we will apply the *no-arbitrage* market condition. In the next section we will consider the much more complicated case of an energy commodity.

Under the no-arbitrage assumption we must be indifferent between two scenarios where one involves the purchase of the forward on the stock and the other involves the purchase of the stock. In the first scenario, we enter into a forward contract. At the time of the forward contract expiration, we pay the cash we agreed on in the forward price contract and obtain the stock. We immediately sell the stock in the marketplace. Under the second scenario, we borrow the money from the bank and we use it to purchase the stock today and hold it until the same time as the forward expiration. At that point, we sell the stock and we pay the bank what we owe it: the original principal plus the interest.

Under both scenarios the net cash flow at origination time, t, is zero. In the first scenario we simply agree to purchase the stock at future time T for an amount of the forward price, $F_{t,T}$. No cash is exchanged at origination time. In the second scenario, we purchase the stock for the market price S_t at origination time t, and we therefore borrow the principal amount S_t from the bank. The net cash flow in the second scenario is also zero at time t, since we get the same amount from the bank as we use to purchase the stock.

Since we are indifferent between the two scenarios, the cash flow from the first scenario at expiration time T must be the same as the cash flow from the second scenario at time T. Under the first scenario at expiration we pay out the amount $F_{t,T}$ for the stock. We get the stock and sell it in the marketplace for S_T. Hence, in the first scenario, the cash flow at time T is given by $(S_T - F_{t,T})$. Under the second scenario, we sell the stock and we pay back the bank for the principal amount and the interest. In this case, the cash flow at time T is given by $(S_T - S_t\, e^{r(T-t)})$, where $S_t\, e^{r(T-t)}$ is both the principal and the interest owed to the bank, the interest compounded continuously at a risk-free rate. Under the no-arbitrage condition the two cash flows must be the same, giving us a solution for the forward price in terms of the spot price, both at origination time t:

$$F_{t,T} = S_t\, e^{r(T-t)} \qquad (5-1)$$

where: $F_{t,T}$ = forward price observed at time t, with expiration at time T
S_t = spot price at time t
t = time of observation
T = time of expiration
r = risk-free rate, continuously compounded

The forward price is thus given by the stock price at the time of the origination, which is then compounded at the risk-free rate over the forward price expiration time.

We can now use Equation 5–1 to relate the forward price to the expected stock price, as seen at the time of forward price contract origination, t. If the stock earns an expected return, μ, then the expected price of the stock at expiration time T, but as calculated at time t, is given by:

$$E_t[S_T] = S_t\, e^{\mu(T-t)} \qquad (5-2)$$

where: μ = the expected return on the stock, continuously compounded

Given Equation 5–1 for the forward price in terms of the stock price at origination time t, we can express the forward price in terms of the expected stock price at the time of expiration:

$$F_{t,T} = E_t[\widetilde{S}_T]\, e^{(r-\mu)(T-t)} \qquad (5-3)$$

The forward price is proportional to the expected spot price at the time of expiration but not—as a rule—equal to it. The forward price is equal to the expected spot price adjusted for the market cost of risk, where we define the market cost of risk, λ, as following:[2]

$$\lambda = \frac{(\mu - r)}{\sigma} \qquad (5-4)$$

In other words, for a traded asset, the risk-free rate is equal to the expected rate of return on the asset minus the market cost of risk times the volatility for that asset.

$$r = \mu - \lambda\sigma \qquad (5-5)$$

where: λ = market cost of risk, and
σ = volatility of the asset price.

By replacing the r term in Equation 5–3 using Equation 5–5, we generate Equation 5–6. The forward price is equal to the expected spot price adjusted for the market cost of risk:

$$F_{t,T} = E_t[\widetilde{S}_T]\, e^{-\lambda\sigma(T-t)} \qquad (5-6)$$

While the above arbitrage-free derivation of the forward price in terms of the expected spot price at expiration was applied to the simplest case of a stock price that pays no dividends, we can use the definition of the market cost of risk and the intuitive expectation of the forward price being proportional to the expected stock price to guide us in the analysis of the more complicated forward price markets.

5.6.2. Going from Spot Price Models to Forward Price Models

The case above was simple enough to be treated through a simple cash-flow analysis. A more general application of the arbitrage-free market condition is the creation of a risk-free portfolio consisting of the commodity product and its hedges. The modeling steps include the creation of the risk-free portfolio consisting of the forward price and all market hedges necessary to make the portfolio risk-free, the incorporation of pricing models for the market hedges, and the derivation of the forward price model given boundary market conditions.

5.6.3. The Risk-Free Portfolio

We can start with the process of creating a risk-free portfolio for a simple case, and we will build up to the skill level necessary to model forward prices on energy commodities. The risk-free portfolio approach has been used for the derivations of pricing models for options on stocks. Defining differential equations for forward prices is no different. Hence, as we go along, if you are familiar with the option price differential equations you will find that the forward price differential equations really look very similar, only with a different boundary condition at the expiration time.

First we will assume that the stock does not pay any dividends, and that the stock follows a simple lognormal model, with a rate of return μ, and a volatility σ:

$$d\widetilde{S}_t = \mu S_t dt + \sigma S_t d\widetilde{z} \qquad (5-7)$$

where: μ = mean rate of return
σ = volatility
dt = the time period over which the change in the price is observed
$d\widetilde{z}$ = random stochastic variable with mean of zero and standard deviation of dt

Secondly, we assume that the forward price's randomness comes purely from the underlying stock price randomness. Hence, a risk-free portfolio can be constructed such that it consists of the forward and some number of shares of the underlying stock:

$$\Pi_t \equiv F_{t,T} + nS_t \tag{5-8}$$

where: Π = portfolio value
$F_{t,T}$ = forward price expiring at time T
n = number of stocks in the portfolio
S = spot price

Since the changes in the forward price are due only to the changes in the stock price and the passage of time, for the change in the portfolio value over time dt, we have the following:

$$F_{t,T} = f(S_t,t) \tag{5-9}$$
$$d\Pi_t = dF_{t,T} + ndS_t$$

The above equation specifies the change in the value of the portfolio at time t over some time period dt. The value of the portfolio at any time t is defined as the value of the forward price plus the value of the stocks at time t.

The value of the portfolio should not be confused with the initial cash investment in the portfolio. Since the forward contracts require no payment from either side entering into the contract at origination, and there is no exchange of payment for delivery of stock until the forward contract expiration, the portfolio cash investment at origination consists only of the money necessary for entering into the stock position of n shares.

We still have to figure out just exactly how many shares of the stock we need to hold in the portfolio (hence either buy or sell) in order to make the portfolio risk-free. Since we have yet to define the value of n, we do not know if it is indeed a positive or a negative stock position. If the stock position is positive, it means that we are *long* the stock, i.e., that we had to purchase the stock. Hence, we would have to borrow money to do so, as our portfolio cash flow at origination would be positive. On the other hand, if it turns out that the value of n is negative, we would be sellers of the stock (*short* the stock), and hence our investment cash flow would be negative, resulting in our putting the money into the bank at contract origination.

We know that a risk-free portfolio ought to earn (or pay) the risk-free rate of return, r:

$$d\Pi_t = rnS_t dt \tag{5-10}$$

Given a risk-free portfolio investment, I would pay the bank the risk-free rate for borrowing the money for the investment if my overall investment value is positive, and I would receive from the bank the risk-free rate for depositing the money from the investment if my overall investment value is negative. Since the forward contract does not cost any money—as it is an agreement to be settled at the forward expiration date—I only need to worry about the cost of money on the stock position. Hence, for this to be a zero-sum game, my risk-free investment must earn the risk-free rate. Hence the above equation.

Using Ito's Lemma (discussed in chapter 2) for the expansion of the change in the portfolio value over time dt into its subcomponent parts, and by substituting the value of dS_t from Equation 5–7 into the above Equations 5–9 and 5–10, we obtain the following differential equation for the option price:

$$\left(\frac{\partial F_{t,T}}{\partial S_t}\mu S_t + \frac{1}{2}\frac{\partial^2 F_{t,T}}{\partial S_t^2}\sigma^2 S_t^2 + \frac{\partial F_{t,T}}{\partial t} + n\mu S_t - rnS_t\right)dt + \left(\frac{\partial F_{t,T}}{\partial S_t} + n\right)\sigma S_t d\widetilde{z}_t = 0 \qquad (5\text{–}11)$$

Since we want the portfolio to be risk-free, we want to make the stochastic term (the term multiplied by the stochastic variable $d\widetilde{z}_t$) zero. By doing so we obtain the number of shares of the stock that we need to hold in the portfolio:

$$n = -\frac{\partial F_{t,T}}{\partial S_t} \qquad (5\text{–}12)$$

For the portfolio to be risk-free it turns out that we need to sell stock, since n is negative. Plugging the solution to n back in to the differential equation, we obtain the final equation to be solved for the forward price:

$$\frac{\partial F}{\partial t} + \left(r\frac{\partial F}{\partial S} + \frac{1}{2}\frac{\partial^2 F}{\partial S^2}\sigma^2 S^2\right) = 0 \qquad (5\text{–}13)$$

If we assume that the forward price is linear in S, the solution for the forward price—given the above differential equation, and given the end condition, which requires that at the time of expiration the forward price is equal to the spot price—is given by

$$F_{t,T} = e^{r(T-t)}S_t \qquad (5\text{–}14)$$

Hence, we obtain the same result as when showing that the forward price is not equal to the expected spot price.

5.6.4. Effect of Dividends

If we relax the assumption that the stock price pays no dividends, then the differential equation must be adjusted for this. In this case, we have two different stock price return formulations, one for the holder of a stock position, and one for a nonholder of a stock position. The non-holder of a stock position does not capture the value of the dividend payments, and hence she observes the stock price drop after dividend payments by the exact amount of those payments. If we assume that the dividends, δ, are paid continuously, then we have:

$$d\widetilde{S}_t^{non-holder} = S_t(\mu - \delta)dt + S_t\sigma d\widetilde{z}_t \qquad (5\text{–}15)$$

On the other hand, a holder of a stock position does capture the dividend values. We will make the assumption that the holder immediately turns around and reinvests the dividends back into the stock. Hence, to such a stock holder, the stock return is given by:

$$d\widetilde{S}_t^{holder} = S_t\mu dt + S_t\sigma d\widetilde{z}_t \qquad (5\text{–}16)$$

This distinction is important, because a holder of a forward on a stock is a nonholder of the stock until the forward expiration date. Hence, even though the market value of the forward price will change with the stock price change, it will do so as it would for a nonholder, because we would not see the dividend flow as holders of a forward position.

Now we need to answer two questions: How does the payment of the dividend affect what the risk-free portfolio ought to earn over time dt? and How does the payment of the dividend affect our cost of money in setting up the portfolio? The solution to this problem is particularly relevant to energy commodities, as the convenience yield value to the holder of the commodity acts just like the dividend value to the holder of a dividend-paying stock.

As always, the net sum game for a risk-free portfolio where I finance the portfolio through the bank must be zero. On one side I have the difference in the value of the portfolio and on the other I have the cost of money for putting on this portfolio. This has not changed. However, while my stock position does capture the dividend, my forward position does not, hence the change in the market portfolio value is now given by:

$$d\Pi_t = \frac{\partial F_{t,T}}{\partial S_t} dS_t^{non\text{-}holder} + \frac{1}{2} \frac{\partial^2 F_{t,T}}{\partial S_t^2} (dS_t^{non\text{-}holder})^2 + \frac{\partial F_{t,T}}{\partial t} dt + ndS_t^{holder} \qquad (5-17)$$

$$d\Pi_t = \left(\frac{\partial F_{t,T}}{\partial S_t} (\mu - \delta)S_t + \frac{1}{2} \frac{\partial^2 F_{t,T}}{\partial S_t^2} \sigma^2 S_t^2 + \frac{\partial F_{t,T}}{\partial t} + n\mu S_t \right) dt + \left(\frac{\partial F_{t,T}}{\partial S_t} + n \right) \sigma S_t d\tilde{z}_t \qquad (5-18)$$

On the financing side, nothing has changed, since we still have to finance the original investment, which has not changed in value. Furthermore, if we make the portfolio risk-free, then this investment's financing rate must be the risk-free rate.

$$d\Pi = rnS_t dt \qquad (5-19)$$

and in order to zero out the portfolio risk, the position in the stock must once again be

$$n = - \frac{\partial F_{t,T}}{\partial S_t} \qquad (5-20)$$

Again applying Ito's Lemma we obtain the differential equation for the case where the forward is on a dividend-paying stock:

$$\frac{\partial F_{t,T}}{\partial t} + (r - \delta) \frac{\partial F_{t,T}}{\partial S_t} S_t + \frac{1}{2} \frac{\partial^2 F_{t,T}}{\partial S_t^2} \sigma^2 S_t^2 = 0 \qquad (5-21)$$

5.6.5. Equivalence Between Dividends and the Convenience Yield

So far we have worked with a forward on a dividend-paying stock. How do we then translate the above to a differential equation for the forward price on an energy commodity? In order to perform this transformation, we need to recognize the difference between a stock price and the spot price of an energy commodity. The transformation of the dividend-paying stock price into an energy spot price yields the following transformation of Equation 5–19:

$$dS_t^{non-holder} = (\mu - Cy)S_t dt + \sigma S_t d\tilde{z}_t \qquad (5-22)$$

where the spot price S_t now refers to the spot price of the commodity, and where the dividend value has been replaced by the convenience yield value of the commodity. Again, applying Ito's lemma provides us with a partial differential equation for the forward price:

$$\frac{\partial F_{t,T}}{\partial t} + (r - Cy)\frac{\partial F_{t,T}}{\partial S_t}S_t + \frac{1}{2}\frac{\partial^2 F_{t,T}}{\partial S_t^2}\sigma^2 S_t^2 = 0 \qquad (5-23)$$

We have to solve Equation 5–23 to obtain the forward price model as a function of spot price and time. Where the forward price market is driven by more than a single factor, such as the spot price, we would have to incorporate the additional market drivers into the formulation of the risk-free portfolio. A later section will take you through the process of modeling forward prices in the case of a two-factor spot price model.

In order to go ahead and actually solve for the forward price as a function of the market drivers, we have to make some assumptions about how to formulate the convenience yield. There is a huge degree of freedom here, as who is to say that one formulation for the convenience yield is better than another? However, we do have some intuitions to guide us in this process. First of all, setting the convenience yield to a constant would result in a solution to the forward price that would look as follows:

$$F_{t,T} = S_t e^{(r - Cy)(T - t)} \qquad (5-24)$$

This assumption results in forward prices that are either in a contango or in backwardation. The possible forward price market states, where we have backwardation in the front and contango in the back portion of the forward price curve, would simply not be possible under the assumption that the convenience yield is a constant.

If we allow for an introduction of a second factor, the equilibrium price L_t, the above differential equation for the forward price can be generalized to read as follows:

$$\frac{\partial F}{\partial t} + \left((r - Cy)\frac{\partial F}{\partial S} + \frac{1}{2}\frac{\partial^2 F}{\partial S^2}\sigma^2 S^2\right) + \left(r\frac{\partial F}{\partial L} + \frac{1}{2}\frac{\partial^2 F}{\partial L^2}\xi^2 L^2\right)$$
$$+ \frac{\partial^2 F}{\partial S \partial L}\rho\xi L\sigma S = 0 \qquad (5-25)$$

Furthermore, if this equilibrium price is not a traded asset, then the risk-adjusted drift on the equilibrium price[3] has to take the place of the risk-free rate, r:

$$\frac{\partial F}{\partial t} + \left((r - Cy)\frac{\partial F}{\partial S} + \frac{1}{2}\frac{\partial^2 F}{\partial S^2}\sigma^2 S^2\right) + \left((\mu - \lambda\xi)\frac{\partial F}{\partial L} + \frac{1}{2}\frac{\partial^2 F}{\partial L^2}\xi^2 L^2\right)$$
$$+ \frac{\partial^2 F}{\partial S \partial L}\rho\xi L\sigma S = 0 \qquad (5-26)$$

Next, we have to define the convenience yield, Cy. The convenience yield can be either positive or negative, as the relative benefits of holding the energy fuel versus simply purchasing it in the spot market are a function of the general state of the spot market supply and demand. Hence, it would appear reasonable to tie the convenience yield to the relative difference between the current spot price and its equilibrium value as a reflection on the balance between the supply and the demand. Tied to this intuition is also the fact that the convenience yield appears to diminish with increasing forward price expirations. (This would be consistent with a mean-reverting model, where the spot prices approach the equilibrium level prices, resulting in a spot price to equilibrium price spread diminishing, and hence the actual convenience yield value also diminishing.)

Putting the above convenience yield characteristics all together would result in the following two examples of possible functional definitions. The first is a convenience yield as a function of the log of the ratio of the equilibrium price to the spot price:[4]

$$Cy(t) = \delta(t) + \gamma \ln\left(\frac{S_t}{L_t}\right) \tag{5-27}$$

Another example of a possible functional definition is very similar to the above, only instead of using the log of the equilibrium to the spot price ratio, it uses the difference between the spot price and the equilibrium price as a percentage of the spot price:

$$Cy(t) = \delta(t) + \gamma\left(\frac{S_t - L_t}{S_t}\right) \tag{5-28}$$

We will be using the latter case in the following section, where we go through the steps of solving for the forward price from the differential Equation 5–26.

Given the partial differential equation for the forward price, and given the formulation of the convenience yield, we need only one more thing before we can solve for the forward price: the boundary condition. At expiration, the forward price converges to the spot price. Hence, we must have the following condition hold:

$$F_{T,T} = S_T \tag{5-29}$$

5.6.6. Seasonality

Before we proceed toward the final step of solving the differential equation, there is one more issue that we have not yet discussed: seasonality. If you think that the above was complicated, the inclusion of seasonality contributions into the partial differential equation would make the derivation of the forward price model even more difficult. The valuation expert does have the choice of treating seasonality terms either within this level of modeling or within the implementation stage. In the following case study we will leave the seasonality contribution to the implementation stage rather than within the spot price modeling for the sake of simplicity.

We will look into the case of a two-factor spot price model where the spot prices mean-revert toward the equilibrium level, which is assumed to be lognormally distributed. This will be the underlying spot price model. This underlying spot price model will lead us to the solution for the underlying forward price model. The seasonality contribution will be added on top of this forward price model to give us the full solution for the forward prices:

$$F_{t,T} = F_{t,T}^{Und} + \text{seasonality contribution} \tag{5-30}$$

where: F = the market forward price
F^{Und} = the underlying forward price (stripped of seasonality)

5.7. THE TWO-FACTOR MEAN-REVERTING MODEL (PILIPOVIC)

Our final step toward the forward price solution is to go from a spot price model to a forward price model.

Equation 5–26 defines the differential equation for the forward price in case of a two-factor model. We need to solve this differential equation for F subject to the boundary constraint:

$$F_{T,T} = S_T \tag{5-31}$$

We will assume that the spot prices follow the two-factor price mean-reverting model (Pilipovic) introduced in chapter 4:

$$d\widetilde{S}_t = \alpha(L_t - \widetilde{S}_t)dt + S_t\sigma d\widetilde{z}_t \tag{5-32}$$

$$d\widetilde{L}_t = \mu L_t dt + \xi L_t d\widetilde{w}_t \tag{5-33}$$

where: $d\widetilde{z}_t \sim N(0,dt)$
$d\widetilde{w}_t \sim N(0,dt)$
$\rho_{z\widetilde{w}} = 0 =$ correlation between z and w
S = spot price
L = long-term equilibrium price
α = rate of mean reversion
σ = spot price volatility
ξ = equilibrium price volatility

The above Equations 5–32 and 5–33 can be used to solve for the spot price, obtaining the following:

$$\widetilde{S}_t\Big|_o = S_0 e^{-(\alpha+1/2\sigma^2)t+\sigma\widetilde{z}_t} + \alpha L_0 e^{-(\alpha+1/2\sigma^2)t+\sigma\widetilde{z}_t} \int_0^t e^{(\mu-1/2\xi^2)x+\xi\widetilde{w}_x} e^{(\alpha+1/2\sigma^2)x+\sigma\widetilde{z}_x} dx \tag{5-34}$$

By taking the expected value of the right-hand side of the above equation, we obtain the expected value of the spot price at time t, conditional on time $t = 0$:

$$E_0[\widetilde{S}_t] = S_0 e^{-\alpha t} + \frac{\alpha}{(\alpha+\mu)} L_0(e^{\mu t} - e^{-\alpha t}) \tag{5-35}$$

Following an intuitive expectation that, while the forward prices are not equal to the expected spot prices, we can define the forward price to be proportional to the expected spot price:

$$F_{t,T} = \beta(\tau) \cdot E_t[S_T] \tag{5-35}$$

where we have introduced a function of time to define this proportionality:

$\beta = $ function of time
$\tau = T - t$

Since the forward prices are now assumed to be linear in the spot and equilibrium price, the differential equation for the forward price simplifies into the following:

$$(Cy_t - r_t)S_t \partial_S F_{t,T} = (\mu - \lambda\xi)L_t \partial_L F_{t,T} - \partial_\tau F_{t,T} \tag{5-36}$$

By applying the boundary condition on the forward price at the time of its expiration, we obtain the boundary condition for the function β:

$$\beta(\tau = 0) = 1 \tag{5-37}$$

Using Equation 5–28 to define the convenience yield Cy:

$$Cy_t = \delta_t + \frac{\gamma(S_t - L_t)}{S_t} \tag{5-38}$$

When we plug this back into the differential equation for the forward price, Equation 5–29, we obtain the following sets of equations to be solved for β, δ, and γ:

$$\lambda\xi\beta + \partial_\tau\beta = 0 \tag{5-39}$$

$$S_t\{\delta_t\beta - r_t\beta + \gamma\beta + \partial_\tau\beta - \alpha\beta\} + L_t\{-\gamma\beta + \alpha\beta\} = 0 \tag{5-40}$$

which results in the following:

$$\beta(\tau) = e^{-\lambda\xi\tau} \tag{5-41}$$

$$\gamma = \alpha \tag{5-42}$$

$$\delta_t = \lambda\xi + r_t \tag{5-43}$$

We thus obtain the following formulation for the forward price, as a function of both the spot price and the equilibrium price:

$$F_{t,T} = \left(S_t - \left(\frac{\alpha}{\alpha + \mu}\right)L_t\right)e^{-(\alpha + \lambda\xi)\tau} + \left(\frac{\alpha}{\alpha + \mu}\right)L_t e^{(\mu - \lambda\xi)\tau} \tag{5-44}$$

Note that in the typical case for energy markets the drift on the equilibrium price is typically much smaller than the mean-reverting rate, allowing us to make the following approximation:

$$\left(\frac{\alpha}{\alpha + \mu}\right) \approx 1 \tag{5-45}$$

which further simplifies the formulation for the forward price:

$$F_{t,T} \approx (S_t - L_t)e^{-(\alpha + \lambda\xi)\tau} + L_t e^{(\mu - \lambda\xi)\tau} \tag{5-46}$$

The two terms that define the forward price $F_{t,T}$ also determine the look of the forward price curve in terms of the near-term and long-term curve backwardation and/or contango. In the case that the spot price is greater than the equilibrium price—giving a positive convenience yield—the near-term portion of the curve is in backwardation. If the spot price was greater than the equilibrium price, just the opposite would be true: The near-term portion of the forward price curve would be in contango. If the market cost of risk on the equilibrium price was greater than the equilibrium price drift, then the long-term portion of the curve would be in backwardation. But if the opposite was true, the long-term portion of the curve would show a contango market.

Finally, the above formulation can also be generalized to include a long-term equilibrium price convenience yield, which might arise due to long-term costs of production or storage.

5.8. TESTING THE SPOT PRICE MODEL ON FORWARD PRICE DATA

Once the forward price model has been defined, the ultimate test of the model is how well it fits the actual forward price markets. In the case where the forward prices are extremely illiquid and infrequently observed, we are forced to rely to a good extent on the validity of the spot price models and forward price modeling assumptions. In the case where the forward price markets have enough of a history to be used as a test of the forward price theoretical model, we would look for the model parameters to be as stable as possible for a test of forward price model validity.

E N D N O T E S

1. See Hull, *Options, Futures and Other Derivative Securities,* pp. 56–57 and 78–79.
2. Ibid., p. 276.
3. The drift on the equilibrium price, μ, can be generalized to include long-term convenience yield effects, such as the cost of storage. However, if the energy is "in the ground," it may be argued that the cost of storage is, in fact, zero.
4. Gabillon, "Analyzing the Forward Curve," p. 36.

CHAPTER 6

Volatilities

6.1. INTRODUCTION

Volatility is one of the price characteristics that defines the behavior of the price process. There are many different types of volatility measures. Spot price volatility tells us about how much randomness there is in the spot price returns over very small time intervals. Option volatility tells us about the randomness of the option's underlying price over the lifetime of the option. All volatility measures are estimates of to what degree randomness plays a role in price behavior.

When we think about the price of a commodity and how it is going to change from today to tomorrow, there are two very specific things we need to know: What change do we expect to see, and just how wrong may this expectation turn out to be? This relates to the concept that every price change has a deterministic term and a stochastic term, as discussed in chapter 2. The stochastic term represents the randomness in the price over some time period. The volatility tells us the magnitude of this randomness. Similarly, if we were to plot a histogram of price returns, the width of the distribution would be directly related to the volatility of price returns: the greater the volatility, the greater is the width of the distribution.

Since the volatilities tell us about a very important aspect of price behavior, they are used as an important input in the valuation and risk management of a trading book. In option pricing, the width of the price distribution determines the probability of the option expiring in-the-money. If the price distribution is very wide, then the option has a chance of expiring very far in-the-money. Thus, the greater the volatility, the greater is the value of an option. In portfolio analysis and value-at-risk analysis (VAR), volatility is also important in the simulation or estimation of the portfolio value distribution.

Volatility can be very volatile. In fact, volatility in most energy markets is a function of time, exhibiting a combination of deterministic and random behavior. In other words, we see "volatility term structure" in energy markets. This, of course, is a fact that many people choose to ignore. Constant or "flat" volatilities are "easier" to handle in modeling. Unfortunately, this simplifying assumption can wreak havoc with valuation and risk management in energy markets.

In this chapter we will introduce volatility; explain how to calculate historical, market-implied, and model-implied volatilities; and bring together all the concepts as we develop the

kind of discrete volatility matrix required for much of the valuation and risk management required by energy markets.

6.2. MEASURING RANDOMNESS

It would probably be very useful to first explain the difference between three terms: variance,
standard deviation, and volatility. All three measure the magnitude of randomness in a price
process, but each of these measures is expressed within a different framework.

6.2.1. Standard Deviation and Variance

Let's assume that we have a time series of spot prices, and a corresponding time series of spot
price returns, which we will analyze. The standard deviation is a measure of the width of the
probability distribution of the price returns:

$$STD\left(\frac{d\widetilde{S}}{S}\right) = \sqrt{E\left[\left(\frac{d\widetilde{S}}{S}\right)^2\right] - \left(E\left[\frac{d\widetilde{S}}{S}\right]\right)^2} \qquad (6-1)$$

And the variance is simply the standard deviation squared:

$$Variance = \left(STD\left(\frac{d\widetilde{S}}{S}\right)\right)^2 \qquad (6-2)$$

As such, both the standard deviation and the variance are specific to the time period over which
the price returns have been observed. If we take the same spot price process, and look at the
standard deviations or variances of the cumulative price returns at different points in time, we
will get different measures of standard deviation as well as of variance. Therefore, using standard deviations to compare two different distributions would not be meaningful unless we en-
sured that the two distributions covered the exact same overall time period. And the same is
true for the variances.

6.2.2. Volatility Defined

This problem of comparing apples to oranges motivated the definition of volatilities. Volatility,
σ, is simply the price returns' standard deviation normalized by time with time expressed in annual terms:

$$\sigma = \frac{STD\left(\frac{d\widetilde{S}}{S}\right)}{\sqrt{dt}} \qquad (6-3)$$

The volatilities give us a very intuitive measure of the magnitude of price randomness.
The volatility roughly represents the percentage of the price range within which we can expect
to see the prices 66% of the time. For example, if the spot price volatility is 0.1, or 10%, and if

the spot price is currently $20, then over the next year we can—very roughly—expect the price to be within the $18 to $22 range 66% of the time.

6.2.3. Comparing Variance and Volatility

Volatility is the annualized standard deviation of price returns. Comparing distribution volatilities instead of standard deviations ensures that we are always comparing apples to apples. There is one more difference between volatilities and standard deviations. The volatility of a price process is always assumed to measure the annualized distribution width of price returns. Standard deviations, on the other hand, are much more general and do not necessarily measure the width of the price return distributions only, but the width of any distribution you choose. Thus we can have standard deviations of price returns or of prices, for example.

Hence, while the variance grows with the time period used in obtaining the price return, the volatility measure is always expressed in annualized terms. This normalization of the price return's variance into volatilities allows us to compare different markets or models through a consistent measure of magnitudes of random behavior and saves us from the potential mistake of trying to compare apples to oranges. Or, to put it another way, given a normally distributed process with a constant volatility, the variance of the price returns will grow with time. Hence, if we were to compare two such processes, we need to compare either the standard deviations over the exact same time periods, or we can translate the standard deviations into volatilities and compare these standardized measures of randomness magnitudes.

6.2.4. Variance and Volatility in Spot Price Models

Typically, the spot price models assume that the price returns have a stochastic component that is normally distributed. We will use the lognormal model from chapter 4's Equation 4–1—as the simplest with the assumption of flat volatilities—to explain the stochastic behavior characteristics of the spot price:

$$d\widetilde{S} = S\mu dt + \sigma S d\widetilde{z} \tag{6-4}$$

where: S = spot price
μ = spot price rate of return
σ = spot price volatility
$d\widetilde{z}$ = normally distributed random variable with a mean of 0 and a variance of dt

The stochastic term's proportionality to the stock price ensures that the prices always remain positive. If we take the expected value of the price return's stochastic term squared, we obtain the price return's variance (applying Ito's Lemma):

$$E\left[\left(\frac{d\widetilde{S}}{S}\right)^2\right] = \left(E\left[\frac{d\widetilde{S}}{S}\right]\right)^2 + \sigma^2 dt \tag{6-5}$$

Please note that the volatility term, $\sigma^2 dt$, is proportional to the time period over which the price return is calculated.

The volatility is obtained by dividing the variance with time, and then taking the square root of that quantity.

$$\sigma = \sqrt{\frac{E\left[\left(\frac{d\widetilde{S}}{S}\right)^2\right] - \left(E\left[\frac{d\widetilde{S}}{S}\right]\right)^2}{dt}} \qquad (6-6)$$

If we allow the time period between the price observations to be extremely small (close to zero), we obtain an approximation for the volatility that is purely a function of the price returns squared:

$$\sigma \cong \sqrt{\frac{E\left[\left(\frac{d\widetilde{S}}{S}\right)^2\right]}{dt}} \qquad (6-7)$$

By letting dt go to zero, we can omit subtracting the drift term, as it is of order dt, and thus insignificant. One way that this approximation can be tested is through the comparison of volatilities estimated using different models. These volatility estimates tend to be very close to each other despite the fact that different drift terms are assumed by the different models. This tells us that the drift terms are relatively insignificant as compared to the stochastic terms, and that measuring the volatility purely through the use of Equation 6–7 is a good approximation.

6.3. THE STOCHASTIC TERM

In order to be able to understand how to define volatilities over a period of time, and how to re-late the average volatility over a period of time to the shorter-term volatilities that were ob-served within that period of time, we need to understand the properties of the random variable $d\widetilde{z}_t$ within the stochastic term. Again, using the lognormal model, the stochastic component is the $\sigma d\widetilde{z}_t$ term.

Recall from Section 2.6.2.1 that the random variable, $d\widetilde{z}_t$, is normally distributed, with a mean value of zero and a standard deviation of dt:

$$d\widetilde{z}_t \sim \aleph(0, dt) \qquad (6-8)$$

This is equivalent to saying that the expected value of the random variable is zero, while the expected value of the random variable squared is exactly dt. Now let's use this knowledge about the random variable $d\widetilde{z}_t$ to define the behavior of the stochastic term in the equation for the price return, $\sigma d\widetilde{z}_t$. The expected value of this stochastic term is zero, because the expected value of the random variable $d\widetilde{z}_t$ is zero.

Similarly, the expected value of the stochastic term squared is $\sigma^2 dt$. This means that the standard deviation of the price returns is proportional to both the volatility and the square root of the time period between price observations. The greater the time period be-tween observations, the greater is the standard deviation of the price returns. Note that so far we have assumed that the volatility is constant and does not change. Hence the volatility of price returns can remain constant as we allow the time period between the observations to change, while the variance of price returns is proportional to the time period between observations.

6.3.1. Case of Constant Volatility

Now that we understand how the stochastic term's variance grows with the time period between observations, what we still need to know is how the randomness of two consecutive time periods relates to the randomness measured as the sum of the two periods. In this case we can use the fact that under the random walk, the overall path the random variable has taken is simply a sum of the individual random steps (see Figure 6–1):

$$\sigma \tilde{z}_{0,t_N} = \sigma \tilde{z}_{0,t_1} + \sigma \tilde{z}_{t_1,t_2} + ... + \sigma \tilde{z}_{t_{N-1},t_N} \qquad (6-9)$$

where we will assume that the *n-th* step was made corresponding to time period t_n to t_{n+1}, hence each step has a variance of $(t_{n+1} - t_n)$. The expected value of the overall path, $\tilde{z}_{0,t_N}$, is zero, because each of the steps is a random variable with an expected value of zero. Similarly, the variance of the overall path is the sum of the individual steps' variance, given by:

$$\sigma^2 t_n = \sigma^2 t_1 + \sigma^2 (t_2 - t_1) + ... + \sigma^2 (t_N - t_{N-1}) = \sum_{n=0}^{N-1} \sigma^2 (t_{n+1} - t_n) \qquad (6-10)$$

This result was derived by incorporating the fact that in a true random walk, the autocorrelation between the steps is zero, hence each step is independent of other steps and shows zero correlation with the other steps.

6.3.2. Case of Volatilities with Term Structure

The above relationship for the variance of a whole path can be generalized for the case where the volatilities are not the same for each step (i.e., they have term structure). In this case, each

---

FIGURE 6–1

Sample Random Price Path

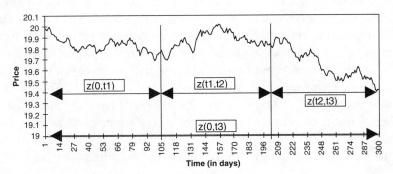

step might have a variance of a different magnitude, $\sigma_{t_n, t_{n+1}}$. The path's variance is then given by:

$$\sigma^2_{0, t_n} \, t_n = \sigma^2_{t_0, t_1} \, t_1 + \sigma^2_{t_1, t_2} (t_2 - t_1) + \dots + \sigma^2_{t_{N-1}, t_N} (t_N - t_{N-1}) = \sum_{n=0}^{N-1} \sigma^2_{t_n, t_{n+1}} (t_{n+1} - t_n) \quad (6-11)$$

The volatility of the path is then given by the square root of the variance of the path divided by the time it took to complete the path:

$$\sigma_{0, t_N} = \sqrt{\frac{\sum_{n=0}^{N-1} \sigma^2_{t_n, t_{n+1}} (t_{n+1} - t_n)}{t_N}} \quad (6-12)$$

It is important to understand this relationship, as it can be extremely useful in allowing us to go from defining volatilities over short periods of time to average volatilities over longer periods of time.

6.4. MEASURING HISTORICAL VOLATILITIES

We can measure the volatility of historical time series of prices; the values generated are called *historical volatilities*. Note that these values are average volatilities for the period analyzed.

6.4.1. Simple Techniques

Volatilities can be observed from historical data of spot or forward prices. Following the pattern of the previous section, we can simply use price returns to obtain the volatility estimates:

$$\sigma^2 dt = E\left[(d\widetilde{S} \, / \, S)^2 \right] \quad (6-13)$$

or rather, for a data set of N price returns, we have:

$$\sigma = \left\{ (1 \, / \, N) \sum_{n=1}^{N} (d\widetilde{S}_n \, / \, S_n)^2 / dt \right\}^{1/2} \quad (6-14)$$

Note that the *1/dt* term is the time normalization of the price return variance. In the cases where the prices returns were calculated using calendar daily prices, this term would equal *1/365*, for 365 days in the year. If, on the other hand, the price returns were weekly, then this term would be *1/52*, for 52 weeks in the year. When historical price data cover only the business days, and not the weekends, we have a choice of how to annualize the volatilities. One alternative is to ignore the weekend effect and simply let *1/dt* equal *1/252* for 252 business days in the year, thus making the assumption that the weekends have no additional impact on the prices. Another choice is to treat the price returns over the weekends by normalizing these returns with *3/365*, while all the other price returns are normalized with *1/365*, thus treating price returns over the weekends differently from the price returns during the week.

6.4.2. More-Complex Techniques

There are more-sophisticated means of obtaining volatility estimates from historical price data. While the above volatility estimation involves daily price observations, such as close of day or daily settlement prices, another alternative is to use not only the closing price, but also the daily high and the low prices of the commodity. The estimation process in this case involves correcting for the bias that results in the use of the high and the low prices over the day. However, once the bias is taken care of, the resulting volatility measure carries less of a sampling error than would the simple close-to-close volatility estimate. This technique is primarily limited to analyzing data from futures markets, where the exchanges report highs, lows, and closing prices that are all readily observed by the marketplace and available to the public as historical data. Most of the over-the-counter (OTC) energy markets do not have this kind of luxury in data availability. In these cases, we are lucky if we can just get our hands on the daily settlement price data in order to do simple volatility estimates.

Once we have volatility estimates for relatively short time periods, such as on a per-week or per-month basis, we can perform time series analysis of these estimates in order to capture volatility term structure behavior, and in order to be able to provide volatility forecasts. Such volatility forecasts are particularly important in the markets where the options are not very liquid and obtaining market-implied volatility information is practically impossible.

6.5. MARKET-IMPLIED VOLATILITIES

This section will discuss volatilities implied by current market prices of an option, a series of options, caplets, and options on average prices. These market-implied volatilities tell us something about the future, whereas historical volatilities only describe the past.

6.5.1. Option-Implied Volatilities

The option volatility is the volatility we input in order to get the option price. However, we can also go the other way. If we have the option price, we can back out the volatility used in getting the option price. Such option-implied volatility can be very different in value from the historical volatility. Historical volatilities are calculated based purely on the historical underlying market price. As such, the historical volatilities have nothing to do with the traded option prices. The traded option prices, instead, imply what the market thinks the option volatilities ought to be going forward in time. As with historical average volatilities, we will be backing out a single, average volatility implied by the market option price(s).

The volatility implied from the market option prices, called the *market-implied volatility*, can be very different from the historical volatility. The reason for this difference is that the option-implied volatility looks forward in time, while the historical volatility looks backward through time. The historical volatility uses historical price data in its calculation, thus it is a volatility measure of already-past price behavior. The market-implied option volatility, on the other hand, represents what the market expects the option underlying price uncertainty to be over the time period from today until the option expiration date. Market-implied volatility "looks" forward in time, and as such is a reflection on how volatile the market believes the prices will be over the time period till the option's expiration.

In order to measure the implied volatility from a single option price, the most practical method ito use is the simple search method: try many different values of volatility in the option pricing formula. The volatility that provides the desired option price would be considered the model-implied volatility.

When we refer to the Black-Scholes equivalent volatility, we simply mean that we have used the Black-Scholes option pricing model in backing out the implied flat or constant volatility, given the option price. Because Black-Scholes is based on a lognormal price process, the Black-Scholes equivalent volatility is also the lognormal equivalent volatility.

When we have market prices for European options—which settle on discrete prices, such as a single spot or a single forward price on a specific date—then the option price can be used to imply the volatility of the discrete price. This option-implied volatility represents the average volatility of the price from today to the option's expiration date.

6.5.2. Implied Volatilities from a Series of Options

If we have a series of European options with discrete price settlement and with increasing expiration times, we can use these options to back out the rudimentary term structure of such time-averaged volatilities of discrete prices. If you have a series of options that are based on the same settlement price, then you have enough information to begin seeing the underlying volatility term structure specific to that settlement price.

For example, if we have three European options, one with an expiration in a month, the second in two months, and the third in three months, and all the options are on the same three-month forward price—which we will assume to be lognormal—then we can use these option prices to back out the term structure of the forward price volatilities over the first three months. In this case, since all three volatilities measure the randomness of the exact same point on the forward price curve, we can use this information to back out the volatility of the forward price for each of the three months. The one-month option price implies the volatility of the forward price over the first month:

$$\sigma_{0,1} = \sigma_{0,1}^{Option} \qquad (6-15)$$

where: $\sigma_{0,1}$ = the first month's volatility

$\sigma_{0,1}^{Option}$ = the 1-month option-implied volatility

The two-month option volatility is the average volatility of the same forward price but over the first and the second month:

$$\sigma_{0,2}^{Option} = \sqrt{\left(\frac{(\sigma_{0,1}^2 + \sigma_{1,2}^2)}{2}\right)} \qquad (6-16)$$

The two-month option-implied volatility is the average of the first month's volatility and the second month's volatility, the averaging being done as defined by the above equation. Since we already have the first month's volatility and we have the two-month option volatility, we can back out the second month's volatility of the forward price:

$$\sigma_{1,2} = \sqrt{2(\sigma_{0,2}^{Option})^2 - \sigma_{0,1}^2} \tag{6-17}$$

Finally, the three-month option volatility is the average of the first, second, and third month's volatilities:

$$\sigma_{0,3}^{Option} = \sqrt{\left(\frac{(\sigma_{0,1}^2 + \sigma_{1,2}^2 + \sigma_{2,3}^2)}{3}\right)} \tag{6-18}$$

This provides the solution for the third month's volatility of the forward price:

$$\sigma_{2,3} = \sqrt{3(\sigma_{0,3}^{Option})^2 - \sigma_{0,1}^2 - \sigma_{1,2}^2} \tag{6-19}$$

In the case where we do not have a series of single option prices on the same discrete forward price, as in the above example, but instead have cap or floor prices (still settled on discrete prices), the job of backing out the volatility term structure of the underlying price(s) becomes more difficult. This particular problem is handled in the following section.

6.5.3. Calibrating Caplet Volatility Term Structure

Option contracts that are commonly called "caps" and "floors" also provide us with information to calibrate volatility term structure.

A cap or a floor is a series of options all priced together, with their prices summed up to give a single cap or floor price. (A cap is a series of call options; a floor is a series of put options.) A cap or a floor has a tenor associated with it. The tenor refers to the expiration date differential between the options within the cap or the floor. For example, a one-year cap with a monthly tenor consists of twelve individual options, referred to as caplets, with the first caplet expiring in a month, the second in two months, the third in three, etc., with the last caplet expiring in one year. So, given a series of cap or floor prices instead of individual option prices, the process of backing out volatility term structures, specifically for individual options, becomes more difficult.

6.5.3.1. Motivation

You may wonder why in the case of caps or floors we need to bother with backing out the individual caplet option volatilities. Why not just back out the cap-specific volatilities? And you would be right to make this comment in a world where the volatilities are indeed constant or do not have a strong term structure.

Unfortunately, this is not the case in the real world of energies. By backing out only the cap volatilities we would be making the incorrect assumption that the option volatility is constant throughout the cap lifetime. Furthermore, we would find many limitations in the process, including possibly obtaining negative forward variances—a topic that we will get into in the following sections. Volatilities do indeed have a term structure—typically a very obvious and strong term structure in the energy markets—suggesting that the volatilities at which the options of different expirations should be valued will possibly be very different.

Ignoring term structure in caplet volatilities would impact not only the pricing of the options, but also the hedging. By not recognizing and backing out this caplet volatility term structure, the trading operation would allow for the existence of arbitrage within its books. Let me give you an example here. Suppose that I back out and use only the cap-implied volatilities in the trading and hedging of my cap books. I might use a volatility of 25% for pricing the one-year monthly tenor cap, and a volatility of 15% for pricing the two-year monthly tenor cap. If I did this, my pricing would be inconsistent, not to mention the hedging.

Why is this a problem? Well, the one-year cap consists of the first twelve caplet options, the first with an expiration in one month and the last with an expiration in one year. The two-year cap consists of the twenty-four options, the first with an expiration in one month, and the last with an expiration in two years. Hence, the two-year cap consists of the one-year cap plus the additional twelve options, with expirations past the first year. And yet, by using the two different cap volatilities I would be pricing this one-year cap—on its own—at the 28% volatility, and I would be pricing it—as a part of the two-year cap—at the 22% volatility (see Figure 6–2). This is obviously inconsistent pricing, not to mention that my hedging of the first-year cap within the two different deals would also be very different, when in fact it should be the same. The only way of getting around this problem is to indeed back out the caplet, or the individual option volatilities, in order to obtain the true volatility term structure, which will allow consistent pricing and hedging between caps and floors. I should be using the exact same caplet volatility curve to price the two caps in the example (see Figure 6–3).

6.5.3.2. Calibration Techniques

Suppose that you have the three-month cap, the one-year cap, and the two-year cap, all of monthly tenor. This means that the first cap consists of three caplets or options. The second cap consists of twelve caplets, the first three being identical to the caplets in the first cap. The third cap consists of twenty-four caplets, the first twelve of which are identical to the caplets in the one-year cap. We are trying to back out the volatilities corresponding to each caplet such that

F I G U R E   6–2

Incorrect Treatment of Caplet Volatilities

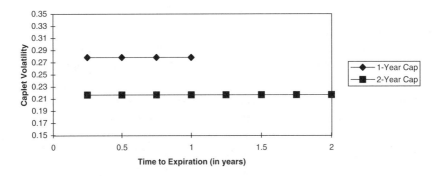

FIGURE 6–3

Correct Treatment of Caplet Volatilities

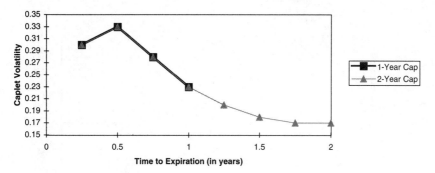

we retain the market price of the three caps while at the same time we use the same volatilities to price the same caplets. The cap prices are then given by:

$$CAP_1 = C(F_1,\sigma_1,T_1) + C(F_2,\sigma_2,T_2) + C(F_3,\sigma_3,T_3) \tag{6-20}$$

$$CAP_2 = C(F_1,\sigma_1,T_1) + C(F_2,\sigma_2,T_2) + ... + C(F_{12},\sigma_{12},T_{12}) \tag{6-21}$$

$$CAP_3 = C(F_1,\sigma_1,T_1) + C(F_2,\sigma_2,T_2) + ... + C(F_{24},\sigma_{24},T_{24}) \tag{6-22}$$

where $C(F_T,\sigma_T,T)$ equals the call option price of the caplet calculated as a function of the forward price F_T, using the volatility σ_T, and with the expiration time of T. We try to estimate all the caplet volatilities, σ_T, such that we preserve the market prices of caps, CAP_1, CAP_2, and CAP_3.[1]

An example of what such a caplet volatility term structure might look like is given in Figure 6–4. The graph shows the volatilities increasing from the current spot price out to the three-month point. Such a volatility term structure is typical of a market where there is an expectation of an event, such as volatility in the weather, this expectation being reflected in volatilities increasing before they begin declining toward more of the volatility equilibrium levels in the long-term portion of the volatility curve.

6.5.4. Implied Volatilities from Options on the Average of Price

We discussed the complications of backing out volatilities when the market quotes caps and floors instead of individual options on discrete prices. Here we will discuss an additional complication: that of pricing options where the settlement is based on an average of prices rather than a discrete price. In this case, we need to ensure that our option model can indeed handle the averaging effects, so that we end up with a volatility term structure consistent with discrete price volatilities. If we do not go through this additional trouble, we might have to carry volatility term structures for all kinds of possible averages, such as monthly average of daily prices, quarterly average of daily prices, annual average of weekly prices, etc. Even more im-

F I G U R E   6-4

Caplet Volatilities with Event Expectation

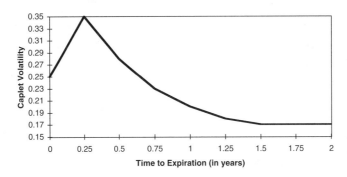

portantly, by not translating the volatilities back to the discrete price level we will lose the possibility of linking the volatilities of different types of averages, which will result once again in an inconsistent treatment of the pricing of options on different types of averages. Figures 6–5 and 6–6 show the effects of averaging on option volatilities. The first graph shows the case of flat discrete price volatilities, and the second graph shows the case of discrete price volatilities with term structure.

In the energy markets, the OTC options markets tend to trade quite a bit of caps and floors on averages of prices. In trying to back out the option volatility term structures for discrete prices in the energy markets, we need to worry both about the treatment of caps vs. caplets and the treatment of options on discrete vs. average price settlements. Obviously, this can be quite a job, and the actual development process requires a good amount of organizational thought.

F I G U R E   6-5

Average Price Option Vols for Flat Caplet Volatilities

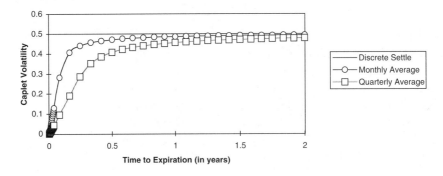

FIGURE 6-6

Average Price Option Vols for a Term Structure of Caplet Volatilities

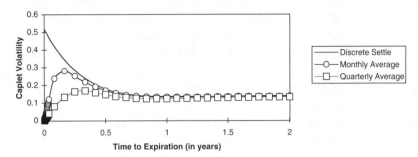

6.5.5. The Volatility Smile

Last, but not least, is the problem of capturing the *volatility smile*. The volatility smile is a phenomenon that shows the lognormal equivalent volatilities for options of the same time to expiration and on the same settlement price to be different across different strikes. When the actual price distribution has fatter tails than the lognormal model distribution does, the out-of-the-money calls and puts tend to show volatilities that increase as the option strikes make the options go further and further out-of-the-money. Such volatility strike structure ends up looking like a smile, hence the name.

In reality, the volatility strike structure does not have to be a smile. It can take on various shapes, depending on what the actual price distribution is, compared to the lognormal price distribution. As you might have already guessed, if the option pricing model is built to incorporate the exact price distribution, the volatility strike structure would be flat, i.e., the same volatility would reflect all the options of the same expiration time but of varying strike prices. Unfortunately, it is difficult to come up with such an option pricing model that incorporates all the price distribution characteristics. Thus the traders are forced to incorporate the strike structure volatility effects in the implementation of the option methodology: the traders maintain the volatilities for various out-of-the-money and in-the-money options.

6.6. MODEL-IMPLIED VOLATILITIES

In this section we are going to introduce the third set of volatility calculations: the model-implied volatilities. Given model parameters, we can calculate the model-implied volatilities. We will use the three price models introduced in chapters 2 through 5 to back out model-specific volatility term structures and correlation matrices:

- the single-factor lognormal
- a single-factor log-of-price mean-reverting models
- the two-factor price mean-reverting model

The assumptions we make—through models—about the market spot price behavior impacts the behavior of forward prices, and both of these impact the look of volatility term structures and correlation matrices. Given the models for the spot and forward price behavior, we can estimate their model-implied volatilities and correlations. We can use historical data to observe the historical volatilities and correlations. Similarly, we can use the historical data to calibrate the model parameters, and then use these to obtain model-implied volatilities and correlations. The comparison between the historical volatilities and correlations and their model-implied counterparts provides us with yet another means of benchmarking between models.

While these model-implied volatilities and correlations provide us with another set of tests on model appropriateness, they also may come in use in the case where the options market is highly illiquid, if not almost nonexistent. In such a market, the options on the books still need to be valued regardless of how sporadic and infrequent the option deals are. The model-implied volatilities can be used in such cases to support whatever market information there is and allow the pricing and hedging calculations for the illiquid options.

6.6.1. The Lognormal Model

The single-factor lognormal model was defined by Equation 4–1, and it is repeated below:

$$d\widetilde{S}_t = \mu S_t dt + \sigma S_t d\widetilde{z}_t \tag{6-23}$$

The volatility is the same as the Black-Scholes implied volatility, as Black-Scholes assumes that Equation 6–23 is the option's settlement-price behavior. This volatility is assumed to be constant over time, and is exactly the same for the spot price as for all the forward prices on the forward price curve:

$$\sigma_t^s = \sqrt{\frac{E_t\left[\left(\frac{d\widetilde{S}_t}{S_t}\right)^2\right]}{dt}} = \sigma \tag{6-24}$$

$$\sigma_t^{F_{t,T}} = \sqrt{\frac{E_t\left[\left(\frac{d\widetilde{F}_{t,T}}{F_{t,T}}\right)^2\right]}{dt}} = \sigma \tag{6-25}$$

The model-implied volatility term structure is flat. In addition, the single-factor lognormal model implies that the forward prices are perfectly correlated with the spot prices and also with each other:

$$\rho_{S_t,F_{t,T}} = \frac{E_t\left[\frac{d\widetilde{S}_t}{S_t}\frac{d\widetilde{F}_{t,T}}{F_{t,T}}\right]}{\sigma^{S_t}\sigma^{F_{t,T}}dt} = 1 \tag{6-26}$$

$$\rho_{F_{t,T1},F_{t,T2}} = \frac{E_t\left[\frac{d\widetilde{F}_{t,T1}}{F_{t,T1}}\frac{d\widetilde{F}_{t,T2}}{F_{t,T2}}\right]}{\sigma^{F_{t,T1}}\sigma^{F_{t,T2}}dt} = 1 \tag{6-27}$$

Since the energy spot and forward price volatilities exhibit strong decaying term structure across the forward prices, and nonperfect correlations, the single-factor lognormal model is not consistent with reality.

6.6.2. The Log-of-Price Mean-Reverting Model

In the single-factor version of the log-of-price mean-reverting model, the mean reversion impacts the volatility term structure by giving it a decreasing effect over time. As discussed to a great extent in the previous chapters, mean reversion has a dampening effect on spot price volatility, estimated from spot distributions over time. The greater the time, the more we see this dampening effect when compared to what the lognormal model would exhibit with the exact same spot price volatility.

When dealing with forward prices—whose behavior is a function of the spot price behavior, the volatility dampening effect is also of importance. In fact, in a single-factor mean-reverting model, the volatility of the forward prices approaches zero as the forward price expiration date is allowed to grow to infinity. Specifically, the volatility of the spot and forward prices in a single-factor mean-reverting model, where the mean reversion is in the log of the spot price, is given by:

$$\sigma_t^s = \sqrt{\frac{E_t\left[\left(\frac{d\widetilde{S}_t}{S_t}\right)^2\right]}{dt}} = \sigma \tag{6-28}$$

$$\sigma_t^{F_{t,T}} = \sqrt{\frac{E_t\left[\left(\frac{d\widetilde{F}_{t,T}}{F_{t,T}}\right)^2\right]}{dt}} = e^{-\alpha(T-t)}\sigma \tag{6-29}$$

Note that while the spot price volatility is constant over time, the volatility of the forward price decreases exponentially the greater the forward price time to expiration, T, is.

Now the interesting thing about this single-factor mean-reverting model, with the mean-reversion in the log of the price, is that while the volatilities are indeed functions of the forward price time to expiration and have a term structure that decreases over time toward zero, the correlations are not a function of the forward price time to expiration. In fact, the correlations remain perfect between all points on the forward price curve:

$$\rho_{S_t,F_{t,T2}} = \frac{E_t\left[\frac{d\widetilde{S}_t}{S_t}\frac{d\widetilde{F}_{t,T}}{F_{t,T}}\right]}{\sigma^{S_t}\sigma^{F_{t,T}}dt} = 1 \tag{6-30}$$

$$\rho_{F_{t,T1},F_{t,T2}} = \frac{E_t\left[\frac{d\widetilde{F}_{t,T1}}{F_{t,T1}}\frac{d\widetilde{F}_{t,T2}}{F_{t,T2}}\right]}{\sigma^{F_{t,T1}}\sigma^{F_{t,T2}}dt} = 1 \tag{6-31}$$

The correlations retain the characteristics of a lognormal model with no mean-reversion effects. This is due to the fact that we are working with a single-factor model. The next case, which looks at the two-factor price mean-reverting model, will have a different correlation result.

6.6.3. The Price Mean-Reverting Model

In the two-factor price mean-reverting model (Pilipovic), we find that the volatilities of the forward prices and the correlations as well are functions of the forward price time to expiration and follow a mean reverting process to the equilibrium price volatility. The stochastic term in the change of the forward price, $dF_{t,T}$, over some time period, dt, is given by:

$$\Delta F_{t,T} - E[\Delta F_{t,T}] \cong S_t \sigma e^{\alpha' \tau} \Delta \widetilde{z} + (e^{\mu' \tau} - e^{-\alpha' \tau}) L_t \xi \Delta \widetilde{w}_t$$

where: S = spot price
$F_{t,T}$ = forward price with expiration T observed at time t
α = rate of mean reversion
α' = risk-adjusted rate of mean reversion = $\alpha - \lambda \xi$
λ = cost of risk
τ = time to expiration = $T - t$
σ = spot price volatility
μ' = risk-adjusted drift rate
ξ = equilibrium price volatility
$d\widetilde{z}_t$ = random stochastic variable in the spot price return
$d\widetilde{w}_t$ = random stochastic variable in the equilibrium price return

Assuming that the spot price and the equilibrium price have a correlation of ρ, we have the spot and the forward price model-implied volatilities defined as follows:

$$\sigma_t^s = \sqrt{\dfrac{E_t\left[\left(\dfrac{d\widetilde{S}_t}{S_t}\right)^2\right]}{dt}} = \sigma \tag{6-32}$$

$$\sigma_t^{F_{t,T}} = \sqrt{\dfrac{E_t\left[\left(\dfrac{d\widetilde{F}_{t,T}}{F_{t,T}}\right)^2\right]}{dt}}$$

$$= \sqrt{\dfrac{e^{-2\alpha'(T-t)}\sigma^2 S_t^2 + \left(\left\{\dfrac{\alpha}{\alpha+\mu}\right\}\{e^{\mu'(T-t)} - e^{-\alpha'(T-t)}\}\right)^2 \xi^2 L_t^2}{F_{t,T}^2}} \tag{6-33}$$

While the spot price volatility remains constant over time, the forward price volatility is defined by both the spot price volatility and the long-term equilibrium price volatility. The weighting of the forward price volatility on the spot price volatility decreases, while the weighting on the long-term equilibrium price increases as the forward price expiration time increases. The long-term forward prices have volatilities converging toward the equilibrium price volatility. As the forward price expiration date goes to infinity, its volatility approaches and is almost entirely defined by the long-term equilibrium price volatility.

Similarly, for the correlations, we obtain:

$$\rho_{S_t, F_{t,T2}} = \frac{E_t\left[\dfrac{d\widetilde{S}_t}{S_t}\dfrac{d\widetilde{F}_{t,T}}{F_{t,T}}\right]}{\sigma^{S_t}\sigma^{F_{t,T}}dt} = e^{-\alpha'(T-t)}\frac{\sigma S_t}{\sigma_t^{F_{t,T}}F_{t,T}} \tag{6-34}$$

$$\rho_{F_{t,T1}, F_{t,T2}} = \frac{E_t\left[\dfrac{d\widetilde{F}_{t,T1}}{F_{t,T1}}\dfrac{d\widetilde{F}_{t,T2}}{F_{t,T2}}\right]}{\sigma^{F_{t,T1}}\sigma^{F_{t,T2}}dt}$$

$$= \frac{\left(e^{-\alpha(T_1-t)}e^{-\alpha(T_2-t)}\sigma^2 S_t^2 + \left(\dfrac{\alpha}{\alpha+\mu}\right)^2 (e^{\mu(T_1-t)}-e^{-\alpha'(T_1-t)})(e^{\mu'(T_2-t)}-e^{-\alpha'(T_2-t)})\xi^2 L_t^2\right)}{\sigma^{F_{t,T_1}}F_{t,T_1}\sigma^{F_{t,T_2}}F_{t,T_2}} \tag{6-35}$$

As long as the volatility of the long-term equilibrium price, ξ, is nonzero—i.e., the long-term equilibrium price is allowed to exhibit a stochastic behavior—the correlation between the forward prices of different expiration dates, and also the correlation between the spot and forward prices will be less than one.

If the two-factor price mean-reverting model is reduced to a single-factor model, the above correlations will become one, as ξ is set to zero. While a single-factor mean-reverting model can capture the decreasing volatility term structure typical of the energy markets, a second factor in the spot price model is necessary to capture the nonperfect correlations between the spot and the forward prices and also between the forward prices of differing expiration times.

We can simplify the above expression for volatility and correlation by approximating the spot price with the equilibrium price and assuming that the drift term on the equilibrium price is much smaller than the mean-reverting parameter:

$$\sigma_F^2 \cong \sigma^2 e^{-2\alpha'\tau} + (1 - e^{-\alpha'\tau})^2\xi^2 + 2\rho\sigma\xi e^{-\alpha'\tau}(1 - e^{-\alpha'\tau}) \tag{6-36}$$

where: $\alpha' = \alpha - \lambda\xi$

and where we have allowed the spot and the equilibrium price to exhibit a nonzero currelation, ρ

We can also simplify the correlation formulation:

$$E\left[\frac{d\widetilde{F}_{0,T_1}}{F_{0,T_1}}, \frac{d\widetilde{F}_{0,T_2}}{F_{0,T_2}}\right] \cong e^{-\alpha'(T_1+T_2)}\sigma^2 + (1 - e^{-\alpha'T_1})(1 - e^{\alpha'T_2})\xi^2$$

$$+ (e^{-\alpha'T_1}(1 - e^{-\alpha'T_2}) + e^{-\alpha'T_2}(1 - e^{-\alpha'T_1}))\rho\sigma\xi \tag{6-37}$$

Figures 6–7 through 6–12 demonstrate that, when compared to historical volatilities in

F I G U R E   6–7

Comparison of Model Implied to Historical WTI Volatilities

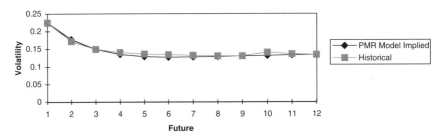

F I G U R E   6–8

Comparison of Model Implied to Historical Natural Gas Volatilities

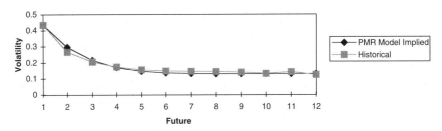

F I G U R E   6–9

WTI Historical Correlations

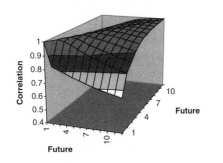

F I G U R E   6–10

WTI Model Implied Correlations

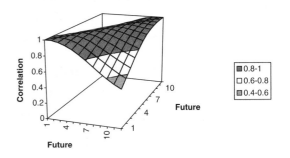

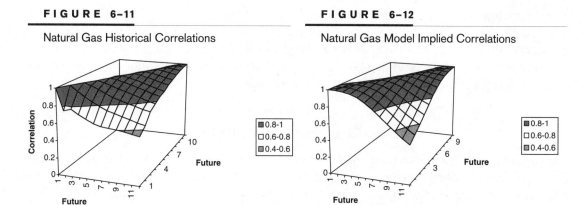

FIGURE 6-11

Natural Gas Historical Correlations

FIGURE 6-12

Natural Gas Model Implied Correlations

the natural gas and WTI markets, the two-factor price mean-reverting model does well in capturing the behavior of forward prices.

The practical implication of the two-factor model is that every forward price point on the curve ends up having its own volatility term structure. The two-factor model forces us to look at volatilities not across a single-dimension—time—but across two dimensions—time and forward price. Thus we go from the single-volatility term structure—corresponding to single-factor models—to the two-dimensional matrix of volatilities.

6.7. BUILDING THE VOLATILITY MATRIX

To truly understand the implications of having forward prices which have individual volatility term structures, we will go through the process of building a volatility matrix. Building the volatility matrix depends on all the intuition and techniques introduced so far in this chapter. The technique represents a new, comprehensive methodology.[1]

Any market that exhibits a split personality in the forward prices—as measured by short-term forward prices vs. long-term forward prices, with correlation being significantly less than one between the short- and long-term forward prices—needs to be treated with a volatility matrix instead of a single volatility curve. In other words, any market that has a true nature of being driven by two factors (if not more) needs to have a volatility matrix structure rather than a one-dimensional volatility term structure.

6.7.1. Introduction to the Forward Volatility Matrix

The volatility matrix provides the lowest common denominator volatilities that can be combined in many different ways to capture the pricing of a variety of different types of options in a trading book. These lowest common denominators represent the smallest volatility blocks necessary to provide a consistent volatility framework for the various types of options in the book, and for capturing the specific characteristics of a particular marketplace (see Figure 6–1). Each cell could represent a discrete volatility or the volatility of the particular time bucket.

In this volatility matrix framework, we have a means of defining discrete, or very short-term, volatilities for every forward price at any point in time in the future. The volatility matrix has two dimensions: the first is the time dimension, starting with today, and the second is the forward price, starting with the spot price. All the elements in this volatility matrix are thus short-term volatilities, representing the volatilities of forward prices with different expirations and at different points in time, but always over some short time period, dt.

6.7.2. Discrete Volatilities

We can define the discrete volatility at time t specific to the forward price with expiration time T, $F_{t,T}$, as $\sigma_{t,\tau}^{Discrete}$, where τ equals $T - t$, i.e., the forward price time to expiration relative to the time of observation t. (See Figure 6–13.) Now suppose that we can forecast these discrete volatilities at regular and discrete time periods, starting with time $t = 0$, then dt, $2dt$, $3dt$, etc. For each of these times we will have a set of discrete volatilities corresponding to all the forward prices. Hence, for time $t = 0$, we will have the current discrete volatilities $\sigma_{0,\tau}^{Discrete}$, across all the forward prices, where τ is the time to expiration. At time dt, we will have the first discrete period's discrete volatilities, again $\sigma_{dt,\tau}^{Discrete}$ across all the forward prices but as observed at time dt, and so on. Now, if we let the expiration times τ of all the forward prices also be defined in discrete time terms, we obtain a matrix of discrete volatilities, with the vertical axis representing the time t, and the horizontal axis representing the forward expiration time—expressed relative to time t. A three dimensional example of such a volatility matrix is shown in Figure 6–14. Figure 6–15 shows another example of a volatility matrix under event expectations.

The volatility forecast for the spot price at some time ndt in the future would then be given by $\sigma_{ndt,0}$, where the first index refers to the time of the volatility forecast, and the second index refers to the point on the forward price curve (in the case of the spot price it is the 0-th point). In Figure 6–13, the spot price discrete volatility term structure is given by the first column. If we take a snapshot of the current discrete volatility for all the points on the forward price curve, these volatilities would be given by $\sigma_{0,ndt}$. The first index is given the value zero because we are

F I G U R E   6–13

Discrete Volatility Matrix by Time Buckets

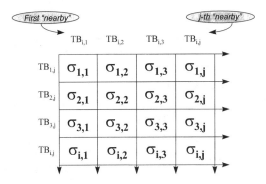

FIGURE 6–14

Sample Discrete Volatility Matrix

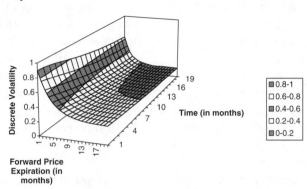

taking the discrete volatility snapshot today, at time $t = 0$, and the second index, *ndt*, refers to the forward price point on the curve with expiration time of *ndt* relative to today.

Hence, $\sigma_{ndt,mdt}$ refers to the volatility at time *ndt* from today, of the forward price, which expires at time *mdt* relative to *ndt*. The volatility term structure of the same forward price point on the forward price curve would be given by one of the columns in Figure 6–13. On the other hand, if we wanted to find out what the discrete volatilities are at some time *t* for all the points on the forward price curve, starting with the spot price, we would look at a particular row of the matrix that corresponds to the time of interest.

6.7.3. Tying In Caplet Volatilities

We are using discrete, or short-term, volatilities to build this matrix, in order to ensure that we have the least-common-denominator volatilities, which can be used in many different ways to ultimately value a diverse set of derivative products. We will go through the steps of how these

FIGURE 6–15

Sample Effect of Event Expectations on Discrete Volatilities

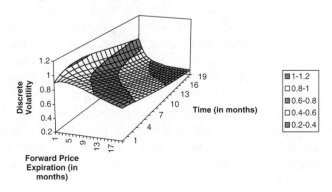

volatilities relate to the particular option volatilities in the later sections of this chapter. But first it would be insightful to take you through the steps of how these discrete volatilities might equate to Black-Scholes equivalent volatilities in the case of a European option on a forward price.

Suppose that at time $t = 0$ we purchase an option on a forward price with the expiration time of $3dt$, and the option expires at the same time as the forward price, at time $t = 3dt$. During the first time period, $t = dt$, the forward price moves down the forward price curve, from the expiration of $3dt$ at the start of the period to the expiration of $2dt$ at the end of the period. During the second time period, $t = 2dt$, the forward price keeps moving down the forward price curve, from the expiration of $2dt$ at the start of the period to the expiration of dt at the end of the period. Finally, during the third and also the last time period, $t = 3dt$, the forward price moves from the point of expiration of dt down the curve until it converges with the spot price at the very end of the third period.

In terms of the volatility matrix, the discrete volatilities, which correspond to each of the periods, lie along a "cross-diagonal" line: the discrete volatility corresponding to the first period is found in the first row and third column of the volatility matrix, the discrete volatility corresponding to the second period is in the second row and second column, while the third-period discrete volatility lies in the third row and first column of the discrete volatility matrix. The average volatility across all three periods relates to these discrete volatilities as follows:

$$\sigma_{0,3} = \sqrt{\frac{(\sigma_{1,3}^2 + \sigma_{2,2}^2 + \sigma_{3,1}^2)}{3}} \qquad (6-38)$$

European options with discrete forward price settlement will have average option volatilities that are the average across the cross-diagonal of the discrete volatility matrix. The calculation of these average volatilities can be generalized so that for the option that expires in N months we have:

$$\sigma_{0,N} = \sqrt{\frac{(\sigma_{1,N}^2 + \sigma_{2,N-1}^2 + ... + \sigma_{N,1}^2)}{N}} \qquad (6-39)$$

Note that if the volatility of the near-term portion of the forward price curve tends to be much greater than the volatility of the long-term portion of the curve, the forward price discrete volatilities across time—as the forward converges toward the spot price and we come closer and closer to the option expiration—will grow. Figure 6-16 shows a sample path that the discrete volatilities of a forward price might follow as it converges to spot.

In volatility markets, where the spot price volatility is significantly greater than the long-term forward price volatility, this market characteristic translates into options that capture most of their volatility value close to the expiration. Another way of saying this is that the option decay is the greatest close to the option expiration. Finally, this fact of increasing discrete volatilities as the forward price converges toward the spot price has a big impact on the hedging calculations. Thus, an option model that uses the average option volatility will do just fine in terms of the price. However, it will do very poorly in terms of providing the appropriate hedges. Instead, an option model that incorporates the discrete volatility term structure will provide both the correct price and the correct hedges.

FIGURE 6-16

Discrete Volatilities Defining the 5-Month Caplet Volatility

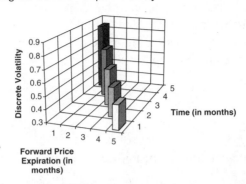

6.7.4. Two-Dimensional Approach to Volatility Term Structure

The discrete volatility matrix approach allows us to build in market characteristics that a single-volatility term structure would not allow us to do. (A "single-volatility term structure" is captured by a vector of volatilities rather than a matrix.) As discussed above, the capture of market characteristics through modeling can have a big impact on the appropriate hedging and risk management of options. One such characteristic is that the near-term portion of the forward price curve has very little correlation with the long-term portion of the forward price curve. It is only intuitive, then, that the near-term portion of the forward price curve has a volatility term structure that can be very different from the volatility term structure of the long-term portion of the forward price curve.

Similarly, incorporating the mean-reverting tendencies in the spot price results in the spot price and near-term forward price volatility term structures, which decay over time toward much lower levels. This possibly very strong decay—when the mean reversion is very strong—is not seen in the long-term portion of the forward price curve, which tends to have much flatter volatility term structure. Similarly, expectations of eventful markets might give spot and near-term forward price volatilities a term structure with a "hump." The existence of such an event hump in the volatility term structure of the long-term forward prices is very unlikely, unless there are events that are expected to affect both the short-term and the long-term market prices.

However, even in markets where the mean reversion is relatively small, such as the interest rate markets, there is a market condition under which a single-volatility term structure would yield what should be impossible results: The resulting discrete variances calculated under the single-volatility term structure framework can turn out to be negative. The single-volatility term structure framework is equivalent to the matrix approach where all the rows of the volatility matrix are equivalent to the very first row. In other words, in the single-volatility term structure framework we are making the assumption that the volatilities of individual forward price points are constant over time.

Let's work through two examples of single-volatility term structure applications. First we will look at a case where the single-volatility term structure approach yields positive discrete volatilities, and then we will look at a market condition where the resulting discrete volatilities turn out to be mathematically imaginary. If the market quotes only caps and floors, the transformation from the cap volatilities to the caplet volatilities needs to be performed first. Once the caplet volatilities are available, we can proceed to back out the discrete volatilities.

Consider the following market situation. Suppose that you have caplet volatilities for the one-month, two-month, and three-month caplets:

$$\sigma_1^{CAPLET} = 40\%$$
$$\sigma_2^{CAPLET} = 30\%$$
$$\sigma_3^{CAPLET} = 23\%$$

The first month's discrete volatility is then given by the first month's caplet volatility:

$$\sigma_1 = \sigma_1^{CAPLET} = 40\%$$

In order to get the second month's discrete volatility, we need to do a bit of calculation:

$$\sigma_2 = \sqrt{2(\sigma_2^{CAPLET})^2 - \sigma_1^2} = \sqrt{2(0.3)^2 - (0.4)^2} = 14.14\% \tag{6-40}$$

Now that we have both the first and the second month's discrete volatilities, we can calculate the third month's discrete volatility:

$$\sigma_3 = \sqrt{3(\sigma_3^{CAPLET})^2 - \sigma_2^2 - \sigma_1^2} = \sqrt{3(0.252) - 0.42 - 0.14142} = 8.66\% \tag{6-41}$$

Thus, the discrete volatilities that correspond to the caplet volatilities of 40%, 30%, and 25%, are given by 40%, 14.14%, and 8.66%. These discrete volatilities would then be incorporated in the pricing and hedging of options, as is discussed in chapter 8 on option pricing.

But now let's take a look at a slightly different market scenario, which actually is not that different in the caplet volatility values but is very different in the discrete volatility results we obtain. Suppose that the one-month forward price market is just a little more eventful, resulting in the one-month caplet having a volatility of 45% rather than 40%. We now have the one-month discrete volatility given by:

$$\sigma_1 = \sigma_1^{CAPLET} = 45\% \tag{6-42}$$

but now the second month discrete volatility is given by:

$$\sigma_2 = \sqrt{2(\sigma_2^{CAPLET})^2 - \sigma_1^2} = \sqrt{2(0.3)^2 - (0.45)^2} = \sqrt{-0.0225} \tag{6-43}$$

an imaginary number! You might ask, how can this be? The problem is that while the volatility of the one-month forward price is currently at 45%, it is not going to remain at that level. Instead, it might drop down to 40% in just a month. Thus, the volatility of that one-month forward price in a month will drop back to the noneventful levels, resulting in a two-month caplet volatility, which is priced assuming the drop from the 45% to the 40% volatility level.

The above example forces us to treat discrete volatilities within a two-dimensional matrix rather than within a single-volatility term structure. This latter market scenario is very common in eventful energy markets, where the caplet volatility drop-off can be quite significant.

6.7.5. Tying In Historical Volatilities

The historical volatilities represent the historical volatility term structure across the forward price points on the forward price curve, which the term structures of all the forward price points ought to approach. In other words, if we built a discrete volatility matrix and let the number of rows of the matrix go to infinity—i.e., if we looked at the discrete volatilities across the forward prices at some infinite time in the future—these discrete volatilities ought to converge to the historical average volatilities.

For example, if the first month's forward price currently has a volatility of 300%, but historically has an average volatility of 200%, then over time we ought to see the 300% volatility of the first month's forward price drop down to 200%. This expectation of the current discrete volatilities approaching the historical volatilities over time should hold for all the forward prices. As we look across the rows of the volatility matrix, we should see the discrete volatilities across rows approach the historical volatility term structure.

6.7.6. Tying In Caplet and Swaption Prices

We have already gone through an example of how a European option volatility would be translated into the discrete volatilities of the volatility matrix. Specifically, the caplet volatility with an expiration time of $N\Delta t$ would be a function of the discrete volatilities as follows:

$$(\sigma_{caplet})^2 \, N\Delta t = \sum_{n=1}^{N} \sigma_{n, N-n+1}^2 \, \Delta t \qquad (6-44)$$

where: $\sigma_{n, N-n+1}$ = the discrete volatility corresponding to the *n-th* row and $N - n + 1$ *th* column of the volatility matrix. Figure 6–17 shows the relationship between discrete volatility paths of several forward prices and their corresponding caplet volatilities.

FIGURE 6–17

From Discrete Volatilities to Caplet Volatility

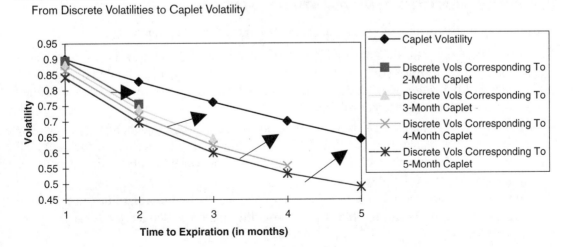

F I G U R E   6–18

Discrete Volatilities Defining the 4-Month Swaption into a 2-Month Swap

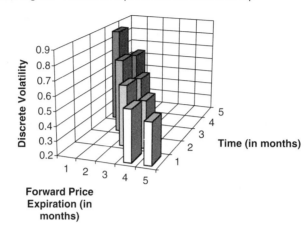

In the case of swaptions, we would also need to have a correlation matrix available for re-lating the discrete volatilities to the swaption volatility. The process is a bit more complicated, but the end results retain consistency between the caplet (and therefore cap) and swaption prices and volatilities. Figure 6–18 shows the discrete volatility paths followed by the two for-ward prices for the case of a four-month swaption into a two-month swap with monthly tenor. Such a swap is a weighted average of forward prices, with the weights being a function of discounting factors and quantities to be delivered, and the swaption volatility comprising of discrete volatilities and correlations across all the forward prices defining the swap price.

6.8. IMPLEMENTING THE VOLATILITY MATRIX

The volatility matrix methodology can be calculated in the following three steps:

- Step 1: Set $\sigma_{1,1}$ to the first month caplet volatility and set $\sigma_{T,1}$ to the historical one-month forward price volatility (see Figure 6–19). Fill in the rest of column 1 (see Fig-ure 6–20), using a sensible forecasting method.[3] In such a way you will have defined the first column of discrete volatilities.

- Step 2: Using the "cross-diagonal" relationship defined by Equation 6–44, calculate $\sigma_{1,2}$ from the caplet two-month volatility (see Figure 6–21). Set $\sigma_{T,2}$ to the historical volatility of the two-month forward price. Again, interpolate to obtain the second col-umn of discrete volatilities.

- Step 3: Repeat the second step for each column of discrete volatilities until all the columns are filled and the full discrete volatility matrix is defined (see Figures 6–22 and 6–23).

FIGURE 6-19

Historical and Equilibrium Volatilities as End Conditions

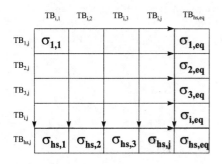

FIGURE 6-20

Filling in First Time Bucket

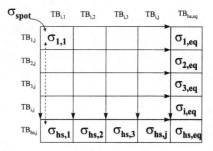

FIGURE 6-21

Applying Single "Cross-Diagonal" Relationship

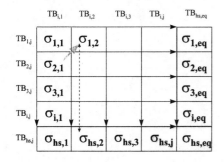

FIGURE 6-22

Applying Multiple "Cross-Diagonal" Relationship

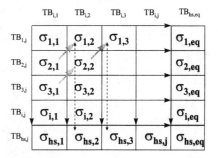

FIGURE 6-23

Abstract of Full Matrix Method Process

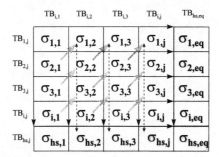

ENDNOTES

1. In my professional practice I have implemented this technique trademarked as the *Univol* methodology.
2. This process will require the use of a statistical search routine and possibly some assumptions about volatility term structure!
3. Possible techniques include ARIMA, VARIMA, ARCH, GARCH or other volatility forecasting methodology based on historical data.

CHAPTER 7

Overview of Option Pricing for Energies

7.1. INTRODUCTION

Options exist all around us, from the financial markets to everyday life. Any insurance you get, whether it is for your car, or health, or house, is a type of option. When you bought your first house, did you know that the mortgage you obtained contained an embedded prepayment option? So options need not scare the energy professional. The secret lies with understanding the option valuation and risk management issues.

In money markets, the typical financial options have the advantage of generally being plain-vanilla options, with well-understood pricing methodologies and modeling choices. Unfortunately, what is considered exotic in the money markets is usually considered plain vanilla in the energy markets. Issues of proper option pricing for energies do not stop with valuation concerns; the proper option underlying price model guides the hedging and portfolio analysis as well. Certain valuation models can be "fudged" to generate a pretty good option pricing methodology, but the same may not be true for hedging. For illiquid option markets, one must develop a good model to simulate the "option underlying" market. In the ideal case, the model captures actual market behavior.

The next two chapters will focus on those aspects of option pricing that are relevant—or peculiar—to energy markets.[1] This chapter will introduce the basic concepts and problems that every risk manager should understand. Chapter 8 will follow with the details, particularly with regard to the valuation of "exotic" options that traders routinely trade in the energy markets.

7.2. BASIC CONCEPTS OF OPTION PRICING

Every option is a right to do something. As a purchaser of an option I buy the right to do something at some future date based on the terms of the contract. As a holder of a *call* option I have the right to purchase an asset for some fixed price—determined at the time of the purchase—at some future period in time. The asset is referred to as the *option underlying* and the fixed price is referred to as the *strike price*. Similarly, as a holder of a *put* option, I have the right to sell the option underlying at the strike price.

The holder of an option pays for the right the option gives her. This payment is the option premium. The right does not have to be exercised. When the right is exercised, then the option is "exercised." In a typical option contract, when the option is exercised, it also expires. When the right is not exercised, then the option expires.

What determines whether an option will be exercised or not is the relative value of the option underlying price—at the time of the option exercise—to the strike price. Whenever the option underlying price is greater than the option's strike price, the option is referred to as being *in-the-money*. On the other hand, when the strike price is greater than the option underlying price, then the option is referred to as being *out-of-the-money*. Finally, when the strike price is the same as the option underlying price, the option is *at-the-money*.

7.2.1. Parity Value

The difference between the underlying price and the strike price is referred to as the option's *parity value*. At option expiration or at the option exercise, the parity value represents the value of the option. For a call option, this is simply the difference between the option underlying price and the strike price—when the option is in-the-money, and it is zero otherwise (see Figure 7–1):

$$Call\ Parity\ Value = max(0,\ U_t - K) \qquad (7-1)$$

For a put option, this is the difference between the strike price and the option underlying price—when the option is in-the-money—and it is zero otherwise (see Figure 7–2):

$$Put\ Parity\ Value = max(0,\ K - U_t) \qquad (7-2)$$

Note that we can relate the put parity value to the call parity value as follows:

$$Call\ Parity\ Value - Put\ Parity\ Value = U_t - K \qquad (7-3)$$

FIGURE 7–1

Call Parity Value

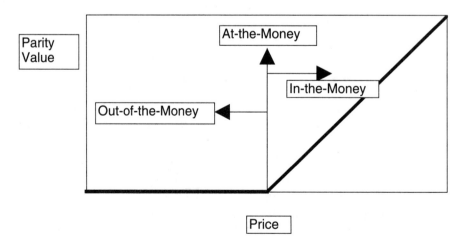

FIGURE 7-2

Put Parity Value

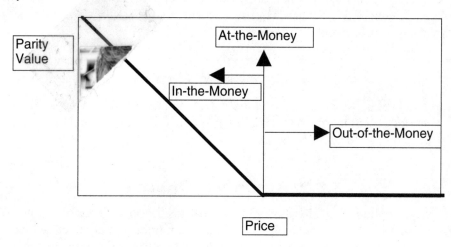

In other words, given the same type of option and given the same strike price, if the call option is in-the-money, then the put option is out-of-the-money, and vice versa. This relationship must always hold, and it is referred to as the *put-call parity*.

7.2.2. Settlement

When exercised, an option can be *settled* either through the delivery of a commodity or the exchange of cash. The exercise of an option "for delivery" requires that the option underlying asset is delivered as defined by the option contract. In turn, the receiving party has to pay the strike price for the delivery. Specifically, a call option holder would pay the strike price to receive the option underlying asset. Similarly, a put option holder would deliver the option underlying asset to receive the strike price.

A *cash-settled* option, on the other hand, requires no delivery. Instead, while one party pays the strike price, the other party pays the value of the option underlying asset price at the time of option exercise. In this case, a call option holder would pay the strike price to receive the option underlying asset price at the time of the option exercise. Similarly, a put option holder would in theory pay the option underlying asset price at the time of option exercise and receive the strike price. In practice, only the parity value gets delivered. Since the option holder will exercise the option when this is profitable to her, the option is never exercised unless it is in-the-money. An option holder would exercise only when she can get positive value out of the exercise.

7.3. TYPES OF OPTIONS

There are European-, American-, Asian- and swing-type options in energy markets.[2] In energy markets, Asian options represent the majority of contracts, in large part due to the market's need to provide options on averages of prices.

7.3.1. European Options

A *European* option allows for a single exercise date. On that date, the holder of the option can take advantage of the option right if this is profitable to her. For a European option the exercise date is also the expiration date of the option.

7.3.2. American Options

An *American*-type option allows for more than one date as the possible exercise date. There are American options that allow for a single exercise any day prior to a contract-defined final option expiration date. There are also American options that allow for a single exercise during a particular day in the week or the month until the option expiration. If the option holder exercises her right prior to the final option expiration date, this is referred to as *early exercise*. This is possible only in the case of the American option. Typically, the American option also expires at the time of early exercise.

   A holder of an American option will compare the value she would obtain by exercising the option with the market value of the option if she were to hold on to it and not exercise. Hence, the option parity value is compared to the American option's market value at every instant the holder is allowed to exercise the option. If the parity value is greater than the option market value, then the holder is better off exercising the American option. If this is the case, the holder benefits more by early exercising on that date than by holding on to the option in hopes of a better deal. This is because the American option price at that moment represents all the probabilities of getting a better deal in the future. By comparison, the European option holder will look only at the parity value of the option on the option expiration date to decide whether to exercise or not. If the parity value is positive, she will exercise.

7.3.3. Asian Options: Options on an Average of Price

A special class of path-dependent European options is commonly seen in energy markets: options on an average of price. These options offer average instead of discrete price settlement, and they are also known as average-price or *Asian* options. There are two different kinds of average-price options: one is cash-settled with the expiration at the end of the averaging period, and the other is an option for delivery at some future time period.

   The cash-settled average-price options can be seen in WTI and natural gas over-the-counter markets. At the option's expiration the option settlement price is calculated as an average over some time period as defined by the option's contract. Typically, these options are traded as caps and floors. For example, a one-year cash-settled cap on an average of WTI prices with a quarterly tenor would consist of four caplet options, the first with expiration in three months, the second in six months, the third in nine months, and the fourth in one year. Each of these options would settle on the average WTI price calculated over the three months prior to option expiration.

Another type of average price options also very common in energy markets are for delivery of energy over some time period. These types of options expire prior to such delivery. For example, a one-year call option for a one-month delivery of natural gas following the option expiration would settle on the one-month average forward price at the point of expiration. This is still an average price option, although the average remains a forward price average, i.e., its price has not yet settled.

7.3.4. Swing Options

Swing options can be found in energy contracts that allow the energy quantities delivered or used to swing. There are various types of swing options in the marketplace. However, two distinct groups of swing options exist based on the types of counterparties in question: swing options that are demand-driven, and swing options that are price-driven.

The price-driven swing options can be found when the counterparties can both buy and sell the energy in the marketplace. The fact that both sides of the contract can deal energy allows the option holder side to maximize the swing contract value. By contrast, demand swing options tend to be found in contracts where one of the parties can only take or withhold from taking delivery of the energy commodity, hence that party is only set up to purchase the commodity but not to deliver the commodity. The demand-driven swing options are primarily found in the contracts between the dealers and the retail sector of the marketplace. However, the industrial users may also enter into these kinds of demand-driven contracts.

The price-driven swing contracts can take on various shapes and forms. The basic swing contract allows the base load of energy delivered to swing a certain amount, with daily and monthly maximum and minimum quantity amounts defined. In addition, the swing option holder may be limited as to how many times the quantity is allowed to swing from the base load. Another spin on this is the forward-strike swing option, where the strike of the option is set at some future date rather than today. Multiple-peaking options, which allow the option holder to purchase the same quantity of energy but only for a fixed number of days over some time period (for example, the option can be exercised five times during the summer for next-day energy delivery) are actually a special subset of swing options, with the base load set to zero.

The price-driven swing options can be priced using trees and assuming that there is no arbitrage, i.e., the option holder will indeed maximize the option value. By comparison, the demand-driven swing contracts have to incorporate the functional relationship between the prices and the quantity demanded, as there is no means for one of the sides of the contract to deal in the marketplace. (A good example here is the contract between the natural gas providers and residential homes: the homes are set up to take delivery of natural gas, but cannot turn around and participate in the marketplace.) These demand-driven swing options are sometimes allowed to swing without bounds (in theory), and sometimes have the minimum and maximum quantities to be delivered defined. The pricing of these swing options takes knowledge of pricing methodologies as well as some amount of creativity.

7.4. EFFECT OF UNDERLYING BEHAVIOR

We have already introduced the concept of option parity value at the time of option expiration. In order to price an option we need to also know the price behavior and the characteristics of the price distribution (expressed in risk-adjusted terms) to determine the option price. Figure 7–3 shows the price distribution overlaid across the call parity value with a strike of K. In the case of a European option, the option price is given by the integral of the product of the probability distribution at each value of the underlying price, times the option parity value at that underlying price. The wider the probability distribution, the greater is the probability of having the option expire in-the-money. Similarly, the fatter the option distribution tails—i.e., the greater the kurtosis—the greater is the probability of having the option expire far in-the-money. As you can see, the probability distribution, and thus the assumptions about the option settlement price behavior, directly affect option valuation.

In order to come up with option pricing models, we need to start by understanding the behavior of the option underlying price, which will ultimately determine whether the option will expire in-the-money and by how much as well as the underlying market price behavior, which drives the option underlying price behavior. The two can be the same, but in the energy commodities they are usually not, as the most common energy option is on an average of prices.

If the option underlying is the spot price, then the underlying market behavior is defined by the behavior of the spot price. In this case, the option underlying price is the same as the underlying market behavior. (This makes the option valuation process quite a bit easier.) However, if the option underlying was some predefined average of spot prices—such as, for example, an average of spot prices over a period of three months—then the option underlying

FIGURE 7-3

Call Parity Value and Price Probability Distribution

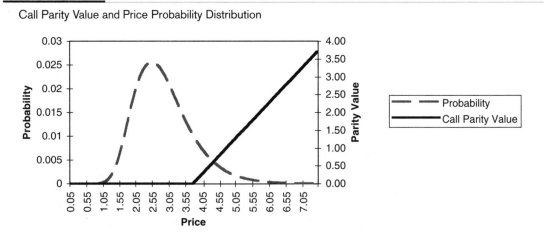

would be the average price, while the spot price would be the underlying market price driving the behavior of the option underlying average price. In this case, users of the option valuation process need to know how the spot prices behave so that they may know how the average of the spot prices behaves, in order to ultimately value the option. This is a more difficult case of option valuation.

In the case where the option underlying is a function of—rather than being equal to—the underlying market price, we have the choice of developing option valuation based on the behavior of the underlying market price or the behavior of the option underlying price. The second is usually the easier, since it is generally easier to model a function of a market price rather than modeling a function of a function. However, if we do decide to go the generally easier way of modeling the option underlying, we still have to ensure that the behavior of the option underlying remains consistent with the behavior of the market underlying price. Unfortunately, imposing this consistency can be as difficult as developing option valuation based on market underlying price behavior.

7.5. OPTION PRICING IMPLEMENTATION TECHNIQUES

Once the actual option underlying process is well defined, either directly or as a function of the underlying market price process, the valuation expert has to decide on how to implement this process to ultimately arrive at a valuation methodology for the option price, hedge, and risk calculations. There are various choices available to use in the implementation. We will cover some of them here. Table 7–1 summarizes the various implementation methodologies across capturing market characteristics and option settlement characteristics.

7.5.1. Closed-Form Solutions

A closed-form solution is the solution to a differential equation that expresses the change in option value relative to all the key variables, subject to hedging assumptions and end conditions. Closed-form solutions for option pricing are the ideal in that they provide us with a

TABLE 7–1

Comparison of Option Pricing Techniques

Issue	Closed-Form Solutions	Simulations	Trees
Difficulty of developing	high	low	medium
American optionality	no	no	yes
Path-dependent option	probably not	yes	no
Multifactor approach	probably not	yes	practical up to two factors
Discrete volatility term structure	probably not	yes	yes

single equation to use in the pricing and risk calculations of options. The Black-Scholes equation is an example of a closed-form solution.

The closed-form solution is the solution to the differential equation that follows the arbitrage-free argument of a risk-free portfolio earning the risk-free rate of return. Hence, we solve for the closed-form solutions to the option price, just as we solved for the forward price closed-form solution in chapter 5: by finding the solution to the differential equation. A closed-form solution is quick and easy to use, and provides a great amount of implementation flexibility. Unfortunately, the more complicated the underlying market process and the more complicated the type of option, the more difficult—if not impossible—it becomes to arrive at the closed-form solutions to option prices. Hence, solving for closed-form solutions often remains the ultimate and yet also the unattainable option valuation technique.

Another choice we have in obtaining the closed-form solution is by taking the expected value of the parity value at the expiration time (see Figure 7–3), given the option underlying price distribution, and present valuing this quantity:

$$O_{t,T} = E_t\left[\max\left((-1)^n(\widetilde{U}_T - K),0\right)\right]e^{-r(T-t)} \qquad (7-4)$$

where: $n = +1$ in the case that the option is a call option
$n = -1$ in the case that it is a put option
U_T = the option underlying asset price at the time of option expiration T
K = the option strike price
r = the risk-free rate

The above is a valid valuation process only if two conditions hold:

* First, the option must be a European option, as we are assuming that the exercise can only occur at the expiration time T.
* Second, the expectation value is taken on a risk-adjusted price distribution. This second condition guarantees that the resulting option valuation will remain arbitrage-free.

If we were to solve for the simple European option using Equation 7–4, assuming that the underlying price is lognormal, we would derive the exact same Black-Scholes option price equation as if we were to do it by solving the arbitrage-free differential equation (see Equation 5–13).

7.5.2. Simulations

Monte Carlo simulations can also be used in option price valuation. This technique simulates either the underlying market prices or the option underlying prices at the time of option expiration. The simulated prices at the option expiration are then used to calculate the expected option parity value at expiration, and then this value is discounted back to obtain the present value of the option. This can be an excellent pricing technique, as all the complexities of multivariable markets can be factored in. With simulations we are not limited to the number of market factors we want to incorporate into describing the price behavior.

However, simulations have two drawbacks. The simulations capture the probability distribution through the sheer number of simulation points. The greater the number of simulations, the more precisely do the simulations converge to the underlying price probability distribution. Unless you have a powerful enough computer don't bother using simulations on a trading desk, where the deals often have to be priced very quickly, or for large portfolio valuation and risk calculations, where the simulations would take a very long time to run through all the deals on the books. This is all the more true when performing mark-to-market calculations.

The second drawback to simulations is that they cannot be used for valuing American options. The problem with applying simulations to value American options has to do with the simple question of early exercise. A holder of an American option will compare the value he would obtain by exercising the option versus the market value of the option at the time. Hence, the option's parity value is compared to the option's market value at every instant the holder is allowed to exercise the option. If we are running the simulations in order to calculate the American option value, we cannot do this parity versus option price comparison within the simulations, given that for each simulated option underlying price we must already have the American option price so that we can decide on early exercise.

While the simulations are no good in the case of American option pricing and in general for day-to-day trading needs, they provide an excellent testing ground for the valuation models considered as candidates for implementation on the trading floor.

7.5.3. Trees

Another implementation methodology is the building of underlying price trees. Like the simulations, the trees also reflect the option underlying price distribution. Unlike the simulations, which converge toward the underlying market distribution through the simulations of a great many prices, the trees have a calculated probability associated with each node in the tree, hence the trees are more precise than the simulations. In addition, unlike the simulations, the trees do provide a means of pricing American-style options. Because the trees provide us with a tree of price levels with associated probabilities, we can move back and forth in time through the tree, allowing us to calculate the American option prices as needed: We compare the American option price at each node of the tree to the parity value at that node in the tree.

While the trees allow us to price American-style options, something that simulations cannot do, they typically fail in the ability to price average price path-dependent options, which is something that the simulations usually can manage. A path-dependent option is one that depends on the underlying prices at different points in time during the life of the option. In a tree, this translates to relating nodes at one time step to nodes at another time step. While this is possible to do, there are so many combinations that one would have to consider, that the practicality of the tree approach quickly diminishes as the number of time steps necessary to combine at the same time increases. This path dependency is something that the simulations are capable of handling through the simulation of underlying paths.

7.5.4. Human Error in Implementation

As we can see from the above discussion, the option valuation implementation may be limited by the type of the option, by the manner in which the valuation is intended to be used—i.e., on the trading floor or for research purposes—and by the complexity of the problem. In addition to these valuation issues, there are also user issues.

As much as sophisticated models can add precision to the option price and risk calculations, so can their use be prone to human error in cases where the traders do not understand how to use them. And it is very important for traders to understand how to use the given option pricing models. For example, a trader who does not understand mean reversion in prices should not be using a mean-reverting option pricing model without a proper support network around him. Since a trader has to be able to convert her views on the existing market situation into the specifics of how it affects the option pricing, she needs to know exactly how the market state translates into model parameters. This is all the more true in illiquid markets, where there is not enough of an options market to give the traders a solid understanding of where everyone else thinks the market is.

7.6. CHOOSING THE RIGHT OPTION PRICING MODEL

Choosing the right option pricing model should be treated in the same way as any business decision-making process. The valuation is an important part of the trading business, particularly under certain trading strategies. Inasmuch as it is a behind-the-scenes aspect of the trading operation, it is still key to a successful trading operation, particularly under the arbitrage-seeking and risk management service provider trading strategies (discussed in detail in chapter 11).

7.6.1. Three Criteria for Evaluating Option Models

In order to make an intelligent decision about which models ought to be ultimately implemented on the trading desk, each option model needs to be evaluated across three areas:

- the ability to capture market reality
- the ease of implementation
- the ease of maintenance

The ease of implementation and the ease of maintenance are important to the degree that they match the kind of trader, valuation, and software expertise and support you have or intend to have in your trading group. There is a give-and-take between pricing and hedging precision and the cost necessary to obtain and maintain these at a high quality level. A huge amount of frustration at all company levels can be avoided by recognizing the reality of the support costs for entering into the more complex option products or option markets up front, and providing such support as necessary. On the other hand, by opting for decreased support, and hence also for low cost of support, the company has to accept the cost of low valuation and hedging precision, which may rear its ugly head in the form of real costs of losses resulting from the inability to properly value the more sophisticated options or even plain-vanilla options in more-complex markets.

In order to evaluate a model for its ability to capture market reality, the particular characteristics of the market reality important to option valuation need to be defined. We have dealt with the building of forward price curves and volatility matrices in the previous chapters. Both of these are inputs to option pricing models. All options have first-order sensitivity to the forward price curves. They also have first-order sensitivity to volatility matrices. But how about correlations between the forward price points? Are these important to the types of option pricing that your trading operation needs to do? What about the capturing of the tails of the particular market price distribution? How important is this characteristic to the types of options you already have or want to have in your trading books? These are just some sample questions you might want to ask in the process of defining which market characteristics are important to your particular options market.

Given a traded options market with at least some option modeling choices, the preceding issues are the ones you need to go through in order to ultimately choose which models best fit your trading needs. But what do you do in the case when the option markets are so illiquid that there is not enough market information to tell you whether the models you are using are precise enough? Unfortunately, in such a case—which, by the way, is more of a norm in the energy options markets—you are forced to use what you have. Spot and forward price historical data may be your only clue for defining volatility matrices. In this case, you need a valuation expert who is as comfortable with data crunching and parameter modeling as with the mathematics of option derivation and implementation techniques.

7.6.2. Investing in Pricing Model vs. Implementation

Given that you probably have a limited budget for option valuation, how much should you invest in the modeling part of the option valuation process and how much in implementation? The answer will generally follow your model choice. The less your option pricing model incorporates the market characteristics, the more you will have to use the implementation of the model to capture the characteristics that the model is missing.

For example, a two-factor option pricing model might need only a single volatility curve to define the volatility of the spot price over time, and the model would imply the rest of the volatility matrix, while a simple lognormal model would need the full volatility matrix to define the volatility term structures for each forward price on the forward price curve. In other words, the two-factor model might imply the whole volatility matrix with many fewer parameters than the lognormal model would require.

In some cases, you do not have much of a choice in the matter. If no models are indeed available for the type of option you need to price, you might end up using the existing option valuation techniques but with implementation adjustments to take care of the biases that might result through this process. When this is the case, you should perform thorough testing of the approximating model in its application on the more complicated option, to ensure that you know all the drawbacks and biases that might result.

7.6.3. A Model Is Only as Good as Its Implementation

While the more sophisticated models might end up explaining a good amount of market behavior that a simpler model might not, it still requires the proper implementation and support for it to give that added value of providing a more precise valuation and hedging means. Having a valuation group that is heavily concentrated on the model mathematics instead of model implementation often results in sophisticated models that are poorly implemented. In fact, running the option pricing models through benchmarking tests will show you that a simple well-implemented model can be more valuable than a sophisticated but poorly implemented model.

By ensuring that a balanced amount of attention is paid to model derivation and model implementation, you can avoid the problem of ending up with an option pricing software that contains bugs. To make things worse, if the traders get used to these bugs, they will perceive an option pricing model that prices correctly as the one that is flawed.

7.7. OPTION VALUATION PROCESS: WHAT SHOULD IT BE?

The option valuation process should follow three steps:

- ◆ Define option underlying market price behavior. Create benchmarks from this behavior for testing alternative models. Make sure forward price and volatility inputs are valid.
- ◆ Test alternative models against benchmarks.
- ◆ Select the most appropriate model.

7.7.1. Defining Underlying Market Price Behavior

The first step to be taken in the option valuation process is to define the underlying market price processes. All option valuation methodologies should be tested against the spot and forward price models that best define the market reality. We can then proceed with defining what types of options need to be valued and how this should be done given the underlying price behavior.

The option models ultimately chosen for implementation will need forward price curves and volatility term structures as inputs, if not also additional options-specific parameters. The question of where all these model parameter values come from needs to be answered prior to implementation. The answer should be part of the understood policies and procedures. The parameters should also be realistic. Do not expect to be reestimating some of the parameters on a weekly basis if your valuation group does not have enough people power to be doing so. Whenever possible, give the traders a feeling for parameter stability and confidence levels. This is particularly important in an illiquid market. Unfortunately, in an illiquid market the data may not be readily available nor extensive. In this case, you have no choice but to do the best you can with what you have and try to draw on the information from similar energy markets that are more liquid.

7.7.2. Testing Alternative Models

Whatever option pricing models are ultimately chosen for implementation, these models ought to be thoroughly tested using simulations and ensuring that the characteristics of the underlying market prices are captured. This test is performed through model benchmarking. If any of the characteristics are not captured, the traders need to be aware of this so that they can ensure a more conservative approach to pricing whenever the missing characteristics do affect the option valuation. Specifically, the models being tested should be ranked by how closely they reflect market reality. Similarly, these same models ought to be ranked by the amount of implementation support necessary and the amount of maintenance support necessary.

No option model will be able to capture all the market characteristics. Given the model limitations, identify which parameters can be "fudged" to obtain more-realistic market prices under certain market scenarios.[3] While this is in general not a good practice to follow, and can be quite dangerous in that it opens the trading business up to fraudulent behavior, chances are that in a developing market all participants will be playing a catch-up game with respect to their valuation and risk management software. However, if managed well, the parameter "fudging" can be a very educational experience for all involved—traders, valuation and risk management experts, and management. However, just as risk limits are set for traders to follow, so should parameter limits be set in the cases where there is a good amount of ambiguity regarding the parameter values. A parameter's going over a limit should trigger a valuation and risk management group discussion and consensus on what needs to be done.

We can learn a lesson here from the mortgage markets. Most mortgage pricing models assumed that the prepayment rate was constant, and most users of such models assumed that there will be no variation in the prepayment rate. Everyone was caught by surprise when indeed the prepayment rate increased drastically in the early 1990s, causing huge changes in portfolio values, particularly in the IO/PO books. The prepayment rate was a parameter that should have been tracked for variation, and the risk limits should have been placed on this risk, even though the models assumed it to be constant over time.

The value of model testing prior to implementation cannot be stressed enough. Ideally, the option model results are practical to use, intuitive to trade on, and stable enough that maintenance does not require a great amount of support. Unfortunately, the energy markets are illiquid and complicated enough that they make the job of arriving at such model results sometimes quite difficult. Recognizing this fact should not discourage you. Quite the opposite, as in any profession, it is the layman who always thinks that the job should be easy to do. Or to put it another way, the more you know the more you become aware of how much more there is to know. So, do not get discouraged. Remember that everyone else is dealing with the same set of issues—whether they are aware of it or not. The ones who are aware have a distinct advantage, as they are more likely to find the solutions that work. After all, how can you come up with a solution to the problem without realizing that there is a problem?

7.7.3. Selecting the Most Appropriate Option Model

If Steps 1 and 2 are done properly, the managers, traders, and quantitative analysts should have meaningful information with which to evaluate, discuss, and ultimately select the most appropriate model or sets of models.

7.8. DID THAT OPTION MAKE MONEY?

One topic worth discussion is, How do you decide whether an option made money for you or not? Different option trading strategies will require different types of profit-and-loss analysis.

If you bought an option as a treasury or hedging function, in order to minimize risk, you did not enter this contract in order to make money; you entered it in order to reduce the risks of your corporation. In this case, the value that the option brought to you has to be measured in risk terms: How much less was I exposed to the market price swings because of the option I bought as an insurance policy?

If you bought an option in the hopes of profit, you would value the deal differently than the hedging strategy. You probably perceived the option to be undervalued. You wanted to capture the spread between the market price and what you perceived its value to be. Ultimate profit or loss analysis is done in present-value terms and includes the hedging you have entered into to offset option risks along the way.

Specifically, there are two ways that this spread can be captured. One is a short-term strategy where you buy the option and sell it in the market the moment the market makes the correction. The other is delta hedging: You buy the option and you rehedge the delta continuously. In the process, your hedges capture the true volatility of the option underlying price, providing you—on the average—with a capture of the spread between the market volatility you bought the option at and the true volatility captured through your delta hedges. In this second strategy, not including the hedges in the analysis of the value the option brought to you would leave you with an unrealistic picture of what happened.

ENDNOTES

1. My favorite book on options is *Option Pricing* by Jarrow and Rudd from the Irwin Series in Finance, published by Richard D. Irwin, Inc., in 1983. Unfortunately, this text is out of print. Other favorites include Hull, *Options, Futures and Other Derivative Securities,* and Cox and Rubenstein, *Options Markets.*

2. These terms don't really reflect any geographical meaning. "European" and "American" have simply become part of the derivatives lexicon. Once average price contracts became popular, traders continued this "continental drift" by referring to options on average prices as "Asian" options.

3. For example, when pricing an averaging (or Asian) option, one could use Black-Scholes by manipulating the volatility term structure and even making additional corrections for skew and kurtosis effects.

CHAPTER 8

Option Valuation

8.1. INTRODUCTION

There is nothing magical about the valuation of options, just a lot of hard work. The task is to pull together all our knowledge about the markets. In chapter 7 we introduced the basics of option pricing, and in chapter 6 we introduced you to the basics (and not so basic) volatility calculations and issues. In this chapter we will draw on many of the concepts and groundwork of those two previous chapters.

In chapter 5 we described an arbitrage-free pricing framework for forward prices. We can follow a similar approach for pricing options, with the results being closed-form solutions to option prices. Under this arbitrage-free framework, we follow the cash flow at contract origination, and price settlement. At contract origination we pay the option price, while we simply agree to the forward contract without any cash exchange. With options we have the choice of exercising or not exercising at expiration time, while with forward prices we have no such choice: we have to exchange cash for delivery. Compared to the forward price solution, the difference in the cash flow at option contract origination causes the differential equation for the option price to include the cost-of-financing term on the option price. The difference in contract settlement causes the boundary condition for the option price at time of expiration to be very different from that of the forward price.

In this chapter we will introduce you to the choices you have in option implementation and we will take you through the valuation issues and modelling process of some common energy options. The options market is rapidly changing, with new contract types being invented every day. Thus, this chapter will detail select contracts as case studies to demonstrate the thinking and the process behind their pricing.

8.2. DETAILED OPTION MODEL IMPLEMENTATION

Model implementation should not be confused with option model derivation, although with some implementation techniques it is hard to separate the two. Model derivation—in its basic form—is the derivation of the differential equation for the option price. How we get from this differential equation to the option price is what I refer to as the model implementation.

There are a number of implementation techniques. We will concentrate on the most common ones: the closed-form solutions (as exemplified by the famous Black-Scholes and Black equations), approximations to the closed-form solutions, and the tree-building methodologies.

8.3. CLOSED-FORM SOLUTIONS

The closed-form implementation methodology involves the solving of the differential equation for the option price to obtain an equation that defines the option price as a function of the market variables and modeling parameters, which played a role in the definition of the option price differential equation. This is a math-intensive procedure, particularly if the differential equation contains more than one market variable.

8.3.1. Pros

Closed-form solutions for option prices are the ideal implementation methodology. The beauty of closed-form solutions for option prices is that they provide us with a simple equation, which can be easily programmed and implemented on the trading floor. Such equations are easy to use and quick to give us the option value as well as the risk calculations when we need them.

8.3.2. Cons

Unfortunately, the closed-form solutions are typically extremely hard to arrive at. The more complicated the marketplace is, the more complicated is the differential equation for the option price. The more complicated the terms of settlement of the option, the more difficult it becomes to satisfy the boundary condition of the option in solving the differential equation.

In the end, in order to arrive at closed-form solutions, we usually need to make many simplifying assumptions about both the market variables and the option settlement character. The end result of these simplifications is that while providing us with a practical and easy to use option pricing methodology, the closed-form solution may not reflect the reality of the market behavior. Examples of such simplification include assuming that the volatilities are constant over time when they are not, assuming that the underlying market price is lognormal when it is mean reverting, and treating the option settlement price as a discrete price when it is actually an average of discrete prices.

It is such simplifications that force us to calculate corrections to the closed-form option price implementation. The later section on closed-form solutions with corrections will take you through some sample ways of dealing with such simplifications.

Two famous closed-form option pricing models are the Black-Scholes model and the Black model. Both assume that the option settlement prices are lognormal and have constant volatilities. Next, we will take you through the derivations of these models.

8.3.3. The Black-Scholes Model

The Black-Scholes closed-form solution for option prices is probably the most famous option pricing methodology out there. It is so easy to use that it can be implemented on the trading floor by the traders themselves.

The Black-Scholes option valuation assumes that the option settlement price is the spot price at the time of option expiration. It also assumes that the spot prices follow a simple log-normal process with a drift term of μ and a spot price volatility of σ:

$$d\widetilde{S} = \mu S dt + \sigma S d\widetilde{z} \tag{8-1}$$

In this simple world, we make the assumption that an option position can be perfectly hedged with the spot price and that we can use a bank's services to borrow and lend money at a risk-free rate. This leads us to derive the differential equation for the option price:

$$\frac{\partial C}{\partial t} + \frac{1}{2}\frac{\partial^2 C}{\partial S^2}\sigma^2 S^2 + rS\frac{\partial C}{\partial S} - rC = 0 \tag{8-2}$$

where: C = call option price
  S = spot price
  K = strike price
  r = discount (risk-free) rate
  σ = spot price volatility

Solving this differential equation and imposing the boundary constraint that the option price must equal the option parity value at expiration, we obtain (after quite a bit of mathematics) the closed-form solution for the option price:

$$C_{BS} = S\aleph(d_1) - Ke^{-r(T-t)}\aleph(d_2) \tag{8-3}$$

$$d_1 = \frac{\ln(S\,/\,K) + \left(r + \dfrac{\sigma^2}{2}\right)(T - t)}{\sigma\sqrt{T - t}} \tag{8-4}$$

$$d_2 = \frac{\ln(S\,/\,K) + \left(r - \dfrac{\sigma^2}{2}\right)(T - t)}{\sigma\sqrt{T - t}} \tag{8-5}$$

$$d_2 = d_1 - \sigma\sqrt{T - t} \tag{8-6}$$

$$\aleph(x) = \int_{-\infty}^{x} \frac{e^{-\frac{y^2}{2}}}{\sqrt{2\pi}}\,dy \tag{8-7}$$

where: T = time of option expiration
  t = time of option valuation

This is the famous Black-Scholes option solution. It is a function of the current spot price, the spot price volatility, the risk-free rate, option's strike price, and the time to option's expiration.

8.3.4. The Black Model

If, instead, the option settles not on the spot price at the time of the option's expiration, but rather a forward price, we end up using the forward price to hedge the option and not the spot price. As already shown in chapter 5, the forward price on a lognormal spot price, as defined above, is given by:

$$F = Se^{r(T-t)} \tag{8-8}$$

and the change in the forward price over time dt is then given by:

$$dF = (\mu - r)F\,dt \tag{8-9}$$

Since the forward price contract is an agreement that carries no cost of financing, our hedge to the option price requires no borrowing of money from the bank. This changes our option differential equation to look as follows:

$$\frac{\partial C}{\partial t} + \frac{1}{2}\frac{\partial^2 C}{\partial F^2}\sigma^2 F^2 - rC = 0 \tag{8-10}$$

Solving this differential equation for the option price results in the closed-form solution in terms of the forward price rather than the spot price. This is the (also famous) Black option pricing model:

$$C_B = Fe^{-r(T-t)}\aleph(d_1) - Ke^{-r(T-t)}\aleph(d_2) \tag{8-11}$$

$$d_1 = \frac{\ln(F\,/\,K) + \left(\dfrac{\sigma^2}{2}\right)(T-t)}{\sigma\sqrt{T-t}} \tag{8-12}$$

$$d_2 = \frac{\ln(F\,/\,K) + \left(-\dfrac{\sigma^2}{2}\right)(T-t)}{\sigma\sqrt{T-t}} \tag{8-13}$$

$$d_2 = d_1 - \sigma\sqrt{T-t} \tag{8-14}$$

$$\aleph(x) = \int_{-\infty}^{x} \frac{e^{-\frac{y^2}{2}}}{\sqrt{2\pi}}\,dy \tag{8-15}$$

where: T = time of option expiration and forward price expiration
t = time of option valuation

8.4. APPROXIMATIONS TO CLOSED-FORM SOLUTIONS

Making simplifying assumptions in the derivation of closed-form solutions, such as that the option settlement prices are lognormal with a constant volatility—i.e., a flat volatility term structure—and that the settlement price is defined by a single-factor model, when in reality this may not be the case, leads us to come up with approximation and/or correction techniques that allow us to continue using the closed-form solutions, such as Black-Scholes or Black. The emphasis of option valuation thus moves from the actual derivation of closed-form solutions in complex markets, to how we implement the simplistic closed-form solution in complex market environments.[1]

8.4.1. Pros

This approximation technique may be as simple as adjusting the volatility inputs fed into the closed-form solution, to properly reflect the way markets act. Or they may be as complicated as calculating the higher-order correction terms to the closed-form solution to capture the skew or kurtosis effects that the closed-form solution does not capture. Either way, we still end up with an equation for calculating the option prices, and as such it remains relatively easy to program and use on a trading desk.

Such corrections to Black-Scholes or Black option pricing equations allow us to price—fairly easily—all kinds of European-style options, including Asian options on averages of prices, whose settlement price may be path-dependent.

8.4.2. Cons

The potential problem of making adjustments to closed-form solutions is that we have to know when it is OK to do so, and when the corrections simply do not capture all there is to capture. In other words, if the Band-Aid formed by the corrections covers the wound—that is, takes care of the simplifications made by the closed-form solutions—then we are fine. But if the wound is too big for the Band-Aid and cannot be covered fully, then this methodology is no longer appropriate. Thus, such methodology always needs to be used with caution and with an understanding (by the traders) of what its boundaries are.

The model corrections attempt to allow for correct pricing. However, even if we achieve this, we are still left with potentially incorrect risk calculations. This is probably the greatest drawback of this methodology. The tree-building methodology (see Section 8.5) offers a way to get this right as well.

8.4.3. The Volatility Smile

The implied volatility term structure and volatility smiles, discussed in great detail in Chapter 6, are the results of using a model that does not capture the full complexity of the marketplace. In other words, these option-implied volatilities are adjusted to capture the true nature of market behavior. In an ideal world, we can incorporate all the market drivers—such as stochastic volatilities, two-factor models for spot and equilibrium price, and stochastic seasonality factors. But the reality of option implementation, particularly in the case of closed-form solutions, forces us to make simplifying assumptions, such as that the volatilities are constant and prices are lognormal.

While most people in the marketplace have probably come to accept market-implied volatility behavior as something independent of other market variables, the truth is that market-implied volatilities are just as much a function of market behavior as of the models you are using to back these implied volatilities out. Hence, if your models do not capture a certain aspect of market behavior, such as fat distribution tails of the spot prices, then your implied volatilities are bound to show a volatility smile across the option strikes.

8.4.4. The Edgeworth Series Expansion

The Edgeworth series expansion offers a very useful technique of estimating the actual price distribution with an approximating price distribution. This technique can be applied to option pricing, resulting in methodologies that can be used to capture the actual market price behavior while still using the assumption of lognormal price behavior with additional price corrections.

We begin with our old friend, the Taylor series expansion, only in this case it is applied to the distribution probability function. The result is the Edgeworth series expansion, given below:

$$f(P) = a(P) + \frac{c_2}{2!}\frac{\partial^2 a(P)}{\partial P^2} - \frac{c_3}{3!}\frac{\partial^3 a(P)}{\partial P^3} + \frac{c_4}{4!}\frac{\partial^4 a(P)}{\partial P^4} + \varepsilon \qquad (8-16)$$

$$c_2 = \text{STD}_{actual} - \text{STD}_{approx} \qquad (8-17)$$

$$c_3 = \text{SKEW}_{actual} - \text{SKEW}_{approx} \qquad (8-18)$$

$$c_4 = \text{KURTOSIS}_{actual} - \text{KURTOSIS}_{approx} + 3\,c_2^2 \qquad (8-19)$$

where: P = option settlement price
$f(P)$ = actual probability function of the settlement price
$a(P)$ = approximating probability function of the settlement price
ε = higher order corrections to the approximating distribution
STD_{actual}, SKEW_{actual}, KURTOSIS_{actual} = the standard deviation, skew, and kurtosis of the actual settlement price distribution
STD_{approx}, SKEW_{approx}, KURTOSIS_{approx} = the standard deviation, skew, and kurtosis of the approximating settlement price distribution

Equation 8–16 gives us an expression for the actual probability distribution function, f, in terms of the approximating probability function, a. Note that the correction terms are functions of the actual vs. the approximating distributions' standard deviation, skew, and kurtosis.

If we make the further assumption that the approximating distribution is lognormal, we can apply the Edgeworth series expansion to option pricing in the case of a European call option, to obtain the following:

$$C = \left\{ \int_K^{+\infty} (P - K)f(P)dP \right\} / fvd \tag{8-20}$$

$$C = \left\{ \begin{array}{l} \int_K^{+\infty} (P - K)a(P)dP + \\[2mm] \dfrac{c_2}{2!}\dfrac{da(P)}{dP} - \dfrac{c_3}{3!}\dfrac{d^2 a(P)}{dP^2}\bigg|_{P=K} + \dfrac{c_4}{4!}\dfrac{d^3 a(P)}{dP^3}\bigg|_{P=K} \end{array} \right\} / fvd \tag{8-21}$$

where: C = price of the call option
         fvd = future value of a dollar at time of option expiration

Finally, if we use the additional trick of requiring our approximating distribution to have the exact same standard deviation as the actual distribution, we have the following simplifications:

$$c_2 = M_2 - M_{2_{approx}} = 0 \tag{8-22}$$

where: M_2 = actual second moment of the option settlement price
         M_2 = approximating second moment of the option settlement price

Now the second correction term in the option equation goes to zero:

$$\frac{c_2}{2!}\frac{d^2 a(P)}{dP^2} \to 0 \tag{8-23}$$

and we have the second moment of the approximating distribution equal to the second moment of the actual distribution:

$$M_2 = M_{2_{approx}} \tag{8-24}$$

In the case of lognormal distributions, we can calculate explicitly the moments of the distribution. They are given by:

$$M_1 = E[P] \tag{8-25}$$

where the expectation is taken in risk-adjusted terms:

$$M_{2_{approx}} = M_1^2 \, e^{\sigma_{approx}^2 T} \tag{8-26}$$

$$M_{3_{approx}} = M_1^3 \, e^{3\sigma_{approx}^2 T} \tag{8-27}$$

$$M_{4_{approx}} = M_1^4 \, e^{6\sigma_{approx}^2 T} \tag{8-28}$$

From this we can define the approximating lognormal distribution's volatility, which allows the second moment of the lognormal distribution to be exactly equal to the second moment of the actual distribution:

$$M_2 = M_1^2 \, e^{\sigma_{approx}^2 \tau} \tag{8-29}$$

where: σ_{approx} = approximating volatility
τ = time to option expiration

This gives us

$$\sigma_{approx} = \sqrt{\frac{\ln\left(\dfrac{M_2}{M_1^2}\right)}{(T-t)}} \tag{8-30}$$

With the above equations holding, we are left only with the skew and kurtosis correction terms:

$$\frac{c_3}{3!}\frac{d^3 a(P)}{dP^3} + \frac{c_4}{4!}\frac{d^4 a(P)}{dP^4} \tag{8-31}$$

where c_3 and c_4 are now given by:

$$c_3 = (E_{actual}[P^3] - E_{approx}[P^3]) \tag{8-32}$$

$$c_4 = (E_{actual}[P^4] - E_{approx}[P^4]) - 4 \cdot E_{actual}[P] \cdot c_3 \tag{8-33}$$

8.4.5. Pulling It All Together

We are finally ready to apply the Edgeworth series expansion to the call and put pricing problem. The above requirement of the second moments of the actual and approximating distributions being equal results in the call and put option prices given by:

$$C_{actual} = C_{BS}(P, \sigma_{approx}) + \left\{ -\frac{c_3}{3!}\frac{d^2 a(P)}{dP^2}\Big|_{P=K} + \frac{c_4}{4!}\frac{d^3 a(P)}{dP^3}\Big|_{P=K} \right\} / fvd \tag{8-34}$$

where: C_{actual} = the call option price
C_{BS} = the Black-Scholes call option value calculated using the approximating volatility

$$P_{actual} = P_{BS}(P, \sigma_{approx}) + \left\{ -\frac{c_3}{3!}\frac{\partial^2 a(P)}{\partial P^2}\Big|_{P=K} + \frac{c_4}{4!}\frac{\partial^3 a(P)}{\partial P^3}\Big|_{P=K} \right\} / fvd \tag{8-35}$$

where: P_{actual} = the put option price
P_{BS} = the Black-Scholes put option value calculated using the approximating volatility

The above also works for the case where the options are on forward rather than spot prices:

$$C_{actual} = C_B(F, \sigma_{approx}) + \left\{ -\frac{c_3}{3!} \frac{\partial^2 a(F)}{\partial F^2} \Big|_{P=K} + \frac{c_4}{4!} \frac{\partial^3 a(F)}{\partial F^3} \Big|_{F=K} \right\} / fvd \qquad (8-36)$$

$$P_{actual} = P_B(F, \sigma_{approx}) + \left\{ -\frac{c_3}{3!} \frac{\partial^2 a(F)}{\partial F^2} \Big|_{P=K} + \frac{c_4}{4!} \frac{\partial^3 a(F)}{\partial F^3} \Big|_{P=K} \right\} / fvd \qquad (8-37)$$

where: C_B = the Black call option value calculated using the approximating volatility

P_B = the Black put option value calculated using the approximating volatility

In summary, in order to use this methodology we need to calculate the following:

σ_{approx} = approximating volatility

c_3 = third-order correction term, function of third moment, M_3

c_4 = fourth-order correction term, function of fourth moment, M_4

$$V_3 = \frac{d^2 a(P)}{dP^2} \Big|_{F=K} = \text{third-order sensitivity of the approximating distribution} \quad (8-38)$$

$$V_4 = \frac{d^3 a(P)}{dP^3} \Big|_{F=K} = \text{fourth-order sensitivity of the approximating distribution} \quad (8-39)$$

In order to calculate the sensitivities of the approximating distributions, we need the probability function of the lognormal distribution. It is given below:

$$a(P) = \frac{\exp\left(\frac{-\left(\ln\left(\frac{P}{E[P]}\right) + \sigma_p^2 \tau \right)^2}{2\sigma_p^2 \tau} \right)}{P\sqrt{2\pi\sigma_p^2 \tau}} \qquad (8-40)$$

where: a = the probability function for a lognormal distribution

P = the option settlement price

σ_p = the volatility of the option settlement price, hence the approximating volatility

τ = time to option expiration, $T - t$

π = the constant pi (3.14 . . .)

We can take derivatives of this probability function to obtain values for V_3 and V_4.

8.5. THE TREE APPROACH

The last option implementation methodology we will discuss here is the tree-building methodology. The idea is that we build a tree (see Figure 8–1) for the option settlement price that defines the movements, up and down, from node to node, of the option settlement price from now until the time of option expiration.

FIGURE 8-1

Binomial Tree Building

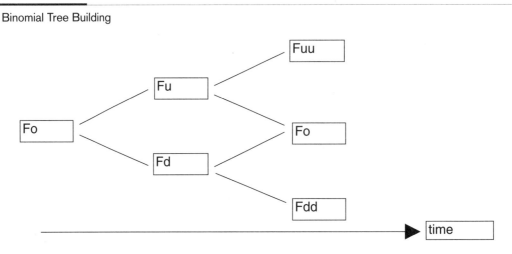

The greater the volatility in the option settlement price, the greater is the up and down jump from node to node. The requirement that there is no arbitrage between current and future value of the settlement price defines the probabilities of going from one node in the tree to another. Thus equipped, we have the values of the settlement price at each node of the tree, as well as the probabilities associated with being at each node of the tree.

In this way we can solve for the option prices backwards: we know what the parity value of the option is at each node of the tree at the expiration time, and we know what the probabilities are. We can then move "backwards" in time through the tree to arrive ultimately at the present value of the option's price.

8.5.1. Pros

Trees can be relatively easy to build and use in option pricing. Furthermore, they allow us to incorporate the volatility term structure within the tree itself and to price American options. Thus, the resulting prices and hedges can both be correct.

8.5.2. Cons

The main drawback of trees is that the Asian path-dependent options, such as options that settle on an average of prices over some time period, cannot practically be priced using trees. The problem is that at the expiration nodes of the tree there are so many possibilities of calculating the average prices backwards from the tree that it becomes so time-consuming to arrive at the solution that it is impractical to use.

One way of dealing with this issue is to combine two methodologies: tree building (for incorporating volatility term structure) and closed-form solutions with corrections (for incorporating the behavior of the average price settlement). In this case the tree is built to the point where the averaging period starts, and at each node at that point in time the closed-form solution with corrections is used to calculate the value of the option price. The rest of the procedure is simple movement backwards in time through the tree to finally obtain the present value of the option price.

8.5.3. Binomial Trees

The building of binomial trees has been covered by many books on option pricing. We will not spend a great deal of time on this methodology here. However, we will summarize the process.

In the simple case of flat volatility term structure, and an option on a forward price, F_0, the tree is built so that the moves up and down are given by $F_0 e^{\sigma \sqrt{dt}}$ and $F_0 e^{-\sigma \sqrt{dt}}$, where dt is the time step between the nodes. The corresponding probability of an up move is then given by:

$$p = \frac{1 - e^{-\sigma \sqrt{\Delta t}}}{e^{\sigma \sqrt{\Delta t}} - e^{-\sigma \sqrt{\Delta t}}} \tag{8-41}$$

The probability of a down move is then $1 - p$.

If we wanted to add the volatility term structure within the binomial tree, we could indeed do so. At every time step, then, the tree would have a different discrete volatility used in deciding the prices along the nodes of the particular time step. The end result is that the tree would in fact imply a form of mean reversion when the volatility term structure is decreasing. (In order to eliminate this mean reversion, you would be forced to go to the trinomial trees.) In this case, the probability of the up move is given by:

$$p = \left[\frac{e^{N(\sigma_0 - \sigma_1)\sqrt{\Delta t}} - e^{-\sigma_1 \sqrt{\Delta t}}}{e^{\sigma_1 \sqrt{\Delta t}} - e^{-\sigma_1 \sqrt{\Delta t}}} \right] \tag{8-42}$$

where $\sigma_0 \equiv \sigma_n$, the volatility at the *n-th* time nodes in the tree $\tag{8-43}$

$\sigma_1 \equiv \sigma_{n+1}$, the volatility at the *n + 1-th* time nodes in the tree $\tag{8-44}$

When volatility curvature is significant, there is a chance that we may end up with negative probabilities. In that case we would be forced to use trinomial trees.

8.5.4. Trinomial Trees

The trinomial trees are built just like the binomial trees, only now instead of the up-and-down move, we have one more degree of freedom: the sideways move (see Figure 8–2). In this case the price moves up and down become $F_0 e^{\sigma \sqrt{3dt}}$ and $F_0 e^{-\sigma \sqrt{3dt}}$, while the side move is really not a move, i.e., F_0 stays at F_0. Now the probability of the up move becomes:

$$p = \frac{(1 - q)\left(1 - e^{-\sigma \sqrt{3\Delta t}}\right)}{e^{\sigma \sqrt{3\Delta t}} - e^{-\sigma \sqrt{3\Delta t}}} \tag{8-45}$$

The parameter q is the probability of the sideways move. Requiring that the second price moment correspond to that of a lognormal price process gives us the value for q:

$$q = 1 - (e^{\sigma^2 \Delta t} - 1)/\left(e^{\sigma \sqrt{3\Delta t}} - e^{-\sigma \sqrt{3\Delta t}}\right)^2 \tag{8-46}$$

And the probability of the down move is $1 - p - q$.

FIGURE 8-2

Trinomial Tree Building

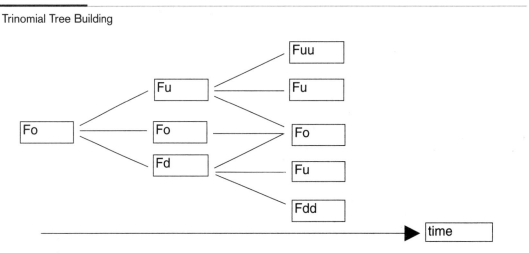

8.6. A SAMPLING OF ENERGY OPTIONS AND THEIR VALUATION

In this section we will use examples for some energy options to show how to apply some of the above option implementation methodologies.

8.6.1. European Options or Caps on Discrete Price Settlement with Mean Reversion Incorporated

The European-style options or caps with a discrete price settlement are typically seen in natural gas and electricity markets. In electricity, the most common caps are the daily settlement caps with the settlements spanning a particular month. In this case, the owner of a cap option has a caplet that expires every day of the month into next day's delivery of electricity.

These are probably the simplest energy options out there. The difficulty is in making sure that the short-term options capture the very strongly decreasing volatility term structures of energy markets. Probably the best approach to pricing these options is through trees, which incorporate the volatility term structures.

8.6.2. European-Style Caps/Floors on Averages of Prices

The cash settled European-type caps and floors, which settle into averages of prices over some period of time, and which expire at the end of the averaging period, are typically seen in WTI and natural gas OTC markets. In order to value the caplets that comprise these caps, we need to include the effects of averaging.

The following will take you through a very simple example here as to how you can do this. I will assume flat volatilities, cash-settlement at the end of the averaging period, and a simple two-price average of prices, which are assumed to be are perfectly correlated—again, for simplicity. Some of these are simplifications that should not be made in the real world (particularly the correlation part), but we do so here for the sake of educational value.

Let the prices be lognormal, with their values at times t_1 and t_2—when the average price observations are taken—be as follows:

$$P_1 = Pe^{-\frac{1}{2}\sigma^2 t_1 + \sigma \tilde{z}_{0,1}} \tag{8-47}$$

$$P_2 = Pe^{-\frac{1}{2}\sigma^2 t_2 + \sigma \tilde{z}_{0,2}} \tag{8-48}$$

where: $t_1 < t_2$

P_1 = price at time t_1
P_2 = price at time t_2
σ = volatility
$\tilde{z}_{0,2}$ = random stochastic variable from time $t = t_0$ to $t = t_2$
$\tilde{z}_{0,1}$ = random stochastic variable from time $t = t_0$ to $t = t_1$
$\tilde{z}_{1,2}$ = random stochastic variable from time $t = t_1$ to $t = t_2$

We have the following relationships between the stochastic variables:

$$\rho(\tilde{z}_{0,1}, \tilde{z}_{1,2}) = 0 \tag{8-49}$$

$$\tilde{z}_{0,2} = \tilde{z}_{0,1} + \tilde{z}_{1,2} \tag{8-50}$$

And the option settlement price is simply the average of two prices:

$$P_A = \frac{(P_1 + P_2)}{2} \tag{8-51}$$

We will now apply the Edgeworth series expansion methodology to calculate the averaging volatility. We begin by calculating the approximating and actual moments of the average price distribution:

$$M_1 = P_A \tag{8-52}$$

$$M_{approx_2} = e^{\sigma^2_{approx} t_2} \tag{8-53}$$

$$M_2 = E[P^2] = E\left[\left(\frac{(P_1 + P_2)}{2}\right)^2\right] \tag{8-54}$$

$$M_2 = \left(\frac{1}{2}\right)^2 (E[P_1^2] + 2E[P_1 P_2] + E[P_2^2]) \tag{8-55}$$

Since we require that the second moments of the actual and approximating distribution equal each other, we obtain the approximating average price volatility:

$$M^2_{approx} = M_2 \tag{8-56}$$

$$e^{\sigma^2_{approx}t_2} = e^{\sigma^2 t_1} \frac{1}{4}(3 + e^{\sigma^2(t_2-t_1)}) \tag{8-57}$$

$$\sigma_{approx} = \frac{1}{\sqrt{t_2}}\left\{ \sigma^2 t_1 + \ln\left(\frac{3 + e^{\sigma^2(t_2-t_1)}}{4}\right)\right\}^{0.5} \tag{8-58}$$

At this point we would value the option price using the Black option model, with the volatility input being the approximating volatility. If we so choose, we could also go on to calculate the higher-order moment corrections for skew and kurtosis, depending on how large these higher-order corrections tend to be for the energy market we are dealing with. It's quite possible that these higher-order corrections are insignificant and do not need to be calculated. However, there is only one way of finding this out: by calculating them at least once.

The above procedure can be generalized for the case where the average is based on N prices instead of just two. Now, the average is given by:

$$P = \frac{1}{N}\sum_{n=1}^{N} P_n \tag{8-59}$$

where

$$t_1 < t_2 < \ldots < t_N \tag{8-60}$$

It turns out that the approximating volatility is then given by:

$$\sigma^2_{approx} = \frac{1}{t_N}\left\{\sigma^2 t_1 + \ln\left(\frac{1}{N^2}\left\{\sum_{n=1}^{N}\sum_{m=1}^{n} e^{(m-1)\sigma^2\Delta t} + \sum_{n=1}^{N-1}(N-n)e^{(n-1)\sigma^2\Delta t}\right\}\right)\right\} \tag{8-61}$$

The above formulation can be further generalized for the case of volatility term structure and nonperfect correlations between the prices comprising the average. The option price would then become sensitive to the correlations between the prices in the average.

8.6.3. Optionality in Cheapest-to-Deliver Forward Prices

The cheapest-to-deliver forward price contract are typically seen in natural gas and electricity markets. Within the contract, the party that delivers the energy has the choice of delivering it at one of two delivery points. These forwards carry embedded optionality. The pricing of a cheapest-to-deliver forward can be done through a closed-form solution:

$$F_{ctd} = F_1(1 - N(h_+^{ctd})) + F_2(N(h_-^{ctd}))$$ (8–62)

$$h_{+/-}^{ctd} = \frac{\ln\left(\dfrac{F_1}{F_2}\right) + /- \left(\dfrac{1}{2}\sigma_{ctd}^2 \tau\right)}{\sigma_{ctd}\sqrt{\tau}}$$ (8–63)

$$\sigma_{ctd}^2 = \sigma_1^2 + \sigma_2^2 - 2\sigma_1\sigma_2\rho$$ (8–64)

where: σ_1 = volatility of F_1
σ_2 = volatility of F_2

Note that the price of the cheapest-to-deliver forward is sensitive to the correlation between the prices at the different points of delivery. Options that settle on such cheapest-to-deliver forward prices can also be derived.[2]

Energy producers carry unique and producer-specific optionality within their books. If they sell a forward contract for delivery of energy at the contract expiration, they have the choice of delivering their own energy—i.e., energy that they produced—or simply buying energy in the market and then delivering it. Thus, the producer carries the cheapest-to-deliver optionality, where the valuation involves comparing the cost function to the market price.

8.6.4. Crack-Spread and Basis-Spread Options

Finally, we will take a look at the crack-spread and basis-spread options. This is the case that (almost) makes the Edgeworth series expansion methodology break down. The problem is that the during the Edgeworth series expansion we have assumed that the approximating distribution is lognormal. The characteristic of a price that is lognormally distributed is that it is always positive. This may not be the case with a spread. Hence, blindly applying the Edgeworth series expansion would give us incorrect prices. Instead, we need to perform an additional "trick."

Suppose we are pricing an option that is based on the difference between the heating oil and WTI crude oil prices. The prices of these commodities at the time of option expiration—again assuming lognormality—are given as follows:

$$P_1 = P_{ho}\, e^{-\frac{1}{2}\sigma_{ho}^2 t + \sigma_{ho}\tilde{z}_1}$$ (8–65)

$$P_2 = P_{wti}\, e^{-\frac{1}{2}\sigma_{wti}^2 t + \sigma_{wti}\tilde{z}_2}$$ (8–66)

where the two commodities have some correlation:

$$E[\tilde{z}_1 \cdot \tilde{z}_2] = \rho t$$ (8–67)

The option then settles on the difference between the two prices:

$$P = (P_1 - P_2) \tag{8-68}$$

It may be useful at this point to define the difference between the correlation and the beta between two commodities. Specifically, the beta of heating oil on WTI is given by:

$$\sigma_{ho}\tilde{z}_{ho} = \beta_{ho,wti}\sigma_{wti}\tilde{z}_{wti} + \sigma_\varepsilon\tilde{z}_\varepsilon \tag{8-69}$$

$$\beta_{ho,wti} = \rho\frac{\sigma_{ho}}{\sigma_{wti}} \tag{8-70}$$

where

$$\sigma_\varepsilon = \sigma_{ho}\sqrt{1 - \rho^2} \tag{8-71}$$

We can now express the heating oil price in terms of the randomness in the WTI price and the residual randomness unique to heating oil:

$$P_1 = P_{ho}\, e^{-\frac{1}{2}\sigma_{ho}^2 t + \sigma_{ho}^2(\rho\tilde{z}_{wti} + \sqrt{1-\rho^2}\tilde{z}_\varepsilon)} \tag{8-72}$$

If we matched the second moments of the actual and the approximating distribution blindly, we would end up with an approximating volatility derived as follows:

$$M_1 = E[P_1] - E[P_2] \tag{8-73}$$

$$M_{approx}^2 = e^{\sigma_{approx}^2 t} \tag{8-74}$$

$$M_2 = E[P_1^2] - 2E[P_1 P_2] + E[P_2^2] \tag{8-75}$$

$$M_{approx}^2 = M_2 \tag{8-76}$$

$$(P_{ho} - P_{wti})^2\, e^{\sigma_{approx}^2 t} = P_{ho}^2\, e^{\sigma_{ho}^2 t} - 2P_{ho}P_{wti}\, e^{\rho\sigma_{wti}\sigma_{ho}t} + P_{wti}^2\, e^{\sigma_{wti}^2 t} \tag{8-77}$$

$$\sigma_{approx} = \frac{1}{\sqrt{t}}\ln\left\{\frac{P_{ho}^2}{S^2}\, e^{\sigma_{ho}^2 t} - 2\frac{P_{ho}P_{wti}}{S^2}\, e^{\rho\sigma_{wti}\sigma_{ho}t} + \frac{P_{wti}^2}{S^2}\, e^{\sigma_{wti}^2 t}\right\}^{0.5} \tag{8-78}$$

It turns out that this gives us prices much higher than they ought to be, simply because the methodology assumed that the spread can never be negative in value.

Instead, we can perform a variable transformation, so that instead of pricing an option on a spread with a particular strike, we price an option on a spread plus some constant, with a strike set at the original strike plus that same constant. In this way we guarantee that the settlement price is indeed always positive. So we introduce a variable Y, such that it equals the spread, S, and some constant, X:

$$Y = S + X \tag{8-79}$$

Now the new approximating volatility is a function of the previously calculated approximating volatility:

$$(\sigma_{approx}^{new}) = \frac{1}{\sqrt{t}} \ln\left\{\left(\frac{S}{Y}\right)^2 e^{\sigma_{approx}^2 t} + \left(\frac{X}{Y}\right)^2 + 2\left(\frac{SX}{Y^2}\right)\right\}^{0.5} \quad (8-80)$$

While this trick provides us with an option-valuation methodology for options on spreads that works extremely well, this is a good example of how one should never apply an option-pricing methodology without fully understanding it and its drawbacks.

E N D N O T E S

1. For an excellant example of this process, see Turnbull & Wakeman (1991).
2. For the mathematically minded, in order to solve for such options, the following relationship is useful:

$$\int_{-\infty}^{\infty} N(A + Bz) \frac{1}{\sqrt{2\pi}} e^{-z^2/2} dz = N\left(\frac{A}{\sqrt{1 + B^2}}\right)$$

Measuring Risk

9.1. INTRODUCTION

In this latter section of the book, we will pull together the valuation techniques introduced in chapters 2–8 and apply them at a higher, "managerial" level. In chapter 9, we will demonstrate how overall risk can be broken down into building blocks. The risks are generally known as the "Greeks," since they are denoted by symbols like Δ (delta) and Γ (gamma). Chapter 10 recombines the building blocks through the application of "portfolio analysis," a process that helps the trading floor either hedge or communicate with the boardroom. Finally, chapter 11 demonstrates how risk managers (and *their* managers) use the tools introduced throughout the book in order to achieve the company's risk/return goals.

9.2. THE RISK/RETURN FRAMEWORK

"Risk management" is the process of achieving the desired balance of risk and return through a particular trading strategy. All quantitative and managerial objectives and tactics should be guided by the desired balance of risk and return. The *risk/return framework* incorporates the full business process of selecting, communicating, valuing, and achieving this balance within the firm's portfolio of assets.

Valuation focuses on the price of individual contracts; risk management focuses on the change in price, both on an individual contract basis and on a portfoliowide basis. A particular company's risk/return balance shifts every time there is "movement," such as when a trader enters a new derivatives contract, or when an underlying market price changes. Rather than just worrying about the valuation of derivatives, risk management is concerned with the "change in price" and its impact on portfolio value. At its very best, risk management practices can serve as a compass among changing currents, pointing out the company's direction and suggesting corrections in course.

Divided into component parts, the term "risk management" suggests two distinct disciplines. The word "risk" suggests defining and quantifying the unknown of how the risk/return balance would change as a function of movement in the total portfolio due to changes in prices, volatility, interest rates, or any other market variables—and time. Quantifying risk requires many tools, both mathematical and statistical.

The word "management," on the other hand, connotes the more general business process. Managing risk requires articulating, communicating, evaluating, and achieving the company's desired balance of risk and return. It should come as a relief that, for most companies, managing risk requires less technical than "business" skills. In fact, in the author's opinion, management issues are equally—if not more—important compared to the technical ones. An effective risk management program must combine technical competency with the kinds of good management required for virtually any business.

As each company selects a unique "risk/return" balance, so does each firm exhibit an individual style of pursuing the ideal balance. The firm's choice of people, models, and systems—as well as the optimized risk and return levels—represents the "risk/return framework." This framework consists of all trading, valuation, and risk management practices.

In an ideal world, a company will adopt and execute policies, procedures, and theoretical models that are consistent throughout the framework. Inconsistencies can introduce risks of their own. From a managerial point of view, a good framework can help to both avoid human risk and optimize the firm's investment in technology. Always remember, risk management is no different from any business function, and we rarely achieve the theoretical ideal, being forced to make practical trade-offs.

9.3. TYPES OF RISK

Risk represents uncertainty. Our task is to identify and quantify all the uncertainty that might affect the value of our portfolio of assets going forward in time. (See Table 9–1 for a list of

TABLE 9–1

Types of Risk

Market	Price
	Volatility
	Correlation
	Liquidity
Commodity	Storage
	Capacity
	Delivery
	Transmission
Human	Trader
	Quant
	Management
	Credit
	Modeling

commonly modeled risks.) While market risks receive the most attention, human risk deserves equal attention.

9.3.1. Market Risk

Market risks dominate our attention. Price uncertainty fuels the entire derivatives and risk management industry. Not only must we model changes in price, we must understand volatilities (or the change in the randomness of price) for individual markets and correlations between different markets. At a higher level, energy players often face the inherent risk of illiquidity. Illiquid markets pose two problems: inadequate price discovery and the lack of adequate hedging opportunities. Risk managers attempt to quantify price risks and determine optimal hedging strategies; illiquidity guarantees that there will be residual risks on the books that cannot be hedged away. Such residual risks are handled on a more managerial level, including the basic decision of whether or not to participate in such illiquid markets.

9.3.2. Commodity Risk

Commodity markets carry physical risks, including storage, delivery, capacity, and transmission. When modeling commodity risk, we ask the questions, How do prices change? and How can we dissect the price risk to understand the impact of fundamental price drivers? As presented in earlier chapters, we see that the fundamental price drivers behind commodity risk express themselves by creating different short- and long-term price processes. Thus, to model commodity risk we must have underlying models that reflect this behavior.

9.3.3. Human Error

As stated earlier, human error represents a major risk. The most infamous cases of derivatives losses began with failed judgment. While rogue traders dominate the news, behind the headlines lurk managerial decisions that created the environment in which the crisis brewed. It is all too easy to blame a single trader for what is truly a poorly managed trading business. Similarly, quantitative analysts can also contribute to problems by becoming "married to a model."

Another uncertainty is "counterparty" or "credit" risk. Credit risk is a relatively new area of quantitative analysis, even in the more mature derivative markets. Energy markets appear to have their hands full with the more elementary issues and will probably begin to incorporate this problem into the risk/return framework over the next two or three years.

9.3.4. Model Risk

Modeling is intended to help reduce risk by providing appropriate hedge calculations. Poor assumptions resulting in inadequate hedges can actually misstate market positions and actually increase risk exposure. Management must insist on adequate benchmarking to continually evaluate the appropriateness of all underlying models.

Model risk also lurks when a firm fails to employ consistent models and methodologies during valuation and portfolio analysis. A common inconsistency lies in the assumptions we make while pricing derivatives and assessing their risk. During the valuation process, we model prices at a *particular point in time.* From this fixed perspective, we can reasonably assume that certain random market variables can be treated as deterministic model parameters. During the risk management process, to the contrary, we cannot make such simple assumptions. "Movement" rests at the heart of risk management; we may not enjoy the convenience of "assuming it away." Valuation forces us to simplify the market, but risk management forces us to recognize the uncertainty in all its glory.

We best see the differences in assumptions in the relationship between "market variables" and "model parameters." Recall from chapter 2 that a market variable has a value that we can observe or imply from the marketplace. A market variable can move around, as a function of the market, with varying degrees of both random and deterministic behavior. A modeling parameter, on the other hand, contains no randomness. A parameter is assumed to be either constant or entirely predictable by some deterministic behavior. For example, time is a parameter: its change is deterministic, as there is no randomness in the progression of the clock.

As seen throughout chapters 4–8, valuation models make varying assumptions about which fundamental drivers should be treated as variables and which should be simplified and handled as parameters. In an ideal world, the valuation models could treat all fundamental drivers as "model variables," effectively harnessing all the market variables and their random characteristics. Unfortunately, in the real world, we must assume certain market characteristics to be constant over time in order to generate practical pricing methodologies to be used within a trading environment. We force market variables to be treated as modeling parameters, which we know very well not to be so.

While such simplifications still yield reasonable valuations *at a particular point in time,* similar "shortcuts" are just not feasible for risk management. A good example is a portfolio of options valued by using the Black-Scholes option pricing model. Recall from chapter 2 that Black-Scholes assumes volatilities to be constant over time. However, we know that volatilities are not constant. While a valuation expert has made this simplifying assumption to arrive at an elegant option pricing methodology, these assumptions cannot protect a trader's portfolio from the very real impact of fluctuating volatilities.

This reinforces the big difference between valuation and risk management. Within valuation, we may make simplifying assumptions by treating some market variables as deterministic modeling parameters that exhibit no randomness in their behavior. Within risk management, we cannot afford to make such simplifications. Any application of such inappropriate simplifying assumption will cause us to omit a real market risk and therefore fail to provide proper hedges, to take advantage of possible market opportunities, or to be honest about the risks taken by the business.

9.4. DEFINITION OF A PORTFOLIO

Portfolios represent a collection of assets and financial positions on these assets.[1] We will introduce the basics of measuring risk by quantifying risk on a portfolio-wide basis. (Note: The concepts introduced here apply also to the most basic portfolio: a single-asset portfolio.)

Mathematically, we represent portfolio value, Π, as the cumulative value of all assets, A, at a particular point in time:

$$\widetilde{\Pi}_t = \sum_{n=1}^{N} (y_n)_t (\widetilde{A}_n)_t \qquad (9-1)$$

where: Π_t = portfolio value at time t
$\quad\quad\quad t$ = time of observation
$\quad\quad\quad A_n$ = *n-th* asset in the portfolio
$\quad\quad\quad N$ = number of assets
$\quad\quad\quad y_n$ = number of units or quantity of *n-th* asset

9.4.1. Change in Portfolio Value

The object of measuring market risk is to determine the distribution of change in either an individual asset or portfolio of assets due to changes in the market. We are concerned with changes resulting from movement in:

- asset price
- volatility
- any other market variable
- time

The general expression for change in portfolio value is:

$$d\widetilde{\Pi} = f(d\widetilde{v}_m, dt) \qquad (9-2)$$

where: $d\widetilde{v}_m$ = the change in the *m-th* market variable.

9.4.2. Time Buckets

Typical portfolios contain contracts of various expirations. A typical portfolio will change in value as forward prices of different expirations change. Similarly, a typical portfolio containing options will also change in value as the volatilities corresponding to different forward prices and time periods change. We need a framework for expressing portfolio value changes in terms of various changes in market variables, such as forward prices and volatilities. We also need a means of understanding how risks vary across the variable term structures, such as across forward prices of different expirations. We handle both needs by breaking the portfolio risks across variables and *time buckets*.

A time bucket is an observation period within the total term covered by a portfolio. A variable risk exposure corresponding to a particular time bucket is the sum of all the risks specific to that variable and specific to the expiration time spanned by the time bucket. For example, if a time bucket covers the time period starting one year out and ending two years out, then the forward price risk corresponding to this time bucket would be the sum of all the forward price risks where the forward prices have expirations of one year to two years out.

Consider a sample portfolio of natural gas and electricity, with both spot and forward price exposure. We can group the exposures by both underlying market and forward price risk time buckets. We will later see how we aggregate the risks represented by each time bucket.

Risk managers should organize time buckets in a meaningful manner. Every time bucket need not represent equal time periods. Looking forward, time should be compartmentalized in a meaningful manner that allows for a smooth transition among our modeling measures. For example, one possible time bucket "structure" might be:

- Weekly time buckets for the first month forward
- Monthly time buckets for the remaining 11 months of the first year forward
- Quarterly time buckets for the second year forward
- Yearly time buckets for years thereafter

Forward price time buckets should be defined by the correlations between the adjoining forward prices along the forward price curve. If the correlation between the forward prices in the near-term portion of the curve is small, then there should be a good number of time buckets covering the near-term portion of the forward price curve in order to capture the independent risks. Similarly, if the correlations between the forward prices in the longer portion of the forward price curve are very high, then there is no need to have many time buckets covering this long-term portion of the forward price curve. These characteristics of low correlations in the short-term and high correlations in the long-term are actually pretty consistent with the energy forward price markets, and thus the time buckets for such markets ought to be numerous in the short term and few in the long term. The time buckets should be spaced so that the risks being measured change in a continuous, sensible manner.

In Figure 9–1, the volatility term structure is steep over the first month and then begins to level off. The treatment of this kind of volatility term structure is consistent with the treatment of forward prices which are not highly correlated in the short term but are highly correlated in the long term. In the corresponding time bucket structure, we might have weekly time buckets for the first month, but then switch to monthly time buckets for the rest of the year. The volatility term

FIGURE 9–1

Sample Caplet Volatility Term Structure

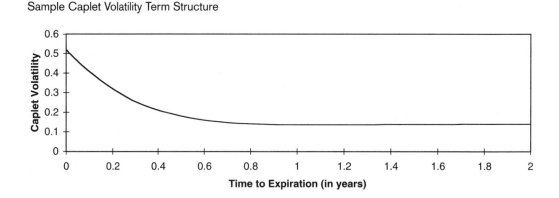

structure appears smoother thereafter, so we simply use annual time buckets for the balance of the portfolio. Generally speaking, this time bucket structure should be applicable to most energy portfolios, but readers are advised to experiment to determine their own (and their market's) preferences.

9.5. MEASURING CHANGES IN PORTFOLIO VALUE

The first step in portfolio analysis, therefore, is to define all the market variables that exhibit random behavior, and thus contribute to a wider portfolio profit and loss distribution, regardless of whether these variables were assumed to be random or deterministic by our underlying valuation models. Specifically, we need to express the changes in our overall portfolio value, over some time period dt, in terms of changes in the market variables—which contain a random, risky component—and also in terms of the change in time. This section will show you how we go about this task.

9.5.1. Taylor Series

The Taylor series was explained in chapter 2 on modeling principles. We will apply it here to the particular case of portfolio value and how this value changes over time. We can use a Taylor series to specifically express the portfolio at time $t + dt$ in terms of the portfolio value at time t plus the component parts of the portfolio value change due to the changes in market variables as well as time:

$$\Pi(t + dt) = \Pi(t) + d\Pi = \Pi(t) + \sum \frac{\partial \Pi}{\partial v_n} dv_n$$

$$+ \frac{1}{2}\sum\sum \left(\frac{\partial^2 \Pi}{\partial \tilde{v}_n \partial \tilde{v}_m}\right)d\tilde{v}_n d\tilde{v}_m + \frac{\partial \Pi}{\partial t} + O(dt) \qquad (9-3)$$

where: $\dfrac{\partial P}{\partial \tilde{v}_n}$ = the first derivative of the portfolio value with respect to n-th variable

$\dfrac{\partial^2 P}{\partial \tilde{v}_n \partial \tilde{v}_m}$ = the second derivative of the portfolio value with respect to n-th and m-th variables

$O(dt)$ = higher-order terms of dt

From the above equation we can obtain the change in the portfolio value over time dt, $d\Pi$, in terms of the market variable changes and the time change:

$$d\Pi = \sum\frac{\partial \Pi}{\partial \tilde{v}_n}d\tilde{v}_n + \frac{1}{2}\sum\sum\left(\frac{\partial^2 \Pi}{\partial \tilde{v}_n \partial \tilde{v}_m}\right)d\tilde{v}_n d\tilde{v}_m + \frac{\partial \Pi}{\partial t} + O(dt) \qquad (9-4)$$

The Taylor series expansion is based on the assumption that when dt is small, $dt << 1$, the function of such a small value of dt can be expressed as a function evaluated at time t plus correction terms. These correction terms are of various orders in dt: $dt^{1/2}$, dt, $dt^{3/2}$, etc. Under the assumption that dt is so small that any term multiplied with dt raised to a power greater than one is insignificant, the above Taylor expansion can be truncated to include only the terms of order dt or less. Specifically, $O(dt)$ refers to the higher-order terms in dt, which are assumed to go to zero with dt being very small.

9.6. PORTFOLIO SENSITIVITY: THE "GREEKS"

The derivatives (those from calculus) of the portfolio value represent the sensitivity of the portfolio to market variables and time. The first-order derivatives are also referred to as the first-order risks, and they are typically associated with the greatest amount of uncertainty in future portfolio value.[2] Some well-known first-order derivatives include *delta*, *vega*, and *theta*. The second-order derivatives of the portfolio represent the sensitivity of the first-order derivatives of the portfolio value to the changes in the variables. *Gamma* is the well-known second-order derivative, which the traders tend to track and worry about.

9.6.1. Delta: Sensitivity to Price Change

The delta measures the sensitivity of the portfolio value change to the change in the spot prices or the forward prices:

$$\Delta_t^{spot} = \frac{\partial P_t}{\partial S_t} \tag{9-5}$$

$$\Delta_t^{forward} = \frac{\partial F_t}{\partial S_t} \tag{9-6}$$

For a one-dollar change in the spot price, for example, the spot price delta of the portfolio would tell us the dollar change in the overall portfolio. Officially, the deltas are the first-order derivatives of the portfolio value with respect to either the spot or the forward price. As such, they are unitless. To obtain the portfolio delta risk in dollar terms for some tick amount in the spot or forward price change, the following transformation needs to be performed:

$$\Delta_{dollar} = \Delta \times \text{tick amount} \tag{9-7}$$

Such a delta expressed in dollars would reflect the dollar change in the portfolio per tick change in the spot or forward price. The tick amount is often set to be one dollar, but is in general a function of how the spot prices are quoted in the marketplace. Natural gas prices, for example, are in the range of two dollars, and the typical daily moves are only a fraction of a dollar. In the case of natural gas it would not make sense to make the tick amount one dollar. Instead, a one-cent move would be much more appropriate.

Note that a portfolio that includes both spot and forward prices will have a whole sequence of deltas. These deltas are generally grouped across markets and also across time buckets. Hence, if I have a portfolio that is a function of both natural gas and electricity markets, for example, I will have a series of deltas arranged across time buckets for each natural gas and electricity market. Thus, the first-order price risks will be expressed across time as well as across markets.

Basis risk represents the uncertainty of using one market to hedge another. It is a special case of delta risk. For example, companies often use futures from the New York Mercantile Exchange (NYMEX) to hedge their oil, natural gas, and (to a lesser extent) electricity exposure. Risk arises from the fact that the futures contracts specify delivery at geographic locations that may be very different from the delivery points being hedged.

Basis risk can be expressed in terms of two delta risks across two markets, and in the following case, two spot markets:

$$B = S_1 - S_2 \tag{9-8}$$

$$\Delta_B = \Delta_1 - \Delta_2 \tag{9-9}$$

The basis delta can thus be spread into the two market deltas.

Similarly, the deltas of my portfolio, with respect to all forward prices that have expirations greater than one month out and less then two months out, would be summed up and put into the second monthly delta time bucket, and so on. This grouping allows traders to simplify the delta risks into groups that tend to have their own particular behavioral aspects.

9.6.2. Vega: Sensitivity to Volatility Change

Vega risk represents the portfolio value change due to unit change in the volatilities.[2] This first-order risk is calculated by taking the first derivative of the portfolio value with respect to the volatility:

$$V_{t,T}^{product} = \frac{\partial \Pi_t}{\partial \sigma_{t,T}^{product}} \tag{9-10}$$

where: V = vega risk

The portfolio vega tells us the dollar change in the overall portfolio for a move in volatility of one, or 100%. Since this is not generally a reasonable daily move in volatility, typically the portfolio vega is expressed in terms of a one-volatility-point change. Assuming that the volatility moves up by one volatility point such that the new volatility is the old volatility plus 0.01, or 1%, we obtain the following portfolio vega calculation for a single volatility point move:

$$V_{0.01} = V \times 0.01 \tag{9-11}$$

Such a vega is expressed in dollars and reflects the dollar change in the portfolio for a 1% up move in the volatility.

As in the case of deltas, a portfolio that is a function of various markets and products will have a whole sequence of vegas. And like the deltas, these vegas are generally grouped across markets, across time buckets, and sometimes also across products. For example, if I have a portfolio that is a function of both natural gas and electricity markets, I will have a series of vegas arranged across time buckets for each of the two markets. The time buckets grouping allows the vegas per market to be analyzed across the various volatility values across the volatility term structure. In fact, the same reasoning that decides on the time buckets for deltas should decide on the time buckets for vega. Therefore, the delta and the vega time buckets ought to be exactly the same.

Unfortunately, the vega risk calculations are more difficult to aggregate when the models used for pricing the various types of options make different and perhaps even inconsistent assumptions about volatilities. In the case where the book contains swaptions as well as caps and floors, and the swaption volatilities are treated as independent from the cap and floor volatilities, there will be no means of relating the two types of volatility risks without developing the framework of the least common denominator volatilities. Unfortunately, the inability to relate one type of product volatility to another can give rise to inefficiencies in volatility risk management and hedging.

Linking vegas represents a terrific opportunity for creating a strong "fabric" to support companywide risk management and hedging. A building-block approach, based on some unified, least common denominator for volatilities of all the option-type products in the books would allow the vega risks to be grouped across markets, time buckets, and product types. To help accomplish this, we proposed the volatility framework in chapter 6, in the section on volatility matrices.

Finally, it is worth noting that in case of the Black or Black-Scholes option, the vega for an option can be related to the "gamma," the second-order risk that represents uncertainty arising from changes in delta. While we will explain gamma in a later section, we will briefly note that we can rearrange mathematical terms and express option vega by using gamma. (This relationship will help us collect terms later while performing portfolio analysis.)

For an option on spot price, priced using Black Scholes, the vega can be reexpressed as:

$$V_s = \Gamma_s S^2 \sigma_s \sqrt{\tau} \qquad (9-12)$$

where: Γ = gamma risk
S = spot price
σ = spot price volatility
τ = time to expiration $(T - t)$

Similarly, for an option on a future the vega is given by:

$$V_F = \Gamma_F F^2 \sigma_F \sqrt{\tau} \qquad (9-13)$$

9.6.3. Theta: Sensitivity to Time

Option portfolios lose value over time due to a phenomenon called *time decay* (with all the market variables held fixed). The closer an option is to expiration, the less time remains for the option to expire in-the-money, or further in-the-money. In the case of options, time is money! The time decay is particularly relevant because the option premium converges toward the option parity value as the time to expiration draws closer and closer. In other words, an option will have less chance of expiring in-the-money or further in-the-money the less time there is to the option expiration date. The strength of such "time decay" is measured by theta.

The time decay of a portfolio is not a risk, although it is a first-order derivative of the portfolio. It is a derivative with respect to time, and hence it tells us about the deterministic change in the portfolio value (rather than random change, as is the case with delta and vega). The time decay of the portfolio is called the theta, Θ, and is defined as follows:

$$\Theta = \frac{\partial \Pi_t}{\partial t} \tag{9-14}$$

Theta represents the change in the portfolio purely due to the passage of time. It is in dollar-per-time units, and unless it is normalized, it will be in annualized terms. In order to normalize it for some shorter time period, we need to do the following:

$$\Theta_{t,t+dt} = \frac{\partial \Pi}{\partial t} \times dt \tag{9-15}$$

Note that dt may be one calendar day (*1/365*), one business day (*1/252*), one week (*1/52*), or one month (*1/12*). The main thing is to select a dt that is consistent with time periods used in hedging.

The theta of a portfolio is important in tracking the overall daily changes in the portfolio value and ensuring that all the subcomponents to the portfolio value changes indeed match very much in the same way that pieces of a puzzle match to give us a large and clear picture. As seen in Figure 9–2, theta changes dramatically, particularly when there is a strong volatility term structure and when an option sits at-the-money close to expiration. The section on marking the portfolio to market and on capturing the portfolio daily price changes will discuss how the portfolio theta and the other risk components add up to give a larger picture of daily portfolio value changes.

FIGURE 9-2

European Call Option Theta (Using Figure 9–1 Caplet Volatility)

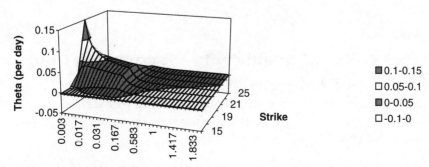

Time to Expiration (in years)

F I G U R E   9-3

Call Theta One Day Before Expiration

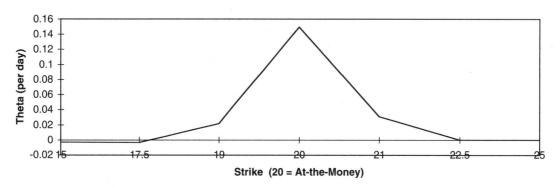

Time decay is the greatest close to expiration and for at-the-money options. Figure 9–3 shows the theta strike structure for an option close to expiration.

As we did with vega, we can express the theta of an option in terms of gamma, in the case of the Black-Scholes option model. This theta to gamma relationship also incorporates the portfolio sensitivity to the discounting rate, r:

$$\Theta_{Call,S} = -\left\{\frac{1}{2}S^2\sigma_S^2\Gamma_S + \frac{\partial C_S}{\partial r}\left(\frac{r}{\tau}\right)\right\} \qquad (9-16)$$

$$\Theta_{Call,F} = -\left\{\frac{1}{2}F^2\sigma_F^2\Gamma_F + \frac{\partial C_F}{\partial r}\left(\frac{r}{\tau}\right)\right\} \qquad (9-17)$$

$$P_S = C_S - S + Ke^{-r\tau} \qquad (9-18)$$

$$P_F = C_F + (K - F)e^{-r\tau} \qquad (9-19)$$

$$\Theta_{Put} = \Theta_{Call} + rKe^{-r\tau} \qquad (9-20)$$

9.6.4. Rho: Sensitivity to Discounting Rates

Rho measures portfolio value change due to a unit change in the discounting or interest rate. Today's energy risk managers rarely measure rho but we will include it to demonstrate the full range of risks. Rho is determined by taking the first-order derivative of the portfolio value relative to the discounting rate:

$$rho_{t,T}^{product} = \frac{\partial \Pi_t}{\partial r_{t,T}^{product}} \qquad (9-21)$$

9.6.5. Gamma: Sensitivity to Changes in Delta

The first-order risks of delta, vega, theta, and rho all represent sensitivities to change. Portfolios also respond to "changes in change," or what are known as "second-order" risks (derived from taking the second derivative of portfolio value relative to a given market variable). Generally small, the most important second-order risks include *gamma* and *cross-gamma* risks. Gamma measures sensitivity to the change in delta. All other second-order derivatives yield measures so small as to usually be considered insignificant.

Gamma is the derivative of delta with respect to either the spot price or the forward price:

$$\Gamma_t^{spot} = \frac{\partial \Delta_t^{spot}}{\partial S_t} = \frac{\partial^2 \Pi_t}{\partial S_t^2} \tag{9-22}$$

$$\Gamma_{t,T}^{for} = \frac{\partial \Delta_{t,T}^{for}}{\partial F_{t,T}} = \frac{\partial^2 \Pi_t}{\partial F_{t,T}^2} \tag{9-23}$$

Gamma represents the change in the value of the delta of the portfolio given a dollar move in the spot or the forward price.

Options carry gamma risk. Generally speaking, forward prices do not carry gamma risk. Certain forward price contracts can generate gamma risk when they include optionality features embedded inside the contracts. Generally, gamma book risks are small compared to the first-order risks. However, gamma risk occasionally triggers huge loss and/or profit scenarios. Such was the case during the stock market crash of 1987.

9.6.5.1. Gamma in Times of Crisis

We will take you through the steps of what happened to companies that had zero delta risk and yet ended up with huge portfolio profits or losses during a crisis, such as a stock or price crash. Consider the case where one portfolio is long gamma, the other short, but both portfolios are delta neutral, i.e., have zero delta risk. (See Table 9-2.) A buyer of options—regardless of whether the options are puts or call or both—will end up with a portfolio that is long gamma. An example of an option portfolio that is long gamma while also being delta neutral is one that is long both calls and puts (a portfolio of straddles). Similarly, a seller of options will end up

TABLE 9-2

Gamma Impact in Times of Crisis

Portfolio	Pre-Crash		During-Crash ($dS < 0$)			
	Δ_{pre}^{Π}	Γ_{pre}^{Π}	$d\Delta^{\Pi} = \Gamma_{pre}^{\Pi} \times dS$	Δ_{post}^{Π}	$d\Pi_{during} = \Delta_{post}^{\Pi} \times dS$
Long	0	+	−	−	+
Short	0	−	+	+	−

with a portfolio that is short gamma, i.e., has negative gamma exposure, such as being short both calls and puts. Both portfolios are assumed to be delta hedged.

A severe drop in underlying asset prices, however, affects the two portfolios in dramatically different ways. In the long gamma position, the negative change in asset price creates a negative delta. The two negative terms cancel out, resulting in a positive increase in portfolio value.

The exact opposite occurs in the short position. The drop in asset prices is exacerbated by losses due to gamma exposure. Even if we attempt to correct with delta hedging using futures, we will always wind up with gamma exposure (until the market bottoms out).

The sharp price drop created large and ever changing deltas. Portfolios delta-hedged at one moment suddenly became delta-positive (i.e., negative or "short" gamma) or delta-negative (positive or "long" gamma). Traders with positive gamma were lucky: negative deltas in a declining market result in profits. On the other side of the coin, however, those with negative gamma found themselves in a pickle: their deltas were positive in a declining market, resulting in losses.

To make things even worse for these poor "short-gamma" souls, the market dropped so quickly that it was practically impossible to keep rehedging the delta, resulting in the end with huge positive deltas for the unlucky side of the market. What is particularly interesting about this story is that even the houses that thought they had zero delta risk found themselves with large deltas on their hands. Hence, gamma, while not a large risk on a day-to-day basis, is not to be taken for granted during a period of market turmoil.

9.6.5.2. Cross-Gamma

In addition to gamma, there is also the cross-gamma risk. Cross-gamma risk exists in books that have options on averages of forward prices, hence the option price can exhibit simultaneous sensitivity to forward prices of different expiration dates. It is the change in the delta of a portfolio with respect to a particular forward price with expiration time T_1, as the forward price with the expiration at time T_2 moves by one dollar:

$$\gamma_{t,T_1,T_2}^{for} = \frac{\partial \Delta_{t,T_1}^{for}}{\partial F_{t,T_2}} = \frac{\partial^2 \Pi_t}{\partial F_{t,T_1} \partial F_{t,T_2}} \tag{9-24}$$

While gamma is not necessarily a large risk, and may even be ignored by traders on a day-to-day basis, the cross gamma is probably even smaller. However, it is still there, and if a trading operation has the means to capture its risk exposure to the cross gamma, it would be wise to do so.

Similarly, cross-market gamma risk exists in books that contain options on basis spreads or options on crack spreads.

9.7. HEDGING

Hedging is the process of entering into contracts to reduce portfolio risk. *Continuous hedging* involves constant trading to hedge away risks as the market moves. (This of course is both impractical and potentially very expensive.) A primary caveat to hedging is to make sure that the hedges do their job! Hedging an energy exposure at one location with a contract that specifies a different location will work only to the degree that the two delivery points are correlated. Anything less than perfect correlation introduces basis risk. In another case, if you want to hedge gamma, make sure the hedging contract itself carries gamma risk. (For example, forwards do not carry gamma risk and would therefore be inappropriate gamma hedge instruments.) How one hedges can also introduce risk concerns: noncontinuous hedging allows gamma risk to take effect.

9.8. MARKING-TO-MARKET

A book that is *marked-to-market* (MTM) has been valued such that the valuation was consistent with all the available and reasonable market information at the time of valuation. This is the process that attempts to arrive at true market value as opposed to a trader's "view" or opinion of value. If any product in the book exactly matches a traded market price, then that product should be valued exactly at the market price. If there are products in the book that are functions of the products for which there are available market prices, then these products' valuation should use the market prices available. Hence, a marked-to-market book has a value that is consistent with the market prices and market variables at the time of valuation. This value is expresed in "present value" terms.

Ideally, firms should mark their books to market at the end of each trading day. Weekly marking-to-market can prove inadequate. Discovering the problems of an unhedged position is not a fun process. This is not an "ivory tower" standard. While many energy firms have never marked-to-market, or only do so before an audit, those practices need to be upgraded in the changing and growing energy markets.

9.8.1. Information for Marking-to-Market

Firms have two ways of obtaining market information for the end-of-the-day book mark-to-market valuation, and generally use both. When relevant, the first is the use of exchange-traded daily closing prices for futures and options. These exchange-based market quotes provide if not the whole forward price curve structure, at least the near-term portion of it. The exchange-traded options generally do not have very long expiration times, and hence generally provide a means of obtaining the near-term portion of the volatility matrix information.

Broker quotes provide the second side of the market—the over-the-counter (OTC) side. These quotes tend to complement—rather than compete with—the exchange traded market quotes. The broker quotes tend to provide OTC market quotes for forward prices beyond the traded exchange markets and for more customized derivative products. Both of these sets of market information are extremely valuable and should be used as much as possible in obtaining MTM book values.

When a market is illiquid, chances are that only the OTC market exists, and even the broker quotes available may be sporadic and unreliable. In such a case the trader has to be careful in using the broker quotes to the extent that these quotes truly represent the marketplace. One way of getting around this problem is to establish relationships with a number of different brokers and use all of their quoted prices in order to get a better market representation. In such a case, the bid and the ask are also wider than would be seen in a liquid market. Again, the trader has the difficult job of deciding what would be a fair mid-market price given such wide market bid-ask spreads.

9.8.2. Mark-to-Market Valuation

Given a book that is marked-to-market on a daily basis, we can use this MTM valuation to ensure that the book risk calculations capture all the market risks that contribute to the daily MTM book value changes. To do so we go back to the Taylor series, which allows us to express the change in the portfolio value within a single marketplace over time dt in terms of the risky components. For example, if we assume that only the spot and forward prices and the volatility matrix (as defined in chapter 6) explain most of the portfolio daily value changes, then we have for the daily price change at time t and over time dt, the following:

$$d\Pi_t = \left\{ \Delta_t^{spot} dS_t + \sum_{n=1}^{N} \Delta_{n,t}^{for} dF_{n,t} \right\}$$

$$+ \left\{ \frac{1}{2} \Gamma_t^{spot} dS_t^2 + \frac{1}{2} \sum_{n=1}^{N} \Gamma_{n,t}^{for} dF_{n,t}^2 + \right.$$

$$\left. \sum_{n=1}^{N} \Gamma_{n,t}^{spot,for} dF_{n,t} dS_t + \sum_{n=1}^{N} \sum_{m=n+1}^{N} \Gamma_{n,m,t}^{for} dF_{n,t} dF_{m,t} \right\} \quad (9\text{-}25)$$

$$+ \sum_{n=1}^{N} \sum_{m=n+1}^{N} V_{n,m,t} d\sigma_{n,m,t} + \Theta_t$$

where: Π = portfolio value
Δ = delta risk for time bucket and market
S_t = spot price at time t
n = number of forward prices
$F_{n,t}$ = $n\text{-}th$ forward price at time t
$\Gamma_{n,t}$ = gamma risk for time bucket and market
$V_{n,m,t}$ = vega risk for time buckets n and m at time t
$\sigma_{n,m,t}$ = $n\text{-}th$, $m\text{-}th$ discrete volatility at time t
$\Theta_{n,t}$ = theta risk for time bucket and market

The previous day's risk calculations should have provided us with all the delta, gamma, cross-gamma, and theta values; and the daily moves from yesterday to today provided us with the changes in the spot and forward prices as well as with the changes in the volatilities. Using this information, we can calculate the value of the portfolio MTM change from the right-hand side of the above equation. In doing so, we are saying: "If my risk calculations are correct, and if my assumptions about what gives the randomness to my portfolio valuation are correct, then I should be able to tell what the daily portfolio change should be, given the market variable changes."

9.8.3. Testing the Mark-to-Market Process

We can test the calculation against the actual change in the portfolio value. The latter we obtain by simply taking the difference between the portfolio MTM today and yesterday. Hence, we have the actual portfolio MTM change, and what the risk components say the MTM change ought to be. If these are very close—i.e., with a small dollar difference—then our assumptions and calculations are indeed correct. However, if these tend to diverge significantly, then this is a sure sign that either an important risk component is missing or there is a bug in the calculations.

ENDNOTES

1. In fact, an energy firm's total portfolio should ideally be defined as the corporate-wide book value and exposure. Ideally, the risk/return framework should thus link the firm's asset-based value, currency and interest-rate exposure, and energy risk through a continuous "corporate utility function." While we will touch on this topic in chapter 10, application of the corporate utility function to an electric utility or a natural gas producer and trader needs greater research in the future.

2. During implementation, one's measurement technique will be a function of how the contracts composing the portfolio are themselves valued. Three alternative techniques include: a) mathematical methodologies if the contracts are priced using closed-form solutions; b) intra-tree methodologies for options priced with trees; and, c) numerical methods if one cannot use either of the first two techniques.

3. "Vega" is not a Greek letter. Our risk management ancestors probably selected the term because the Greek alphabet did not have a letter for "V" which corresponds to the first letter of volatility.

CHAPTER 10

Portfolio Analysis

10.1. INTRODUCTION

Portfolio analysis is the process of measuring and achieving the desired risk and return inherent in company books. Portfolio analysis includes both the calculation of the existing book risks and the definition of hedging tactics to attain the desired risk/return balance. The modeling principles introduced in chapters 2 and 3, plus the risk management tools introduced in chapter 9, are the building blocks for portfolio analysis. Under the umbrella of portfolio analysis we consider optimal hedging strategies, minimum-variance analysis, value-at-risk (VAR) analysis, and even the more general term of risk management.

This chapter will focus on the portfolio analysis techniques called "minimizing variance." As its name suggests, minimum-variance analysis attempts to determine the hedges required to minimize variance (or put another way, to bring risk as close to zero as possible). We will also introduce the related topic of calculating value-at-risk (VAR). Finally, we will briefly present an alternative to the minimum-variance method in which the risk manager attempts to minimize risk while maximizing return—i.e., achieve the specific risk/return balance as stated by the firm's risk/return framework.

10.2. APPLICATIONS OF PORTFOLIO ANALYSIS

Portfolio analysis can be employed at different levels and areas of the company. In the front office, at the trader level, portfolio analysis can be used to arrive at minimum-variance hedges. (See chapter 11 for a discussion of the "front/middle/back" office organization.) In the middle office, portfolio analysis can be used to perform VAR calculations. Both the front office and the middle office can use portfolio analysis to ensure that the underlying price models are indeed consistent with the way the market acts. Furthermore, if the underlying price models indeed sufficiently capture the underlying price behavior, then the hedges will truly provide a minimum-variance book.

Ideally, portfolio analysis can serve as the platform from which all risk management is driven. Given a particular risk-to-return ratio that the company feels comfortable with, or given an investment amount or maximum risk amount, traders could—in theory—optimize the company's portfolio in order to obtain maximum return per unit of risk. In fact, this is the goal of "maximizing the corporate utility function" (which will be explained at the end of this chapter). While the utopian use of portfolio analysis might sound quite interesting and sophisticated, unfortunately it is far too theoretical to be used effectively. Even the simpler portfolio analysis of defining hedges by minimizing the overall book risks rarely occurs in the less sophisticated energy operations. The basic minimum-variance portfolio analysis dominates the trading scene.

10.3. ANALYZING THE CHANGE IN PORTFOLIO VALUE

Portfolio analysis begins with solving for the expected return and risk. Here we rely heavily on Taylor series expansion, introduced in chapter 2.[1] (We will also utilize the section in Appendix A that discusses taking the expected values of random variables.)

We will make several assumptions during portfolio analysis. While we will concentrate on the math, a fundamental assumption is that in reality a firm could achieve the most efficient risk-return balance. This requires at least some liquidity in the overall energy markets. We are also constrained by the market reality to make more-realistic assumptions about market behavior. The simplifying assumptions made during the valuation must now be replaced. Our job is to reflect the reality of risks as best as we can.

In order to calculate the variance of the portfolio—so that we can indeed perform minimum-variance hedge calculations—we need to be able to extract the stochastic term from the portfolio change. Regardless of what underlying price models are used to model the behavior of the spot and forward prices in the portfolio, we define the stochastic term as the following:

$$Z(d\widetilde{\Pi}_t^I) = d\widetilde{\Pi}_t^I - E[d\widetilde{\Pi}_t^I] \qquad (10-1)$$

In other words, the stochastic, or risky, part of the portfolio behavior is obtained from the portfolio change over time dt by extracting the expected value of that change. In fact, for all three models we have analyzed on energy markets—the lognormal, the log-of-price mean-reverting, and the price mean-reverting models—the stochastic term in the portfolio value change over time dt can be written as follows:

$$Z(d\widetilde{\Pi}) = \sum_n \Delta_n^\pi F_n \sigma_n^{Fut} d\widetilde{z}_n^{Fut} + \frac{1}{2}\sum_n\sum_m \Gamma_{n,m}^\pi F_n F_m \sigma_n^{Fut}\sigma_m^{Fut}(d\widetilde{z}_n^{Fut}d\widetilde{z}_m^{Fut} - \rho_{n,m}dt) \quad (10-2)$$

We have utilized both Taylor series expansion and the nature of the stochastic terms in the three models to obtain the above expression for the random portion in the portfolio value change.

Note that in this equation we did not keep the second order dt (i.e., dt^2) terms, having assumed these higher-order dt terms away as too small to be significant. However, we have applied the Ito's lemma to the second-order $d\widetilde{z}$ terms in the equation. By doing so, we retain the gamma terms in our estimation of portfolio variance. We are thus relaxing the assumption of continuous hedging. (Even the most sophisticated houses cannot achieve this theoretical hedging ideal.) A non-continuously hedged portfolio may be delta neutral, but gamma risk will still remain. The following equation expresses the risks of a non-continuously hedged portfolio with the delta risk just hedged away:

$$Z(d\widetilde{\Pi}_t^H) = \frac{1}{2}\sum_n\sum_m\Gamma_{n,m}F_nF_m\sigma_n^{Fut}\sigma_m^{Fut}(d\widetilde{z}_nd\widetilde{z}_m - \rho_{n,m}dt) \qquad (10\text{--}3)$$

With the vega risk also included, we have the following change in the portfolio value over time dt, and its corresponding stochastic term:

$$d\widetilde{\Pi} = \begin{bmatrix} \displaystyle\sum_n^N\Delta_n^\Pi dF_n + \sum_{n,m}^N\frac{1}{2}\Gamma_{n,m}^\Pi dF_ndF_m \\[2ex] + \displaystyle\sum_{n,m}^N V_{n,m}^\Pi d\sigma_{n,m} + \Theta^\Pi dt \end{bmatrix} \qquad (10\text{--}4)$$

$$Z(d\widetilde{\Pi}) = \begin{bmatrix} \displaystyle\sum_n^N\Delta_n^\Pi\sigma_n^{Fut}F_nd\widetilde{z}_n^{Fut} + \frac{1}{2}\sum_n^N\sum_m^N\Gamma_{n,m}^\Pi F_nF_m\sigma_n^{Fut}\sigma_m^{Fut}(d\widetilde{z}_n^{Fut}dz_m^{Fut} \\[2ex] -\rho_{n,m}\,dt) + \displaystyle\sum_n^N\sum_m^N V_{n,m}^\Pi\sigma_{n,m}\gamma_{n,m}d\widetilde{w}_{n,m} \end{bmatrix} \qquad (10\text{--}5)$$

Note how the vega term, $V_{n,m}$, is expressed in discrete terms. We are also here suggesting that the portfolio analysis ought to be based on the volatility matrix described in chapter 6.

Expected variance, skew, and kurtosis—and therefore also the portfolio distribution moments—can be estimated using the above general formulation for the stochastic term in the change in the portfolio value. By taking the expected values of the stochastic term in the portfolio value change we obtain the distribution moments.

10.4. THE MINIMUM-VARIANCE METHOD

The "minimum-variance method" offers the most practical portfolio analysis technique. Of those energy firms performing portfolio analysis, most rely on the minimum-variance method. Even among these, the majority operate on a deal-by-deal analysis, while a minority employ a portfolio-wide process. The method is a fairly straightforward process:

- ◆ Define an initial portfolio and available hedges
- ◆ Calculate standard deviations for future market moves
- ◆ Calculate the number of new hedges required to keep future risk at an absolute minimum

We will make some major assumptions for the minimum-variance method: We ignore transaction costs associated with entering hedging trades. Transaction costs might include the bid/ask spread, counterparty credit risk, transmission rates and availability, and many other fundamental realities. Finally, we assume that the necessary hedges will be available in the marketplace. (All these assumptions can be relaxed into a more sophisticated model through the "corporate utility function," which will be introduced at the end of this chapter.)

10.4.1. The Hedged Portfolio

We will consider two types of portfolios—initial and hedged. The initial portfolio is assumed to be our starting point, an unhedged collection of futures and options. A hedged portfolio is defined as the initial portfolio plus any hedges available in the marketplace, with the positions defined so as to minimize variance.

The initial (or unhedged) portfolio of forwards, F, and options, O, can be defined as:

$$\Pi_t^I = \sum_n F_n + \sum_n O_n \qquad (10\text{--}6)$$

Given a single hedge, H, the hedged portfolio value would then be given by:

$$\Pi_t^H = \Pi_t^I + nH \qquad (10\text{--}7)$$

where: Π_t^H = hedged portfolio
$\quad\quad\;\; \Pi_t^I$ = initial (unhedged) portfolio
$\quad\quad\;\; H$ = hedge (either forward or option contract)
$\quad\quad\;\; n$ = number of contracts of H

The yet undefined hedge position, n, will be determined such that the hedge gives us the minimum possible variance for the hedged portfolio. We solve for the value of the minimum-variance hedge position by taking the derivative of the variance of the portfolio value change and setting it to zero:

$$\frac{\partial Var(d\Pi_t^H)}{\partial n} = 0 \qquad (10\text{--}8)$$

where

$$d\Pi_t^H = d\Pi_t^I + ndH \qquad (10\text{--}9)$$

The portfolio variance will be a function of n^2, resulting in variance as a function of the hedge contract positions shown in Figure 10–1. Note that there is a well-defined minimum for the portfolio variance as a function of the hedge position. This minimum is exactly defined by Equation 10–8.

10.4.2. Per-Deal Hedges

We will slowly build up our understanding of minimum variance by applying the method against increasingly complex portfolios. The lowest level at which portfolio analysis can be applied is at a per-deal hedge, which we will treat as a single-asset portfolio. We will consider the relatively simple cases of hedging with forward contracts. Then we will add options for a general model.

10.4.2.1. Hedging with a Single Forward Contract
Consider a hedged portfolio of a single deal, asset A, plus some number of units of a forward contract hedge:[2]

FIGURE 10-1

Portfolio Variance as a Function of Hedge Position

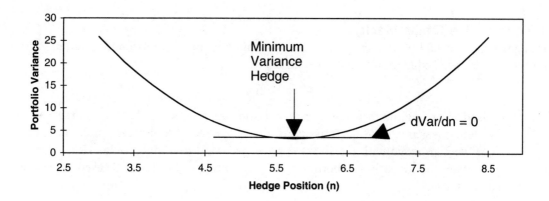

$$\Pi_t^{HF} = A_t + nF_t \tag{10-10}$$

where: Π_t^{HF} = single-asset portfolio hedged by a forward at time t
A_t = asset value at time t
F_t = forward contract at time t
n = number of forward contracts required for minimum variance hedge

The change in the single-asset portfolio value over some time is then given by:

$$d\Pi_t^{HF} = d\Pi_t^I + ndF_t = dA_t + ndF_t \tag{10-11}$$

The solution to the following equation then provides the minimum per-deal risk hedge:

$$\frac{\partial Var(d\Pi_t^{HF})}{dn} = 0 \tag{10-12}$$

Letting delta and gamma be defined for the asset A in terms of the forward contract we are using as a hedge,

$$\frac{\partial A}{\partial F} = \Delta \tag{10-13}$$

$$\Gamma = \frac{\partial^2 A}{\partial F} \tag{10-14}$$

and by applying Taylor series expansion, Equation 10-12 reduces to:

$$\frac{\partial}{dn}\left((\Delta + n)^2 F^2 \sigma^2 dt + \frac{1}{2}\Gamma^2 F^4 \sigma^4 dt^2\right) = 0 \tag{10-15}$$

By taking the derivative with respect to the contract position, we have:

$$2(\Delta + n)F^2\sigma^2 dt = 0 \tag{10-16}$$

10.4.2.2. The Delta Hedge

Using the above equation we can finally express the number of forward contracts required for a minimum-variance hedge for a single-asset portfolio:

$$n = -\Delta \tag{10-17}$$

Surprised? The minimum-variance hedge is obtained by selling delta contracts of the hedge. The delta measures how much the portfolio will move if the forward price moves by a dollar. Since we can hedge with the forward price, we want to eliminate this risk, which requires us to offset the move in the portfolio with the move in the forward, used as a hedge. Thus the delta hedge.

10.4.2.3. Hedging a Forward with Another Forward

Now consider a portfolio with a single forward contract with expiration T_1. We will hedge this portfolio with a second forward contract that has a different expiration T_2—a hedging practice that is very common in illiquid energy markets:

$$\Pi_t^I = F_{t,T_1}^A \tag{10-18}$$

$$H = F_{t,T_2}^H \tag{10-19}$$

$$\Pi_t^H = F_{t,T_1}^A + nF_{t,T_2}^H \tag{10-20}$$

In this case, the variance of the hedged portfolio would be as follows:

$$Var(d\Pi_t^H) = \begin{pmatrix} F_{t,T_1}^A (\sigma_t^A)^2 \, dt + \\ 2nF_{t,T_1}^A F_{t,T_2}^H \sigma_t^A \sigma_t^H \rho_{A,H} dt + \\ n^2(F_{t,T_2}^H)^2(\sigma_t^H)^2 \, dt \end{pmatrix} \tag{10-21}$$

As we did before, we solve for the minimum-variance hedge by taking the differential of the variance with respect to the number of hedge contracts, n, and solve for n by setting the equation to zero.

$$\frac{\partial Var(d\Pi_H)}{\partial n} = 0 \tag{10-22}$$

This gives us the following (see Appendix A for derivation):

$$MinVar(d\Pi_t^H) = 2F_1 F_2 \sigma_1 \sigma_2 \rho_{12} dt + 2nF_2^2\sigma_2^2 dt = 0 \tag{10-23}$$

We solve for n to obtain the answer:

$$n = \frac{-F^A_{t,T_1}\,\sigma^A_t}{F^H_{t,T_2}\,\sigma^H_t}\,\rho_{AH} \qquad (10-24)$$

This relationship may look familiar. This is a beta hedge (beta was discussed in chapter 9), with additional normalization for forward price levels. Put another way, the number of hedge forward prices in this case is simply the beta times the ratio of the two forward prices.

$$n = \frac{-F^A_{t,T_1}\,\sigma^A_t}{F^H_{t,T_2}\,\sigma^H_t}\,\rho_{AH} = \left(\frac{-F^A_{t,T_1}}{F^H_{t,T_2}}\right)\left(\frac{\sigma^A_t}{\sigma^H_t}\,\rho_{AH}\right) = \left(\frac{-F^A_{t,T_1}}{F^H_{t,T_2}}\right)\beta_{AH} \qquad (10-25)$$

In most cases, the asset forward contract, F^A_{t,T_1}, and the hedging forward contract, F^H_{t,T_2}, will not be perfectly correlated. As a result, the minimum variance cannot be equal to zero. The hedge will not be perfect and we will be left with a residual risk equal to the value of the minimized variance. This residual risk can be solved for by taking the expected value of the variance of the hedged portfolio (the steps are shown in Appendix A), to obtain:

$$MinVar(d\Pi^H_t) = (F^A_{t,T_1})^2(\sigma^A_t)^2(1 - \rho^2_{AH})dt \qquad (10-26)$$

And from this we obtain the standard deviation of our hedged portfolio:

$$STD(\Pi) = \left[F^A_{t,T_1}\sigma^A_t\,\sqrt{(1 - \rho^2_{AH})}\sqrt{dt}\right] \qquad (10-27)$$

This portfolio standard deviation is plotted against the possible correlation values in Figure 10–2.

If the correlation between the forward price in our original portfolio and the hedging forward is exactly 100% or negative 100%, we are left with zero residual risk. In other words, we are perfectly hedged. However, if the correlation is not perfect, we are left with

F I G U R E   10–2

Residual STD as a Function of Forward Price Correlation

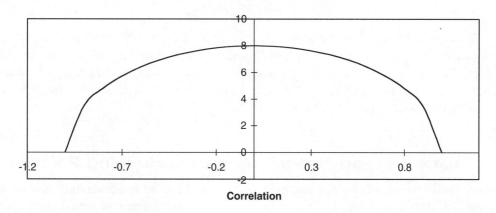

Correlation

residual risk in our books, and there is absolutely nothing we can do about it. It turns out that if we have a well-diversified portfolio, this residual risk gets diversified away (this is discussed in one of the following sections). However, if this is not the case, we have to accept the residual risk for what it is: there to stay, unless we can come up with a hedge that has a higher correlation.

10.4.3. Portfolios with Options

Now we will consider options. We will first analyze the variance of an option. We will then use this understanding to formulate a very general expression of change in portfolio value.

Consider a portfolio that consists of a single option, O_t^A, on a forward price, F_o. We create a hedged portfolio, which consists of the option and some number of forward contracts, F_h. We first calculate the change in the initial portfolio value:

$$d\Pi_t^I = dO_t^A = \Delta dF_O + \frac{1}{2}\Gamma d(F_O)^2 + Vd\sigma + \Theta dt \qquad (10\text{--}28)$$

where we have included the vega risk as well. The variance of this portfolio is then given by:

$$Var(\Pi_t^I) = Var(dO_t^A) = \{\Delta^2(F_O)^2\,\sigma^2 + V^2\sigma^2\xi^2\}dt$$

$$+ \left\{ \begin{array}{l} \dfrac{1}{2}\Gamma^2(F_O)^4\,\sigma^4 + \dfrac{1}{2}\left(\dfrac{\partial V}{\partial\sigma}\right)^2\sigma^4\xi^4 + \\[2ex] \left(\dfrac{\partial\Delta}{\partial\sigma}\right)^2(F_{t,T1}^H)^2\sigma^4\xi^4 \end{array} \right\} dt^2 \quad (10\text{--}29)$$

Note that the above equation includes the first- and the second-order risks. By performing the same exercise of calculating the minimum variance position for the hedged portfolio, we obtain the minimum-variance hedge to be a sale of the following number of forwards:

$$n = \frac{-\Delta\rho_{F_0 F_H}F_0\sigma_0}{F_H\sigma^{F_H}} \qquad (10\text{--}30)$$

The residual hedged portfolio variance includes the residual delta risk as well as the gamma and the vega risks that our forward hedge could do nothing about. As the time period dt goes to zero—i.e., we begin hedging continuously—the gamma and the other higher order components of the hedge position go to zero with dt, and we are left with the residual delta risk and the vega risk.

10.4.4. Lessons from Inadequate Hedging Policies

Let us consider several cases of inadequate hedging to build an understanding of how to perform minimum variance on a complex portfolio. A poor hedge can actually increase risk compared to not hedging at all. Similarly, not hedging does not represent the most risk-averse strategy.

10.4.4.1. Impact of Poor Hedging

We can use the portfolio variance calculations to tell us what happens to risk when we do not have the correct correlation measures between the risk we are trying to offset and the hedge we are trying to use. Let's look at the simplest case of a portfolio of a single forward price, F_1. Suppose that we are trying to use another forward of the same expiration and the same commodity, but at a different delivery point, F_2. In this case, our hedged portfolio is given by:

$$\Pi_H + F_1 + nF_2 \qquad (10-31)$$

Now let's assume that we do not know what the correlation is between the two forward prices, and let's see what happens if we perform a simple one-for-one hedge. This is such a simple and tempting thing to do, after all! Now our portfolio is given by:

$$\Pi_H = F_1 - F_2 \qquad (10-32)$$

And its variance is then given by:

$$Var(d\widetilde{\Pi}_H) = F_1^2\sigma_1^2 dt - 2F_1F_2\sigma_1\sigma_2\rho_{12}dt + F_2^2\sigma_2^2 dt \qquad (10-33)$$

Now we will consider how this one-for-one strategy compares with the minimum-variance strategy we already worked out in one of the above sections, across different values of the correlation between the two forward prices.

If you remember, the variance of the minimum-variance-hedged portfolio is given by:

$$Var(d\widetilde{\Pi}_H) = F_1^2\sigma_1^2 dt(1 - \rho_{12}) \qquad (10-34)$$

Now, what if the correlation is exactly minus 100%:

$$\rho = -1 \qquad (10-35)$$

The variance of our one-for-one hedge portfolio is then given by:

$$Var(d\widetilde{\Pi}_H) = (F_1\sigma_1 + F_2\sigma_2)^2\, dt \qquad (10-36)$$

The variance of the one-for-one hedged portfolio is more than double the variance we would have if we did not use a hedge at all! Meanwhile, the variance of our minimum-variance portfolio is exactly zero:

$$Var(d\widetilde{\Pi}_H) = 0 \qquad (10-37)$$

Now let's see what happens if the correlation is zero:

$$\rho = 0 \qquad (10-38)$$

Now we have the variance of the one-for-one hedged portfolio at roughly double the value of the variance if we did not hedge at all:

$$Var(d\widetilde{\Pi}_H) = (F_1^2\sigma_1^2 + F_2^2\sigma_2^2)dt \qquad (10-39)$$

Meanwhile, the minimum-variance-hedged portfolio would have told us not to do anything, resulting in the minimum possible variance under these conditions, which is simply the variance of our original portfolio:

$$Var(d\widetilde{\Pi}_H) = F_1^2 \sigma_1^2 dt \quad \text{—i.e. NO HEDGE} \tag{10-40}$$

Finally, let's consider the optimistic case of the correlation being exactly one:

$$\rho = +1 \tag{10-41}$$

Even in this case we end up with a nonzero variance in our one-for-one hedged portfolio:

$$Var(d\widetilde{\Pi}_H) = (F_1\sigma_1 - F_2\sigma_2)^2 \, dt \tag{10-42}$$

Meanwhile, our minimum-variance-hedged portfolio gives us zero residual risk, i.e., it is perfectly hedged:

$$Var(d\Pi_H) = 0 \tag{10-43}$$

This last result has to do with the fact that the random moves in prices are proportional to the price levels and volatilities. The higher the prices, the greater are the random moves. The same is true regarding the volatility of prices. Thus, even though two commodities are perfectly correlated, in deciding on the hedge using one versus the other commodity, we still need to normalize this hedge by the relative price and volatility values.

The difference between the variances of the one-for-one strategy and the minimum-variance strategy represents the amount of unnecessary risk that we could have avoided had we been able to do our homework. In the case where the correlation between two forward prices is actually pretty small, and we assume that it is perfect, we may easily end up with more risk than the risk we started out with. The difference between the risk of a "hedged" portfolio that was hedged incorrectly, assuming a perfect correlation, and the risk of a portfolio not hedged at all is given by:

$$(F_1\sigma_1 - F_2\sigma_2\rho)^2 \, dt \tag{10-44}$$

Note that if the correlation is less than the ratio of the forwards and volatilities, as in the following:

$$\rho < \frac{F_2\sigma_2}{F_1\sigma_1} \tag{10-45}$$

Then, what we believe is a hedged portfolio is in fact a portfolio that has more risk than the original, unhedged portfolio.

The poor hedge examples are really not that silly. To this day the natural gas market is not well developed at local delivery points, forcing the market players to hedge longer-term deals using NYMEX futures. The forward prices at local delivery points do not necessarily have a great deal of correlation with the corresponding NYMEX futures prices, possibly resulting in large basis risk. Hence, even the minimum-variance hedges may leave a good amount of residual risk in the books. However, the non-optimal hedges that assume perfect correlations end up potentially not only not reducing portfolio risk but in fact increasing it. It is no surprise, then, that there have been a certain number of tragic natural gas market trading disasters.

10.4.4.2. To Hedge or Not to Hedge

Any trader or manager should ask herself whether the costs of hedging, as captured through the bid/ask spreads and transaction costs, are justified given the reduction in book risks. This is a very reasonable approach to take toward hedging. After all, when you are deciding on how much car insurance coverage you need, you weigh the additional insurance premium against the additional insurance protection to make the decision on the type of insurance coverage. The same should be true here.

Let's once again look at the simple case of a single forward portfolio. If we do not hedge, we end up with the portfolio variance of:

$$Var(d\widetilde{\Pi}_I) = F_1^2\sigma_1^2 dt \tag{10-46}$$

And if we put on a minimum-variance hedge using a single forward for hedging, we are left with the hedged portfolio variance of:

$$Var(d\widetilde{\Pi}_H) = F_1^2\sigma_1^2 dt(1 - \rho^2) \tag{10-47}$$

Specifically, the minimum-variance hedge reduces the portfolio risk by an amount of:

$$F_1^2\sigma_1^2\rho^{dt} \tag{10-48}$$

Now we can ask ourselves, What is the cost of the hedge? Is the "give-and-take" fair? The answer will be a function of both the amounts of risk reduced and the costs of hedging, but it will also be a function of your own individual risk aversion. A person who is more risk-averse than you may be willing to take on higher hedging costs in order to obtain the exact same risk reduction. This is where we are starting to get into what is called the optimization of the corporate utility function: decision making regarding risk and return based on the company's individual risk-aversion.

10.4.4.3. Benefits of Diversification

Finally, before we leave the minimum-variance portfolio approach and move on to VAR and utility function analysis, let's go through the effects of portfolio diversification and how it can work in your favor. Suppose the portfolio risk can be expressed in terms of a single systematic risk, $d\tilde{z}_0$ and in terms of numerous residual, nonsystematic risks, symbolized by $d\epsilon$:

$$Z(d\widetilde{\Pi}) = \Delta_{z_0}^{\Pi}\, d\tilde{z}_0 + \sum_n^N \Delta_{\varepsilon_n}^{\Pi}\, d\tilde{\varepsilon}_n \tag{10-49}$$

We are keeping only the delta terms in the risk definition to make this simple. Let's also assume that we can hedge away the systematic market risk, $\Delta_{z_0}^{\Pi} d\tilde{z}_0$. In this case, we are left with only the residual risks. The relationship of variance to the portfolio returns—i.e., the variance of the portfolio expressed as a percentage of the portfolio value—is then given by:

$$dt(\sigma_\Pi)^2 = \frac{E[(Z(d\Pi)^2)]}{\Pi^2} = \frac{\sum_n^N (\Delta_{\varepsilon_n}^\Pi)^2 \, dt}{\Pi^2} \qquad (10-50)$$

where we have used the fact that, by definition, the residuals are assumed to be independent, i.e., uncorrelated.

Now let's simplify things even more. Suppose that the portfolio consists purely of forward prices:

$$\Pi = \sum w_n F_n \qquad (10-51)$$

and that the residual risks have the same variance, so that the variance of this portfolio with the systematic risk hedged away becomes proportional to:

$$dt(\sigma_\Pi)^2 \propto \frac{\sum w_n^2 F_n^2}{\left(\sum w_n F_n\right)^2} \qquad (10-52)$$

Further making the simplification that we have roughly the same dollar value in each forward price, we are left with a variance of the portfoliowhich is proportional to:

$$dt(\sigma_\Pi)^2 \propto \frac{\sum_{n=1}^N (1)^2}{\left(\sum_{n=1}^N 1\right)^2} = \frac{N}{N^2} = \frac{1}{N} \qquad (10-53)$$

The portfolio variance drops off as $1/N$ as the number of different forward price contracts we have in the books increases!

I am not saying anything here that would surprise a stock trader who trades hundreds of stocks and uses the S&P 500 index to hedge the market systematic risk. Such traders know intuitively the value of portfolio diversification. And we do not have to be constrained to the world of trading to find value in diversification. All insurance companies, whether the policy is for health or for car insurance, benefit from its effects. In fact, the residential electricity suppliers will function a great deal like insurance companies in pricing, with their diversification in residential contract prices.

10.5. THE GENERALIZED MINIMUM-VARIANCE MODEL

The complexity involved in the portfolio analysis of a whole portfolio comes in the multitude of prices, volatilities, and correlations that might all work at the same time to cause portfolio changes. A portfolio that is a function of several different forward price curves, and volatility matrices, would change over time as defined by Equation 10-4.

Hence, the changes in the prices and the volatility matrices drive the changes in the portfolio value. There is also a decay term: the value the portfolio loses due to passage of time. For options, this is a very important component of option value: The longer the time to expiration, the higher is the option price—particularly for an out-of-the-money option—since the greater the time to expiration, the greater is the chance that the option may expire in the money.

Performing minimum-variance analysis of the whole portfolio, including books from a variety of energy markets, requires computers to incorporate the multitude of correlations and risks. Ultimately, solving for multiple minimum-variance hedges reduces to a linear programming problem. In other words, while this may appear as an overwhelming task, it is a doable task.

10.6. CORRELATIONS

Correlations are important both as inputs in deal and portfolio valuation and in portfolio and value-at-risk (VAR) analysis. They can be estimated from historical data, in which case they are stationary over time, i.e., they remain the same until the next time they are reestimated. Or they can be model-implied. A two-factor model can make fundamental price driver assumptions, which translate into volatility matrices as well as correlation matrices for forward prices within a single market (as discussed in chapter 6). In this case, as the model parameters change, so do the model-implied correlations. However, correlations across markets can only be implied to the extent that the models make assumptions about the relationship between the markets.

The forward price correlations must be obtained to value options on averages of prices, to hedge forward price risks across the curve with only the available liquid forward price contracts. Similarly, any VAR analysis will have to assume some relationships between the behavior of forward prices on the same commodity but with different expirations.

The intermarket and interenergy correlations are necessary for cross-hedging between markets and for VAR analysis, given all the books across markets. We are here defining intermarket correlations as the correlations between price returns of the same energy commodity but at different delivery points, or for delivery at different times of the day. An example of intermarket correlations would be the correlations between natural gas prices at different delivery points, or electricity prices at the same delivery point but for delivery at different times of the day. The interenergy correlations we are defining as correlations of price returns of different energies. These cross-market correlations can also be implied from the cheapest-to-deliver forward prices. However, the likelihood of finding a cheapest-to-deliver forward price market liquid enough to be practically used is very small.

10.7. VALUE-AT-RISK (VAR) ANALYSIS

Value-at-risk (VAR) analysis extends portfolio analysis into a specific type of reporting. Rather then solving for optimal hedges, we are trying to obtain the distribution of the overall portfolio value. The results of VAR analysis ultimately gives the management a sense of what could happen over a period of time with certain probability measures attached to the various scenarios. (Note: There are a growing number of books and seminars on VAR; as with the rest of the book, this section will focus on those aspects of the topic that are unique to energies.)

As in many business processes, there exists no single VAR methodology; in fact, a debate rages that questions the relevance of the practice in energies. Until the market creates something more realistic, however, VAR is here to stay because the technique offers one of the few opportunities to communicate risk directly to management in a simplified (even if a little misleading) manner. In this section, we will first discuss the general nature of VAR and then describe some of the available methods:

- fixed-scenario stress simulations
- Monte Carlo simulations
- variance-covariance method
- historical "simulations"

Equation 10–4, which was used in the portfolio optimization, can be applied to VAR analysis as well, given that the time period for which the VAR analysis is performed is not too long for the Taylor expansion to require more terms. Generally, if the VAR calculation is made for a period up to one month, the higher-order dt terms remain insignificant. For such short time periods, Equation 10–4 can be used to approximate the portfolio value distribution moments, and hence avoid the typically time-consuming process of running VAR simulations.

In order to obtain a more precise measure of VAR, and without any time period constraints, market simulations are generally performed. In this case the difficulty is not in the simulations, but rather in determining just exactly what needs to be simulated: should we simulate all the points on the forward price curve, and all the points in the volatility and correlation matrices? The level of information intensity and simulation intensity can increase very quickly to the point where the simulation becomes so time-consuming that, while it is of value in theory, it is of no value in practice. Simulating every single forward price and volatility within a trading book would generally fall into this category of an unusable VAR analysis.

Instead, factor analysis is sometimes used to reduce the degrees of freedom in the portfolio value simulations, allowing for a more practical, although perhaps not as realistic, capture of portfolio value distribution.

Yet another means of reducing the degrees of freedom would be to go back to the underlying price models and use the market drivers expressed within these models as the variables to be simulated. For example, in the case of a two-factor price mean-reverting model, the equilibrium price and the spot price can be simulated, allowing for a multitude of forward price curve behaviors, such as contango and backwardation, while maintaining the intuition of how the market forward price curves ought to look. This also solves the additional problem with simulating every single forward price and volatility the portfolio is sensitive to. Even with proper correlations implemented into the multi-factor simulations, the resulting forward price curves and volatility matrices may end up looking like nothing ever seen in the marketplace.

The last point that should at least be mentioned is the case of a producer who has assets on the overall company book that may directly increase or offset the trading book risks. Hence, if the trading operation is closely tied to the energy production side, then the hedges ought to incorporate the producer's naturally long positions into the overall portfolio optimization. Similarly, the VAR analysis should incorporate the corporation's assets whenever there is any correlation between the assets and the trading book.

10.7.1. Fixed-Scenario Stress Simulations

"Fixed-scenario stress simulation" is the simplest VAR method. The process generates simulations that move the entire forward price curve up and down to represent all the possible moves.

The advantages of the fixed scenario stress simulation method include:

- simple to perform
- good for doing deltas numerically if you cannot generate them theoretically

The disadvantages include:

- misses full distribution
- not based on probabilities
- misses market correlations

10.7.2. Monte Carlo Simulations

"Monte Carlo simulations" represent a good VAR methodology that could be used throughout the markets. Here we simulate the underlying market variables, which are in turn used to generate the various resulting market scenarios.

The advantages include:

- Degree of difficulty varies with the number of variables simulated; hence, simulations are simple if variables are kept to a minimum
- Provides full P&L distribution, including skew and kurtosis effects
- Can simulate lots of variables, including volatilities; helps us judge whether the underlying models used by the firm adequately reflect reality
- Monte Carlo tools available on most software (e.g., spreadsheets)

The disadvantages include:

- Complexity grows with the number of factors simulated
- Does not maintain certain intuition about the forward price curve when multifactor approach is taken
- Does not capture full scope of market risk when only a single factor or two factors are simulated
- May take a long time to run

As mentioned above, one of the advantages of this method is that one can apply different underlying price models during the implementation phase. We will explore two such multifactor cases: lognormal pricing and price mean-reverting pricing.

In the case of multifactor lognormal assumption guiding our simulations of the forward prices, we need to simulate a whole strip of forward prices, where each forward price exhibits correlations with the other forward prices, but also has its own individual risk. In this case the problem reduces to one of implementation, given a possibly very large data set. Appendix A shows you one way of performing this multifactor implementation.

In the case of a two-factor model, it would be recommended to add two additional factors: one for each seasonality factor, as the seasonality factors do move around from day to day. In this case the simulation problem is quite a bit simpler, as only four variables need to be simulated. The range of forward price values will be more limited compared to the multifactor lognormal model, but the forward price curves might also have more intuitive scenarios captured than in the case of the multifactor simulations.

Ultimately, the company has to choose between using the more conservative method of multifactor simulations—which would also take a much longer time to run—and the model methodology, which would have the benefit of much faster simulations but may not be conservative enough.

10.7.3. Estimated Variance-Covariance Method

Another recommended method is the "estimated variance-covariance" technique. Here we calculate the expected change in portfolio value, its variance, skew, and kurtosis. This method is very applicable to energy markets, particularly when performed simultaneously (and compared) with Monte Carlo simulation.

The advantages include:

- Can be simple if only the second moment calculated
  - looked at over a very small time period
- Reliable for small time periods (up to a month)
- Quick calculation

The disadvantages include:

- Can be complicated if higher moments (skew and kurtosis) are calculated
- Unreliable if time period longer

Our goal is to include as many market variables as possible and then calculate the portfolio variance. Given the change in the portfolio value we can calculate everything we need to define its probability distribution characteristics.

10.7.4. Historical "Simulations"

The final method depends on historical data to judge how a portfolio would look given past activity. Historical simulations are appealing but the market-implied information is preferably used when it is available. The problem with historical data is that it represents the past, rather than the future. So if we want to simulate the future, we are much better off using market-implied information about the future, as this is more representative of the future than is historical data. However, when there is very little market information, which is the case with some energy markets, the historical data is pretty much all we can fall back on.

The advantages include:

♦ Just about the only advantage is that historical simulations are relatively simple to do. (Perhaps this attraction introduces the equal disadvantage of seducing unwary end users!)

The disadvantages include:

♦ Historicals take you "backward," not forward
♦ Current market-implied information about the future is not included
♦ The past represents a single "path." Going forward, many paths are possible

The set of historical data ought to represent at least six months of data; ideally one should simulate based on one or two years' worth of data. (A practical extension of this means that firms should start building their databases as soon as possible.)

10.8. SPECIAL CASE OF ELECTRICITY

Electricity is the most complex of all energy markets. Not only does it follow the underlying price mean-reverting process due to the character of events, but it also has extremely strong annual and semiannual seasonality factors. As if this is not enough, electricity spot prices are very different at different times of the day and in fact tend to behave very differently. The on-peak electricity prices tend to show much greater seasonality factors than do the off-peak prices. This makes sense: The summer highs tend to happen primarily during the day rather than during the night. Similarly, since the big events tend to happen primarily in the summer due to temperature spikes, and since the off-peak hours do not generally see these highs to the same degree, events are much less noticeable in the off-peak hours price data and do not play as big a role.

While the actual modeling of electricity prices can be quite difficult, the implementation of portfolio analysis and VAR analysis in a company that trades electricity nationwide can be quite a large number-crunching job. The electricity markets are segmented enough that making simplifying assumptions of perfect correlations between some of the regions is just not right. Similarly, the time-of-day issues require that at least the off- and on-peak prices get their own individual simulation variables, if not every hour of the day, depending on the sensitivity of the deals in the books to specific hours of the day. Things get even more complicated in the case of producers who might be using other energies in the generation of electricity, thus giving them a naturally long electricity position and a naturally short energy-generating position, such as in natural gas or coal.

10.9. THE CORPORATE UTILITY FUNCTION

The future of portfolio analysis lies beyond simply minimizing risk as performed by minimum-variance methods. Our goal will be to add return to the analysis as well. Remember, after all, our ideal of the risk/return framework. Imagine a technique that simultaneously pursues the firm's optimal preference for both risk and return levels.

Modern Portfolio Theory promotes the concept of the "corporate utility function" as the wave of the future. The utility function approach can capture a great deal more information about both the portfolio dollar value distribution and a company's risk-and-return preferences. The corporate utility function is all of the following:

- A measure of the "degree of happiness"
- An expression of the corporation's risk management goals
- Very similar to the economic concept of "marginal utility"

Under this approach we need first to formulate the utility function as a function of the distribution moments of the hedged portfolio's dollar change over time period dt. A very practical example of such a utility function, U, is given by Cox and Rubenstein in their book *Options Markets*. They discuss the constant proportional utility function, which has the following characteristic:

$$b = -\frac{U''R}{U'} \qquad (10\text{--}54)$$

where: b = level of constant proportional risk aversion

In this case, $U(R)$ must take the form:

$$U(R) = \left(\frac{1}{1-b}\right) R^{(1-b)} \qquad (10\text{--}55)$$

Where: R = the portfolio return

The maximization of the utility function results in a set of equations that define the hedge positions as a function of both the hedged portfolios' expected risk, return, and the corporate risk-aversion.

The difference between these results and the results that we would obtain by performing a minimum-variance portfolio analysis would lie in the fact that the utility function approach incorporates both the expected risk and the expected return (if not also the higher-order moments) and gives and takes between the two in order to arrive at the best set of hedges, while the minimum-variance approach knows nothing about the expected return, thus ignoring the fact that putting on one of the hedges might drive the expected return down significantly.

It is hard to implement the utility function methodology. First and foremost, the company's risk and return preferences may be very theoretical and hard to quantify, and this is why this approach is generally not yet used in the marketplace. But also, very few energy companies are at the level of sophistication where they have the quantitative and programming support to take on a company-wide portfolio analysis project.

ENDNOTES

1. In portfolio analysis Taylor series is more appropriate than Ito's Lemma. While arbitrage-free derivation is based on the assumption of continuous hedging, *dt* approaches zero. However, here in portfolio analysis, we can relax this assumption, as in fact nobody hedges truly continuously.

2. We construct this simplified example with only forward contract hedges for two reasons. Forwards not only yield to easier equations for instructional purposes, forwards also do not carry gamma risk. We will add this additional level of complexity when discussing option hedging.

CHAPTER 11

Risk Management Policies

11.1. INTRODUCTION

A company's "risk/return framework" provides a holistic process for expressing and managing the firm's risk and return preferences. The first ten chapters of this book focused on the quantitative concepts, equations, and implementation issues that serve as the technical skeleton of this risk/return framework. But as we stated in chapter 9, human risk is possibly the greatest of risks. We need proper management policies to minimize human error and optimize quantitative operations.

This concluding chapter, therefore, is intended to place the concept of "management" back into "risk management." With luck, we can articulate the business policies and strategic decisions that will drive the risk/return framework so that the quantitative processes will be more meaningful, efficient, and profitable. Our approach will follow these steps:

1. Introduce the benefits of a risk management policy
2. Define the four kinds of risk management trading strategies
3. Provide an evaluation checklist for preparing the policy
4. Explain the "front/middle/back" office paradigm
5. Propose general issues for risk-management policies and reporting
6. Comment on management issues and implementation

11.2. THE CASE FOR A RISK MANAGEMENT POLICY

Every firm involved with derivatives should have a risk-management policy that states the goals and strategies for the relevant business unit. Ideally, the firm commits these policies to paper and updates them on a regular basis. These policies should be as realistic as possible, both in the evaluation of current practices and in the projection of future objectives. The risk-management policy may be incorporated within the firmwide or business unit business plan. The policy and the business plan should be consistent and closely tied together.

Just as good fences make good neighbors, so do good risk-management policies and guidelines make good traders and risk managers. However, this is true only if the risk-management policy is both reflective of the current trading environment and aware of the improvements expected in the near term. Writing a risk-management policy in the expectations of the state of the trading and risk-management group five years from now helps nobody. It only adds to the frustration and the confusion that probably already exists.

To this extent, the risk-management policy is a reflection of the company's understanding of the practical side of the business as well as the future growth. A company that is realistic about its place in the marketplace and its own evaluation of its performance as a trading and risk-management business, will have a realistic risk-management policy, with guidelines for its traders and risk managers that are very concrete and will help speed the company's growth. On the other hand, a company that is not very realistic tends to write a policy that is theoretical rather than practical, and that typically no one follows—not because they do not want to, but because they cannot, given the existing support structure and understanding of the business.

A risk-management policy offers numerous collateral benefits. The very process of writing it forces evaluation of current practices and requires that the various players from different functions communicate. A well-written policy will improve implementation, increasing the likelihood that the personnel, methodologies, and systems are sensibly selected and not redundant. Managers can use the written policy as a basis for communication between many levels of the firm, both with employees and with upper management.

11.2.1. Horror Stories

Much has been written about how derivatives cause financial disasters. So much, in fact, that in many companies derivatives are equated with dangerous and uncontrollable speculation. While this indeed may be true in some cases, we should not be blaming the products for the way some companies have used and abused them.

A couple of points must be made here. First, for as many bad stories that have been heard, there are many more good stories, which typically do not get mentioned by the press. Bad news is always much more interesting than good news. It is probably no surprise that the media tends to concentrate on the bad, as this is typically what gets our emotions going much more effectively than does the good (a rather sad truth, don't you think?). Also, a trading company that has its own proprietary means of successfully capturing value in the marketplace will not exactly be publishing this fact.

A true and well-done risk-management policy aims to actualize a particular combination of risk and return that the company has set as its goal. Under different trading strategies derivatives can be used as return generators and/or risk reducers. Unfortunately, in almost all the bad stories you might have read in the papers about how derivatives caused financial tragedies, the derivatives were used as return generators under the guise of risk reducers. In such cases, the problem was not with the derivatives, but rather with very poor management structure and control of the trading strategy.

A risk manager might wear many hats within a company, including overseeing valuation and risk calculations, trading, and deal execution. However, of all the hats the most important one is the hat of a manager. A risk manager who has never traded or valued a derivative product might still run a successful risk-management trading group with proper procedures and controls in place and given a thorough understanding of what the key issues are.

11.3. RISK-MANAGEMENT GOALS AND STRATEGIES

The first step in devising a risk-management policy is to understand that risk management can be different things to different people. There are different kinds of trading strategies, which achieve very different kinds of risk-and-return goals. Not only can the same firm be following different—if not conflicting—goals, the firm may actually be practicing strategies that do not necessarily fit the desired goals. (Any mismatch between existing and desired trading strategies should be an area of concern and should be treated specifically in the plan statement according to the risk-management policy.)

There are many different approaches to trading strategies, but we can break them down into four distinct groups:

- ◆ speculation
- ◆ arbitrage
- ◆ market maker
- ◆ treasury

While not mutually exclusive, each strategy represents a different balance of risk and return that requires very different types of business processes and management. (See Table 11–1.) A manager would be wise to evaluate her own operation, understand how it could be categorized as one or more of the distinct strategies, and perhaps begin the process of separating the functions in order to evaluate them.

Figure 11–1 plots the four strategies across risk and return. Speculation, arbitrage, and market making are profit-generating strategies, while the treasury strategy is a pure risk-reducing strategy. As will be made clear later, the arbitrage and market-making strategies can be vague in terms of the degree of risk taken and return sought.

TABLE 11–1

Summary of Risk-Management Strategies

Strategy	Risk	Reward	Term	Liquidity
Speculation	High	High	Short	High
Arbitrage	Low	Low	Short-medium	High
Market maker	Low	Low	As required	As available
Treasury	Reducing	Negative	As required	As available

FIGURE 11-1

Trading Strategies

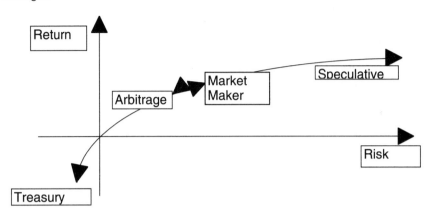

11.3.1. Speculation

A speculative trading strategy is typically a large-return-for-large-risk strategy. It is typically very short-term, in terms of how long the positions are held as well as how far out the traded contracts tend to go. This type of strategy benefits from a great deal of liquidity for greater deal turnover and hence more opportunity. Nonetheless, it can also be seen in illiquid markets, where the deals are held for longer periods of time. The traders asked to generate value in such a strategy are primarily market-driven, as they try to guess the short-term market moves. They take on first-order risks, such as delta and vega, in an attempt to capture value from the underlying prices and volatilities moving up or down.

Some notes on speculation:

- While *speculation* is not a "dirty word," remember that what goes up can just as easily go down
- Unexpected events hurt "double".
- Beware of speculators hiding behind risk management
- Nothing is necessarily wrong with speculation, as long as it is recognized for what it is
- Special case of speculation: not hedging! Without risk management, a firm carries full exposure to market risk

11.3.2. Arbitrage

An arbitrage strategy involves "beating" the marketplace with one's ability to value and hedge derivative products. Sometimes this can be pure arbitrage, where value is captured through a zero-risk pure arbitrage market opportunity. Sometimes this can be "statistical arbitrage," where value is captured by exploiting a market opportunity over a period of time and by doing many trades. The pure arbitrage case is a perfectly hedged value-added deal. An example can be buying a futures contract at the Chicago Board of Trade and simultaneously selling the exact same contract on the Philadelphia exchange but at a higher price than what it was bought for. Obviously, pure arbitrage opportunities carrying no risk are hard to find, and when they are found they do not last for very long.

Statistical arbitrage involves capturing market mispricing, which is obvious only to the players who know something about the market or about product pricing (and the majority do not). A good example of such statistical arbitrage occurs when the market is using too low a volatility in pricing options. To take advantage of such volatility misestimation, the gamma risk is not hedged away but the delta risk is, allowing for the volatility spread to be captured through continuously hedging the options' delta risk. Such statistical arbitrage opportunities do carry a certain amount of risk—the actual level depends on the types of products traded and the hedges available. The risk is typically much smaller than in the case of the speculative strategy. Arbitrage strategies can primarily be found in relatively new and fairly illiquid markets, as these typically provide mispricing opportunities.

Energy producers have an advantage here over the purely cash-settled trading companies. Producers may be able to capture the cost-to-market-price "asset arbitrage," which is unique to the producers of energy commodities. The cost of production of energy is exactly that: how much it costs per unit of energy to get it to the point of delivery. The price, on the other hand, is defined by many other supply-and-demand factors and can be quite a bit different from the cost of production. (A good example here is hydroelectric utilities that have paid off their cost of investment. The cost of production to such a utility is close to zero, and yet the prices at the utility delivery point are typically much greater.) To the producers the "mispricing" is very much related to their cost of production, and hence the arbitrage opportunities are unique across the producers. One way to think about this is that the producers have a natural hedge to use when they perceive a "mispricing" in the marketplace.

11.3.3. Market Maker

Being a risk-management service provider, or market maker, is in theory a zero-risk strategy that captures the bid-ask spread in the marketplace. A market maker is willing to quote a price on almost any deal within a well-defined market-place to its customer. When a customer enters into a deal, the service provider looks for the best hedges for the deal. If the market is liquid and mature, the service provider can hedge off all the first-order risks. When the hedging is assumed continuous, as the first-order risks change due to the market underlying prices and volatilities changing, the service provider immediately rehedges. In such a way, all the risks are brought down to a minimum at all times.

However, the reality is that even in highly liquid markets hedging is not continuous, and hence the service provider is generally left with some small daily risks. Similarly, the hedging costs may be high enough that the risk manager decides that she is better off keeping some risks on the books rather than paying for the hedges. In the case of an illiquid market, not only is the hedging very far from being continuous, it may also be impossible to hedge off certain types of risk. Hence, in both the liquid and the illiquid markets, being a service provider carries a certain amount of risk. One price of good news is that the greater the illiquidity in a market-place, the greater are the bid-ask spreads.

11.3.4. Treasury

Finally, the treasury strategy means providing risk-management service only in-house in order to achieve a particular risk/return combination for the company. This is a one-way strategy, typically consisting of buying certain derivative products to be used as insurance to offset risks. The interest rate derivative products have developed into a huge market because there are so many companies that carry interest rate risks through their loan-based capital that they have a need to manage this risk. The electricity market could also become a large market post deregu-lation for this same reason—there are enough users to generate a need for managing the elec-tricity price risk.

The companies that are purely users of risk-management products typically give their treasury departments the function of entering into derivative transactions in order to minimize some risks or reach a certain risk/return profile. Even as a user, a company should still have a good understanding of the risk-management issues and a management structure that will pro-vide enough controls to ensure that issues that need to be communicated across the managerial levels indeed are communicated.

11.3.5. Mixed Strategies

Many trading places employ one or more of these trading strategies. The typical firm will be exposed to a wide array of risks, returns, terms, and liquidity. We would expect a diverse com-pany to follow diverse strategies. Note in Table 11–1 how the speculative and arbitrage strate-gies have specific terms and liquidities that are necessary, while the market maker and treasury functions follow the market on an "as needed" basis. The manager should make sure she un-derstands "why" her firm is trading and hedging. If the firm "needs" to manage risk, it should follow a treasury function. If the business unit is supposed to be a profit center, one of the other three strategies should be selected. Of course, a pure treasury strategy should never be consid-ered a profit center strategy.

Management confusion tends to creep in when trading strategies are not well defined, or when more than one trading strategy is used and they overlap. Such confusion, resulting from failing to clearly separate the different types of strategies within the organization, is what man-agement should be scared of. A speculative trader can easily hide behind risk-management ser-vices when the top management does not understand the difference between the two types of trading strategies (or turns a blind eye toward such deception). Similarly, if the in-house risk-management services are there to reduce risks rather than to be value generators, then the ex-pectation of large value generation from such a business unit is not only inappropriate, but dan-gerous. Just ask Orange County about this.

Ideally, the manager should build "firewalls" between the trading desks, personnel, and systems employed for any conflicting trading strategies. Yes, this means more work; but managing is the job of managers! Which would be worse, managing a more complex yet meaningful business process, or managing a crisis caused by confused strategies? Requiring separate P&L and risk reporting, and making independent business strategy performance evaluations, constitutes the first step toward separating the trading strategies. Communicating the differences between the strategies by defining trader performance measures that are strategy specific would further ensure that there are no conflicts of interest among the trader ranks, and also within the management business vision.

11.4. INITIAL EVALUATION CHECKLIST

Using the above framework, the energy manager must evaluate the company's current understanding of the risk-management business as well as its potential value within a particular commodity marketplace. A commodity producer will have a different starting position from a commodity user within the marketplace. The producer already has a natural commodity long position, whereas a commodity user has a natural short position. A commodity producer has a very good understanding of many of the market price fundamentals because this understanding is an integral part of the commodity business, whereas the user might not have this benefit.

You need to ask yourself what your current value-added businesses are and how these relate to where you want to go. While this is very much a company-specific discovery process, there are some simple guidelines that should be followed:

- Be realistic about the understanding your company has of the marketplace you wish to enter or are already in. You will be doing your company a disfavor by overestimating its level of expertise or knowledge.
- Define what value or risk reduction your company can generate by following each of the four trading strategies. Do not incorporate what the company could be doing in the future, but rather perform the evaluation of the company as is.
- Ask yourself what makes your company different from other companies in the same commodity marketplace with regard to value-added or hedging capabilities? What is the firm's "core competence," both in general and in the risk-management world? Where are the firm's weaknesses?
- Evaluate the trading, risk-management, and valuation expertise of the company at various managerial and trading levels and across the various trading strategies.
- Evaluate what supporting risk-management and valuation technologies (hardware and software) you currently have to support each of the possible trading strategies.
- Evaluate what risk-management and valuation technologies you have the expertise to develop in-house, given the current professional support.
- Fully understand the current company management structure. Evaluate its efficiency across different trading strategies, particularly in terms of communication channels.
- Understand the historical corporate culture of your company and how flexible it is regarding change.

- Try to evaluate your current risks in the assets you already hold. If you are a producer or a user of a commodity, you already have risks in your books. Even though you might feel comfortable with the levels of risk you have, it is worth the trouble to quantify those risks so that ultimately you can make the big picture decisions.

- Evaluate what risk/return expectations your company management believes that it is experiencing and realizing. Compare these expectations to historical reality, if possible.

Even companies that have traded for a while would benefit from sitting down and reviewing their state of existence. Companies that have never done so are taking a happy-go-lucky attitude. Sometimes this attitude indeed does work out; however, chances are that a happy-go-lucky company will eventually get hurt. Or to put it another way, you are always better off knowing exactly what it is you are doing.

11.4.1. Diagnosing and Selecting Trading Strategies

Which trading strategy does your company follow? Which strategy should it follow? When going through the evaluation checklist, answer within the context of the four different kinds of trading strategies. As you understand the different goals for different activities, it may be necessary to repeat the checklist against the different areas isolated to correspond to the different trading strategies found in the company.

These are very difficult questions, and the answers might change as your company's structure and expertise change. The answers will probably be very much related to what the company has been doing historically and where its expertise is concentrated. A commodity producer who has dealt with commodity price risk for decades might feel very comfortable being a speculative trader. On the other hand, a company that has historically maintained very low risks would not feel comfortable entering into a speculative trading business.

As you are trying to answer these questions, evaluate the current status of your company as well. For example, as a commodity producer you might have been carrying huge price risk for decades. And yet, you may be very scared to enter into derivative transactions, which are contingent on the commodity prices and which might carry much smaller price risk. (Derivatives might also help you hedge away some of the price risk, which you do not necessarily want on your books.) By doing your evaluation fully, you can use your company's current risk/return status as a benchmark for where you want to go. Derivatives and particular trading strategies could be the vehicles that get you there.

11.4.2. Gaps between Existing and Desired Market Position

In order to achieve your target market position you need to define the gaps between your existing market position and where you desire to be. If where you want to be is in fact pretty far away from your current company's reality, then you need to pace yourself: define your goals on a per-year basis. And of course, be realistic about what your company is capable of attaining

given its initial asset base, people base, and company culture. Nothing's wrong with developing a two- to three-year plan. The big energy houses of today were not built overnight. Remember, building on the firm's "core competence" always enhances the probabilities of success.

11.4.3. Corporate Culture

Corporate culture is extremely important in setting and implementing company goals. A company that is defined by a strong vertical hierarchy is less likely to change as easily as a horizontally structured one. This should be kept in mind when the steps for reaching the company goals are defined on a per-year basis.

Also, a company entering the commodity trading and risk-management business for the first time probably ought to reevaluate its corporate culture for efficiency within the scope of the new business. Ideally, the board of directors establishes the general risk/return framework, with varying layers of management handling each level of detail. What if the board or upper management is clueless or has false impressions or expectations? Can the energy risk manager be expected to lead the firm? In such a case, the corporate culture suggests a very slow approach to derivatives!

11.5. THE "FRONT/MIDDLE/BACK OFFICE" PARADIGM

The risk-management policy should clearly state "who does what." Organizational design and personnel functions should be mapped in a clear manner that optimizes the goals and strategies stated by the policy. In this section we will suggest an organizational design based on the "front/middle/back office" paradigm.

Long before the current boom in energy derivatives, the money markets experienced two decades of evolutionary growth. A robust organizational structure evolved in which trading, hedging, and risk-management functions were divided first into a "front" and a "back" office. The front office focused on trading while the back office performed more of an accounting role. More recently, a "middle" office has emerged to perform many of the tasks that populated the gray zone between front and back offices. (See Table 11–2 for a summary of organizational functions.)

Let it be understood that the size of banks and Wall Street houses that have front, middle, and back offices dwarfs the majority of energy firms. Not every energy player needs to replicate the scale of such operations. However, energy firms can learn from the money markets; the front/middle/back office paradigm applies to any risk-management operation, regardless of size.

The front/middle/back office paradigm is more than an "ivory tower" ideal. Energy firms can face the same kinds of human and quantitative risks that the money markets experienced when they too were beginning. Why not learn from their mistakes? If the paradigm seems too complicated, the energy risk manager should acknowledge this as part of the learning curve. Entering new markets always requires new procedures.

Finally, small energy firms face the same risks as large houses but probably on a smaller

TABLE 11-2

The "Front/Middle/Back Office" Paradigm

Function	Front	Middle	Back
Marking-to-market	x		x
Risk reporting	x	x	
Value-at-risk (VAR)		x	
Deal capture	x		x
Risk limit set & monitoring	x	x	

scale; because the smaller firms have more limited staffs, the same person may be performing conflicting functions. While in reality the trading and risk-management operation may reside in a single room—or even a single person—the concept of the front/middle/back office can still be articulated through clearly outlining the individual staff's functions. In the unfortunate situation in which traders mark their own book to market, and there is no additional check performed by the back office, the risk-management policy should at least state this conflict. The presence of conflicts may suggest the need to expand (or curtail) the operation.

11.5.1. Conflicts Between Offices

The front/middle/back office paradigm helps separate the conflicts inherent between the various trading functions. (See Table 11–3.) Conflicts can appear both between offices and within them. Separating people and systems, either literally or figuratively, can help minimize these conflicts as long as management maintains control of the entire process.

TABLE 11-3

Potential Conflicts

Office	Front	Middle	Back
Front	Trading vs. marketing	Assumptions about liquidity	Deal confirmation must be independent of traders Marking-to-market
Middle	Valuation Who's in charge?	Management vs. trading support	Valuation
Back	Marking-to-market Who's in charge?		

By far the most conflicts arise in relation to the trading operation in the front office. In fact, keeping tabs on the traders drove the evolution of the back and later the middle offices. The middle office may assume very different conclusions about valuation, liquidity, and risks relative to the front office. Similarly, the front and back offices may generate very different P&L reports for the same set of books. The back office's lead in deal processing and confirmation represents an important check and balance for controlling traders on a per-deal basis. Conflicts may even occur within the front office. Marketers making promises that the traders cannot keep is a potential problem.

11.5.2. Interoffice Committees

Cross-office committees are a popular and effective method of keeping communication channels open. Every firm involved with derivatives should have a risk-management committee. This committee writes the risk-management policy and evaluates its implementation. Senior personnel (including the chief executive or financial officer) should sit on this committee, along with the lower line staff, including the energy risk manager. If possible, a member of the board of directors should also join. If the firm is large enough to operate a financial (nonenergy) risk-management operation as well, the company should have one unified committee, or at least have representatives of the two groups sitting on the other's group.

One specific concern for the risk-management committee is the whole topic of valuation and risk measurement. The firm needs to keep track of the assumptions and theoretical models being used on the trading floor. Are the models and assumptions appropriate? Are they working? Are there better alternatives available? Larger firms create a special valuation task force. This group not only evaluates and approves valuation techniques but can serve as the authority in case of any conflicts between personnel regarding methodologies between the front, middle, and back office operations.

11.6. THE ENERGY TEAM

Each risk/return framework with its associated mix of goals and strategies will require a different mix of skills from its management and staff. (See Table 11–4.) One of the most difficult tasks a company needs to perform in either starting up or improving an energy commodity trading and risk-management business is hiring people with the right mix of skills, talents, and experience that is needed to arrive at the goals the company has set. The particular mix that is needed is a function of the trading strategies the company wants to follow.

The speculative trading strategy is based on the company's belief that they can predict the market better than the market, i.e., better than the average "Joe" out in the marketplace. Under a speculative trading strategy, the trading expertise is of key importance, while the quantitative expertise is important for valuation purposes, primarily in illiquid markets and when the options used to capture market implied volatility moves need special valuation techniques not readily found in financial literature. Forward price curves in liquid markets are defined by the marketplace. In illiquid markets, the traders might need some help in defining these. The same

T A B L E   11–4

Different Goal, Different Team

Function	Speculation	Arbitrage	Market Maker	Treasury
Trading	Key drivers	Must understand "quants"	Must have diverse, above-average skill set	Emphasis on hedging
Marketing		The client base might provide arbitrage opportunities	Key drivers Must truly understand market and the clients	
Quantitative analysis	Needed in illiquid markets	Key drivers	Must have diverse, above-average skill set	Emphasis on corporate portfolio analysis
Systems	Emphasis on trader limits and risk reporting	Must exceed average	Emphasis on risk reporting, hedging, MTM valuation	
Engineering		Input required for asset-based arbitrage		

is true for volatility matrices. The traders are the bread and butter under this trading strategy. Their instincts about and experiences with the markets to a large extent determine the performance of this particular trading strategy. The systems support is needed to perform book MTM, to calculate the risks, and to ensure that the risks are within the allowable risk limits set by the management.

An arbitrage-based trading strategy requires quite a different focus regarding the experience and skill set needed. Capturing mispricings in the marketplace requires having persons with an above-average set of valuation and hedging skills as part of the trading and risk-management team. The traders in this case need to understand the basic principles behind capturing pure or statistical arbitrage. While the traders under this strategy are extremely important in providing appropriate valuation and hedging deal capture and execution, the strategy can only be as successful as the quality of the quantitative analysis. The actual quantitative methodologies used for valuation and risk management must be more sophisticated and ahead of the marketplace on average.

Providing risk-management services for the company's clients as a market maker requires the most diverse set of skills of the four trading strategies. As a market maker, the risk-management product provider must have the valuation and hedging quantitative skills at least for the standard products within a liquid market. In an illiquid market the quantitative skills are even more important. In either case the trader execution and hedging of deals is important. In illiquid markets the trader risk-management expertise and market instinct play an important role in minimizing risks of newly contracted deals until the time when the more appropriate hedges can be established.

For a market maker, the systems supporting the valuation and risk-management functions are extremely important due to the typically large deal flow, and due to the typically quick response time to client pricing requests. Due to the potentially large number of deals on the books, the trading system's ability to perform mark-to-market and risk calculations quickly and precisely is extremely important. Yet another group of skills is required here, for the marketing and sales of the risk-management products. The marketers have to have a good understanding of the fundamentals of the market price drivers as well as of the products used within the market in order to be effective consultants to their clients in deciding on the appropriate types of products that they need to reduce their energy price risks.

Finally, treasury services require the risk-management expertise from more of a user level than a valuation and portfolio analysis level. Still, a company that uses derivative products to hedge its risks should have an understanding of how to revalue these products, or at least know where to go to get up-to-date valuation and risk calculations for these products. If the derivatives are used more extensively as a risk-management tool, the company ought to consider having a more extensive base of quantitative and market expertise on staff.

For all the trading strategies, having an experienced overall risk manager who understands the risks across all the traded books within the company, including the risks of the non-traded assets, is of great value in reducing the overall company risk exposure and in potentially capturing some of the efficiencies between the traded markets.

11.6.1. Appropriate Knowledge by Organizational Level and Functions

All the levels in a trading company and across the various functions need to know some basics about the trading and risk-management business. A corporate culture that encourages communication across both levels and functions would have an advantage through a more natural framework for sharing knowledge about the business across its employees.

The senior management needs to understand the basic risks and market drivers involved in the trading business and needs to be able to communicate regarding these issues with the middle management of the front, back, and middle offices. The middle management needs to be able to discuss the details of the trading and risk-management business with their employees, as well as be able to talk to the senior management at a company-wide level. Middle management carries the greatest amount of communication responsibility.

The front office needs to understand the specifics of day-to-day trading: the valuation and hedging issues. The traders and quantitative experts need to provide the expertise necessary for the type of trading strategies employed. Their responsibility is to provide middle management with all the necessary information regarding the current state of market drivers, valuation and risk issues, including generating necessary reports. The middle office, on the other hand, needs to be able to perform value-at-risk analysis and to function as a control arm regarding the risk limits and risk-management policy enforcement. As such, they need to provide the necessary value-at-risk reports. Finally, the back office needs to provide the independent control on valuation and to process the contract cash flows.

11.6.2. Management Issues

Managers need not be "quants" or battle-tested traders to run a good operation. We will conclude this book with some special notes for the "generalist," the manager or former engineer who is now in a position of authority.

11.6.2.1. The Role of Senior Management

Senior management can set the vision and define the goals of the trading and risk-management business unit in one of two ways: either by having a strong risk-management leader in charge of the whole business unit, or by having a strong front-office leadership, which drives the rest of the business unit. Of the two choices the first is the ideal, however the second is more likely to be seen in the current commodity marketplace.

A strong risk-management business unit leader has the responsibility of controlling the front, the middle, and the back office development, day-to-day functions, and reporting. She needs to understand the risks in the marketplace, the trading strategy of the company, and the trading, quantitative, and systems support constraints the company deals with in valuation and hedging on a day-to-day basis. While this understanding is very important, her most important job is that of a manager ensuring that the risk-management policies and procedures are carried out. The key to carrying out these duties successfully is to establish an appropriate level of communication down to the front, middle, and back office trenches and up the company ladder to the very top.

In the case where there is a strong front-office leader, senior management must be there to ensure that the middle and back offices retain their objectivity and are capable of following the developments in the front office. By the same token, a strong front office allowed to run free with a weak middle and back office opens the company to the risk of quickly reaching a chaotic state where deals done by the front office cannot be checked by the middle and back offices for risk and valuation calculations. Such situations can be dangerous if the front office in fact does not have the expertise it should have nor the trustworthiness that the senior management believes it has. Problems could arise in cases where the senior management feels that it does not have the time or the skills to provide a detailed level of involvement. (This is often the case in energy companies that have just decided to enter the trading and risk-management world.) When senior management does rely on the departmental heads of the front, middle, and back offices to deal with the day-to-day risk-management issues, they still should maintain a strong managerial hold and demand consistent and regular reporting.

This managerial role is so important that any lack of risk-management understanding by the senior management should not be allowed to defeat it. The worst thing that senior management can do to the company is allow the front office to intimidate it. Instead, senior management should require the front office to treat them as clients, and education on key risk-management issues should be an integral part of the communication.

11.6.2.2. Risk of Management Gaps

When there are no communication and reporting channels defined, the company runs the risk of running a disjointed and mismanaged trading and risk-management business. Requiring reporting of P&L and risk statements from the trading trenches through middle management and up to senior management—with varying degrees of detail, of course—ensures an understanding of the trading strategy risks and performance across various levels of the company and—most importantly—at the very top.

The most common problem that can be seen in the marketplace, particularly in the case of utilities, is that of a senior manager who cannot sleep at night because she does not know what her traders are doing. While this same senior manager would know exactly how to get information from her employees regarding the traditional business she has grown up with, when it comes to the trading and risk-management business she hits a blank wall. The senior manager probably started her career in the trenches of the energy business. Hence, she knows what the traditional business of her company is all about, across all the levels: she can visualize it. But when it comes to this new business of trading and risk management, she does not know where to begin. It was simply plopped into her lap. To the senior managers who feel this way, know that you are not alone. In fact, the senior management of banks has had to deal with these same issues during the deregulation of the banking industry.

11.6.2.3. Reports for Management

The best medicine for such sleeping problems is to set up a communication and reporting framework that will allow the senior managers to get their hands on information coming straight up from the trading trenches. However, the same senior managers who cannot sleep at night will probably also have the problem of understanding just what type of information they should look for from their employees.

Like the risk-management policy, regular written reports for management may appear cumbersome. But the benefits far outweigh the bother. With reporting, problems are brought to management's attention quicker, hopefully before a resulting loss. Managers could insist that the quants and traders report in basic "English"; this would force the staff to focus on the market basics and also allow the managers to emphasize the general rather than technical skills. Finally, staff failure to comply with reporting may flag potential problems.

To start the communication and education process, the initial information should consist of the following:

- P&L reports from both the front office and the back office: daily, month-to-date, year-to-date
- A weekly report on the current market price drivers, the view from the front office: the fundamentals of the marketplace and what is currently driving market prices, including reporting some of the bigger deals with near-term deliveries as well as deals with longer-term deliveries
- Current day-to-day market risks, quantified in dollar terms, from the front office
- Current value-at-risk results from the middle office

Inconsistency between any of the information coming from front, middle, and back offices will point at a lack of unified approaches to valuation and risk management between the three offices. Similarly, any lack of reports and information will point at a lack of necessary trading and risk-management expertise and/or support at some trading and risk-management functions. This is what the senior manager ought to be looking for, while at the same time educating herself about the meaning of the reports and information.

In the worst-case scenario, also not uncommon, the senior manager will not be able to get a majority of the above information. In this case the senior manager's instincts and motivations for losing sleep might be justified. A thorough review of the business and where it stands would in this case be recommended, particularly if the traders were allowed to go on trading with no controls or trading limits. Keep in mind that the good traders will welcome the reporting and the monitoring: how else can they show management just how good a job they are doing? An unwillingness to report trading activities is a clear sign that not all is well in the front office.

11.6.2.4. Capital Allocation and Risk Limits

The capital allocated and the risk limits should be closely linked to the portfolio analysis and value-at-risk analysis. Both portfolio analysis and value-at-risk results can provide a means of defining the distribution of a trading book's dollar value, the first through the calculation of distribution moments and the second through simulations. The defined distribution, in turn, gives the company a means of capturing the whole array of possible market profits and losses, with probability estimates attached to each profit/loss scenario.

When looking at the portfolio value on a day-to-day basis, we have to keep in mind that on the average the value will be centered on the mean of the distribution. However, there will be both ups and downs around this mean. A trading operation has to have pockets deep enough to endure some of these downs if it is to also capture the ups. Hence, the capital allocated to the trading business ought to include such deep pockets, where the traders can go to cover these possible short-term losses.

Each trading strategy will have different-looking distributions. A speculative trading strategy should have a distribution with the highest expected profit. Unfortunately, this distribution will also be the widest; hence, this strategy would require the deepest pockets amongst the four trading strategies.

The pure arbitrage strategy might carry relatively small expected profits on a per-deal basis and given that pure arbitrage is hard to find these days. However, it would also have no risk involved. Statistical arbitrage, on the other hand, could carry a nice expected profit, particularly in somewhat illiquid markets, but it would also show a width of the distribution corresponding to the fact that it is not a zero-risk strategy.

Being a market maker providing risk-management services would carry a relatively small expected profit in a liquid market on a per-deal basis—specifically the bid-ask spread—but the market maker would hopefully make up for this through a good amount of volume. The distribution of this portfolio would be fairly narrow in a liquid market as most of the risk could be hedged away. However, in an illiquid market you would be looking at a slightly higher bid and ask, and hence a slightly higher profit on a per-deal basis, but also a wider distribution due to the greater risks involved in not having a readily available hedge.

One interesting phenomenon we have seen in the market is the "self-policing trader." In several cases, the traders and risk-management departments at electric utilities were leading the way into the new deregulated markets. Their company's upper management and boards of directors literally allowed these new groups a free hand. The surprise was that the traders actually self-imposed their own limits, grooming their operations both to avoid the bright light of a crisis and to prepare for the day when their managers did start asking questions. Self-policing seems remarkable when one considers the typical money market operation, where traders have been known to resist such limits.

11.6.2.5. Managing the Models

Just as models can help the communication between the different levels and functions in the company by providing a common understanding of the fundamental market drivers in the valuation, so can they help when it comes to defining and communicating the market risks. While the markets traded are typically much more complicated than, let's say, a two-factor model might claim, still the two-factor model might provide the basis of discussion as a benchmark and as a point of divergence.

11.6.3. Common Management Misconceptions

Many of the above sections used the phrase "ideal" when proposing how to do things the right way. Before we leave the topic of "management" in "risk management," perhaps we should briefly discuss some common misconceptions by managers about the derivatives market. We will consider the case of acquisitions; reconsider the important issue of hedging vs. speculation; and attempt to dispel the inflated importance of notional amounts.

11.6.3.1. Acquisitions May Not Reduce Risk

Occasionally the trade press reports of a possible or completed acquisition intended as a means of solving implementation problems or capturing energy market risks. I certainly am not an acquisition or a merger expert, but from a pure risk-management point of view, this expensive tactic may not end up being a solution. This provides an excellent case for evaluating how upper-level managerial decisions relate to the risk/return framework.

When management considers an acquisition to reduce risk, then the benefits of the acquisition or a merger should outweigh the negatives. If your motivations for an acquisition are capturing the target's skills, systems, and trading business, compare the costs of the acquisition or merger with the costs of attracting these same skills, purchasing or building a system, and developing the book in-house. Be particularly careful when you are buying a company that is an active trader in one market for the purposes of developing a trading business in yet another market. In this case, chances are that the skills may not be entirely there and the system may need a good deal of adjusting.

Similarly, if there are problems within your company and you cannot seem to attract high-quality people even though you are willing to pay the fair market price, then chances are that the problems will not go away simply with an acquisition or a merger. The last thing you would then want to see happen is that the acquisition goes through and all the quality people simply leave the merged company.

Another reason for purchasing an energy company that companies like to quote is that they want to get exposure to energy price risks and returns, in order to arrive at a particular risk/return portfolio structure. Unfortunately, when a nonenergy company acquires an energy company, what it gets is not a direct exposure to energy price risks and returns, but rather a bunch of stocks. And stock prices, as this book has gone through quite a bit of detail in explaining, do not act the same way energy prices act. Hence, a nonenergy company is better off purchasing energy commodity futures on NYMEX than it is in purchasing an energy company purely to obtain the exposure to energy price risk and return.

11.6.3.2. Hedging vs. Speculation
The topic of hedging versus speculation is important enough to managers to deserve a couple of paragraphs on its own. As mentioned a number of times already, the derivatives-related financial tragedies tend to happen when speculation is masked under the pretense of risk management or hedging. A company that is using derivatives within a speculative strategy has no right to blame derivatives for any resulting losses. A company that is properly using derivatives as hedges will have reduced the company's overall risks, and the chances of such financial tragedies are thereby reduced rather than increased.

When a gap in understanding and communication exists between the company management and the traders, it is very easy for traders to mask speculative plays under hedges for the company or risk-management services for the clients. A manager who does not know what risk reports to ask for or how to read the reports will have no means of control over such trading. A risk-management committee that consists of representatives from the front, middle, and back offices and from management provides a forum for discussion and a means of arriving at a common language and trust.

Finally, management may be even more responsible for the creation of such a financial strategy than just for the lack of the communication and reporting. A bizarre case of codependency develops in a situation where management does not understand exactly how the traders are making money, and yet management is starting to get used to the growing profits of the trading group. Not only does management start depending on these profits growing, but management actually begins putting pressure on the trading staff to make the growth greater and greater year after year. This is a sure prescription for eventual disaster. As we have discussed the different trading strategies at length, we have seen that there is only one trading strategy that is capable of yielding enormous profits. Unfortunately, it comes at a cost: enormous risks tend to accompany enormous profits, and when this strategy is used, management, due to its ignorance, might push the traders into heavier speculation.

11.6.3.3. Irrelevant Notions about Notionals
One other point that is a must to talk about is this idea that floats around in the media regarding "notional amounts," the dollar figure of the underlying asset upon which a derivatives contract is based.

The common perception is that if I tell you what notional amounts I have in my books, then you will know how much risk I have. This is total humbug. While the notional amounts tell us how much volume goes through a trading house, they do nothing to tell us about the amount of risk the trading house has on its books. Hence, deltas, gammas, and vegas would be much more appropriate measures of the risk that a company is currently taking. The company's risk limits on deltas, gammas, and vegas would be much more appropriate measures of how much risk the company is allowing the traders to take on. (Publicly traded companies that operate a trading business should be asked to report the limits of the risks they allow their traders to take, rather than notional amounts, as part of their public annual reporting.)

11.7. IMPLEMENTATION OF RISK-MANAGEMENT POLICIES

How realistic and true to the company environment and state of business the risk-management policy is will be tested in its implementation. A well-designed risk-management policy will be implemented as an integral part of the risk-management day-to-day procedures, functions, reporting, and communication across both horizontal and vertical levels of the trading and risk-management business unit. If all the people within the company necessary for the implementation of the policy fully understand their contributions and responsibilities, know how to go about executing these, and have given their buy-in, then the implementation is half done.

An implementation that is just not happening is a sign that it may be necessary to go back to the drawing board. A full reevaluation of the company's current trading and risk-management business status may be required in order to find the reasons for why the implementation is just not going anywhere.

APPENDIX A: MATHEMATICAL AND STATISTICAL NOTES

A.1. INTRODUCTION

Math? Calculus? Differential equations?

The last time many professionals thought about equations most were wearing jeans and carrying college textbooks. Even those of us lucky enough to earn MBA's probably slipped through without ever solving a differential equation. In this modern age of computers and consultants, most managers can keep their slide rules and calculators in their desks and use a "black box" to do the dirty work.

Unfortunately, very few computer applications exist for energy markets. Even academic journals fail to dedicate much space to the special needs of energy markets. In many instances, the energy risk manager must "do-it-herself" to understand and/or implement a model. Complex math and calculus is a fact of life, and those who can exploit these tools will be one step ahead of the game.

This appendix will detail specific mathematical and calculus techniques that support the concepts introduced by this book. The appendix will go into greater detail than individual chapters and will help minimize the clutter of proofs. We will comment about certain intuitive aspects of these derivations that help underscore the market-based behaviors that we attempt to express through our modeling.

Note: This appendix does not pretend to summarize the basics of advanced mathematics and calculus. For basic calculus you can consult any introductory calculus book. For solving differential equations and for nonstandard integration problems we have found Mathews and Walker, *Mathematical Methods of Physics,* of great value.

A.2. RANDOM VARIABLES

As suggested, the randomly distributed variable (also known as the "random variable") is a key concept used throughout this book and in risk management in general. This section will briefly introduce the general properties that make the concept so useful.

A.2.1. Expected Values of Random Variables

Risk managers will often encounter the problem of taking expected values of random variables, or of equations with embedded random variables. A random variable normally distributed around a mean of zero and with a variance that is proportional to time provides us with convenient properties that help us solve differential equations. (Please see chapter 2 for a complete discussion of random variables.) We denote the random variable's value observed from time t to time T.

$$\widetilde{z}_{t,T} = \aleph(0, T - t) \tag{A-1}$$

The expected value of a random variable is simply zero:

$$E_t[\widetilde{z}_{t,T}] = 0 \tag{A-2}$$

The expected value of the random variable's variance increases with the period of observation. Remember, this variance is usually multiplied with a constant or variable that will give it appropriate magnitude corresponding to the particular process being modeled:

$$E_t[\widetilde{z}_{t,T}^2] = (T - t) \tag{A-3}$$

Like the expected value of the random variable, the third-order expected value is zero because the variable is normally distributed around a mean of zero.

$$E_t[\widetilde{z}_{t,T}^3] = 0 \tag{A-4}$$

Note: all higher-order terms with an odd term (such as 5, 7, etc.) will have an expected value of zero. The even-term higher-order expressions do not equal zero, but we usually only need the expected value of the random variable out to the fourth power:

$$E[\widetilde{z}_{t,T}^4] = 3(T - t)^2 \tag{A-5}$$

A specially useful case is that of taking expected values when the random variable is in the exponential:

$$E_t[e^{a\widetilde{z}_{t,T}}] = e^{(a^2/2)(T-t)} \tag{A-6}$$

A.2.2. Relationship between Two Random Variables

We often build models that include two random variables. For instance, the two-factor Pilipovic Model, introduced in Chapters 4 and 5, depends on a short-term random variable, $\widetilde{z}_{t,T}$, and a long-term random variable, $\widetilde{w}_{t,T}$. The expected value of a product of two random variables is a function of their correlation $\rho_{\widetilde{z},\widetilde{w}}$ and time to "expiration" from observation:

$$E[\widetilde{z}_{t,T}\, \widetilde{w}_{t,T}] = \rho_{\widetilde{z},\widetilde{w}}\, (T - t) \tag{A-7}$$

Note: If the two random variables are not correlated, $\rho_{\widetilde{z},\widetilde{w}} = 0$, the expected value would be zero. If perfectly correlated, $\rho_{\widetilde{z},\widetilde{w}} = 1$, the expected value would be $(T - t)$.

The expected value of the product of two random variables of two forward prices with different expirations would be as follows:

$$E[\tilde{z}_{t,T_1}\tilde{w}_{t,T_2}] = \rho_{\tilde{z}\tilde{w}}\,(\min(T_1,T_2) - t) \qquad (A-9)$$

Another relationship is between the stochastic variables in two forward prices along the same forward price curve.

$$F_1 \text{ s.t. } Z(d\widetilde{F}_1/F_1) = \sigma_1\tilde{z}_1 \qquad (A-10)$$

$$F_2 \text{ s.t. } Z(d\widetilde{F}_2/F_2) = \sigma_2\tilde{z}_2 \qquad (A-11)$$

In this case, we need to worry about the correlation and beta between the two forward prices.

$$Z(d\widetilde{F}_2/F_2) = \beta_{2,1}Z(d\widetilde{F}_1/F_1) + residual \qquad (A-12)$$

$$\sigma_2\tilde{z}_2 = \beta_{2,1}\sigma_1\tilde{z}_1 + \sigma_{\varepsilon_2}\tilde{\varepsilon}_2 \qquad (A-13)$$

The beta and the volatility of the residual term $\tilde{\varepsilon}_2$ can be calculated as functions of the correlation and the volatilities of the two forward prices.

We wish to develop a relationship of $\beta_{2,1}$ in terms of the correlation between $(\rho_{1,2})$ and volatilities of the two forward price curves. (A practical application of this relationship occurs when one hedges one forward contract with another.) We first take the expected values of the two volatilities multiplied by the stochastic variables:

$$E[\sigma_1\tilde{z}_1\sigma_2\tilde{z}_2] = \rho_{2,1}\sigma_1^2 E[\tilde{z}_1^2] + \sigma_1\sigma_{\varepsilon_2} E[\tilde{z}_1\tilde{\varepsilon}_2] \qquad (A-14)$$

We require that the first forward price return and the residual term of the second forward price return are independent of each other, giving us:

$$E[\tilde{z}_1\tilde{\varepsilon}_2] = 0 \qquad (A-15)$$

While correlations are symmetric,

$$\rho_{2,1} = \rho_{1,2} \qquad (A-16)$$

the betas are not,

$$\beta_{1,2} \neq \beta_{2,1} \qquad (A-17)$$

Solving Equation A−14 for the beta gives us:

$$\beta_{2,1} = \rho_{1,2}(\sigma_2/\sigma_1) \qquad (A-18)$$

Similarly, we have:

$$\beta_{1,2} = \rho_{2,1}(\sigma_1/\sigma_2) \qquad (A-19)$$

$$\sigma_{\varepsilon_2} = \sigma_2\sqrt{1 - \rho_{1,2}^2} \qquad (A-20)$$

Finally, the change in the second forward price can be expressed in terms of the change in the first forward price plus an independent residual term:

$$\Delta F_2 = \rho_{1,2}(\sigma_2 F_2 / \sigma_1 F_1)\Delta F_1 + \textit{residual} \tag{A-21}$$

$$\Delta F_2 = \beta_{2,1}(F_2 / F_1)\Delta F_1 + \textit{residual} \tag{A-22}$$

A.3. EXAMPLE OF CALCULATION OF PORTFOL IO VARIANCE

The steps of calculating a sample portfolio's variance, where the portfolio consists of a forward price for some asset with a particular expiration time and a minimum variance hedge forward price, possibly with a different expiration, are as follows:

$$Var(d\Pi_t^H) = E\left[Z\left(dF_{t,T1}^A - \frac{F_{t,T1}^A \sigma_t^A}{F_{t,T2}^H \sigma_t^H} \rho_{AH} dF_{t,T2}^H \right)^2 \right] \tag{A-23}$$

$$Var(d\Pi_t^H) = E\left[\left(\begin{array}{c} F_{t,T1}^A \sigma_t^A dz^A - \\ \frac{F_{t,T1}^A \sigma_t^A}{F_{t,T2}^H \sigma_t^H} \rho_{AH} F_{t,T2}^H \sigma_t^H dz^H \end{array} \right)^2 \right] \tag{A-24}$$

$$Var(d\Pi_t^H) = E\left[\begin{array}{c} (F_{t,T1}^A)^2 (\sigma_t^A)^2 (dz^A)^2 + \\ (F_{t,T1}^A)^2 (\sigma_t^A)^2 (dz^A)^2 \rho_{AH}^2 - \\ 2(F_{t,T1}^A)^2 (\sigma_t^A)^2 (dz^A)^2 \rho_{AH}^2 dz^A dz^H \end{array} \right] \tag{A-25}$$

A.4. REDUCING THE STOCHASTIC TERM

In the case of lognormal prices we can reduce the stochastic terms across a strip of forward prices into systematic and nonsystematic risks in a stepwise manner. The results of this reduction process allow us to further break down the portfolio risks into independent components, or to perform multifactor Monte Carlo simulations.

The following are stochastic terms across forward prices, starting with the spot price and the first nearby forward price:

$$\sigma_0 \tilde{z}_0 \tag{A-26}$$

$$\sigma_1 \tilde{z}_1 = \beta_{1,0}\sigma_0 \tilde{z}_0 + \sigma_1^\varepsilon \tilde{\varepsilon}_1 \tag{A-27}$$

In the above equation, we need to calculate the beta term. In addition, we need to simulate the residual term, $\sigma_1^\varepsilon \tilde{\varepsilon}$.

$$\beta_{1,0} = \rho_{1,0}\frac{\sigma_1}{\sigma_0} \tag{A-28}$$

$$\sigma_1^\varepsilon = \sigma_1 \sqrt{1 - \rho_{1,0}^2} \tag{A-29}$$

For the second nearby forward price, we have:

$$\sigma_2 \tilde{z}_2 = \beta_{2,0} \sigma_0 \tilde{z}_0 + \beta_{2,1} \sigma_1 \tilde{z}_1 + \sigma_{21}^{\varepsilon} \tilde{\varepsilon}_2 \qquad (A-30)$$

$$\beta_{2,1} = \frac{\sigma_2}{\sigma_1} \left(\frac{\rho_{2,1} - \rho_{2,0}\rho_{1,0}}{1 - \rho_{1,0}^2} \right) \qquad (A-31)$$

$$\beta_{2,0} = \frac{\sigma_2}{\sigma_0} \left(\frac{\rho_{2,0} - \rho_{1,0}\rho_{2,1}}{1 - \rho_{1,0}^2} \right) \qquad (A-32)$$

The general solution would be:

$$\sigma_n \tilde{z}_n = \alpha_{n,0} \sigma_0 \tilde{z}_0 + \sum_{m=1}^{n} \alpha_{n,m} \sigma_m^{\varepsilon} \tilde{\varepsilon}_m \qquad (A-33)$$

where n refers to the n-th forward price. Note that the $\sigma_0 \tilde{z}_0$ and $\sigma_m^{\varepsilon} \tilde{z}_m$ terms are independent of each other.

Now let's consider specific cases of varying values of n. For the case of $n = 0$,

$$\alpha_{00} = 1 \qquad (A-34)$$

For an n greater than zero ($n > 0$):

$$\alpha_{n,0} = \sum_{m=0}^{n-1} \beta_{n,m} \alpha_{m,0} \qquad (A-35)$$

For the case of $n > k$:

$$\alpha_{n,k} = \sum_{m=k}^{n-1} \beta_{n,m} \alpha_{m,k} \qquad (A-36)$$

and finally,

$$\alpha_{n,n} = 1 \qquad (A-37)$$

First we calculate all the values of $\alpha_{n,0}$ and slowly build up the alphas as a function of "lower order" alphas:

$$\alpha_{n,0} = \rho_{n,0} \frac{\sigma_n}{\sigma_0} \qquad (A-38)$$

$$\alpha_{n,k} = \frac{1}{(\sigma_k^{\varepsilon})^2} \left\{ \sigma_n \sigma_k \rho_{n,k} - \rho_{n,0}\rho_{k,0} - \sum_{m=1}^{k-1} \alpha_{n,m} \alpha_{k,m} (\sigma_k^{\varepsilon})^2 \right\} \qquad (A-39)$$

where,

$$(\sigma_k^{\varepsilon})^2 = \sigma_n^2 (1 - \rho_{n,0}^2) - \sum_{m=1}^{n-1} \alpha_{n,m}^2 (\sigma_m^{\varepsilon})^2 \qquad (A-40)$$

Finally, we have:

$$\sigma_n \widetilde{z}_n = \rho_{n,0} \sigma_n \widetilde{z}_0 + \sum_{m=1}^{n} \alpha_{n,m} \sigma_m^2 \widetilde{\varepsilon}_m \qquad (A-41)$$

Now we have all the pieces we need in order to perform multifactor Monte Carlo simulations.

APPENDIX B: MODELS FROM INTEREST RATE AND BOND MARKETS

We will briefly present some models seen often in the pricing of bonds and in general in the interest rate markets. We include these essential financial models in this book on energies primarily to give the reader a basis of comparison. (See John Hill's book for complete details.)

All of the models shown here assume that the bond price behavior is driven by the interest rate behavior; i.e., bond prices are a function of the interest rate behavior. This means that the models are first developed for the interest rates and tested against the behavior of the interest rates. Bond price modeling then follows the modeling of the rates.

In solving for the discount bond prices, we have to impose the boundary condition, which requires the bond price with a face value of one dollar to be exactly one dollar at the time of bond price expiration. In fact, bonds are discount instruments, and in using the interest rate models to solve for spot prices for commodities, we would find the formulation to be different. In solving for the spot prices, we would not have the boundary condition imposed the way it is for the bonds. In other words, spot prices are not discount instruments.

B.1. THE VASICEK MODEL

We start with the Vasicek model for interest rates. The Vasicek model assumes that the interest rates are mean-reverting:

$$d\tilde{r}_t = \alpha(b - r_t)dt + \sigma d\tilde{z}_t \tag{B-1}$$

where: t = time of observation
r = short-term interest rate
b = long-term equilibrium value of r
α = speed of mean reversion, the mean-reverting parameter
σ = volatility of the short-term rate (in rate terms and not percentage terms)
$d\tilde{z}$ = random stochastic variable

From the above formulation of the interest rate process we can solve for the discount bond using the relationship defined in the lognormal model in chapter 4 (Equation 4–7) between the short-term rate and the bond price:

$$P_t = e^{-\int_0^T r_t \, dt}$$

(B–2)

where: P = the price of a discount bond.

While this model is very simple to use, it has the main drawback of allowing interest rates to be negative. Note that in this model the stochastic term is not a function of the interest rate's value, but is normally distributed. The exclusion of the interest rate in the stochastic term is what gives the interest rates—under this formulation—the possibility of taking on negative values.

We first solve for the interest rate from Equation B–1 and then for the bond price using Equation B–2, with the additional boundary constraint of the bond price having the value of one dollar at expiration. We thus obtain the following solution for the bond price in the case when alpha does not equal zero:

$$P(t,T) = A(t,T)e^{-B(t,T)r}$$

(B–3)

with the functions $A(t,T)$ and $B(t,T)$ given by:

$$B(t,T) = \frac{1 - e^{-\alpha(T-t)}}{\alpha}$$

(B–4)

$$A(t,T) = \exp\left[\frac{(B(t,T) - T + t)\left(\dfrac{\alpha^2 b - \sigma^2}{2}\right)}{\alpha^2} - \frac{\sigma^2 B(t,T)^2}{4\alpha}\right]$$

(B–5)

B.2. THE COX, INGERSOLL, AND ROSS MODEL

The Cox, Ingersoll, and Ross model deals with the issue of possible negative interest rates by allowing the stochastic term to be proportional to the square root of the interest rate. In this manner, the model preserves the nonnegative nature of interest rates:

$$d\tilde{r} = \alpha(b - r)dt + \sigma\sqrt{r}\,d\tilde{z}$$

(B–6)

where: r = the short-term rate
b = the rate toward which the short-term rates revert
σ = volatility
$d\tilde{z}$ = the normally distributed random variable

In this case, we get the following formulation for the bond prices:

$$P(t,T) = A(t,T)e^{-B(t,T)r}$$

(B–7)

where the following definitions apply:

$$\gamma = \sqrt{\alpha^2 + 2\sigma^2}$$

(B–8)

$$B(t,T) = \frac{2(e^{(\gamma)(T-t)} - 1)}{(\gamma + \alpha)(e^{\gamma(T-t)} - 1) + 2\gamma} \qquad (B-9)$$

$$A(t,T) = \left[\frac{2\gamma e^{(\gamma + \alpha)(T-t)/2}}{(\gamma + \alpha)(e^{\gamma(T-t)} - 1) + 2\gamma} \right]^{\frac{2ab}{\sigma^2}} \qquad (B-10)$$

B.3. THE BLACK, DERMAN, TOY MODEL

Our last interest rate model is the Black, Derman, Toy model. This model is somewhat of a favorite in the interest rate world, where its flexibility in handling numerous complexities of the interest rate curves is a major plus. This model excludes the possibility of negative interest rates by modeling the log of the interest rates rather than the rates themselves:

$$d \ln \tilde{r} = [\theta(t) - \alpha \ln r]dt + \sigma d\tilde{z} \qquad (B-11)$$

where: r = short-term rate
Θ = the value to which the log of the rate reverts; it is allowed to be a function of time, hence it has a term structure
t = time of observation
α = rate of mean reversion
σ = volatility
$d\tilde{z}$ = random stochastic variable

In this case we first must solve for the log of the interest rate, referred to below as a new variable x (see Equation B–12).

$$x = \ln(r) \Rightarrow r_t = e^{x_t} \qquad (B-12)$$

We make this variable substitution in the differential equation for the log of the interest rate, so that the differential equation is now given by Equation B–13.

$$dx = \theta(t)dt - \alpha x dt + \sigma d\tilde{z}_t \qquad (B-13)$$

We solve this differential equation for x.

$$x_t = e^{-\alpha t}x_0 + e^{-\alpha t}\int_0^t e^{\alpha y} \theta(y)dy + e^{-\alpha t}\sigma \int_0^t e^{\alpha y} d\tilde{z}_y \qquad (B-14)$$

From the above formulation of x, we can solve for the expected value of the interest rate:

$$E[\tilde{r}_t] = (r_0)e^{-\alpha t} \times \exp\left(\left[e^{-\alpha t}\int_0^t e^{\alpha y} \theta(y)dy + \frac{\sigma^2}{4\alpha}(1 - e^{-2\alpha t}) \right] \right) \qquad (B-15)$$

Finally, in order to arrive at the bond price, we would first have to fully formulate the interest rate behavior, not just its expected value, and then we would use this to formulate the bond price valuation.

GLOSSARY OF ENERGY RISK MANAGEMENT TERMS

COMMON SYMBOLS

A	Asset
α	Mean-reversion rate
B	Black Model
BS	Black-Scholes Model
$\beta_{1,2}$	Beta of variable 1 on variable 2
β_A	Annual seasonality parameter
β_{SA}	Semi-annual seasonality parameter
c	Correction term
C	Call option
CAP	Cap option
CTD	Cheapest-to-deliver
Cy	Convenience yield
d_1	Intermediary expression in Black-Scholes Model
d_2	Intermediary expression in Black-Scholes Model
δ	Dividend
Δ	Delta of a product or a portfolio
$E(x)$	Expected value of x
ECAR	East Central Reliability Coordination Agreement
ERCOT	Electric Reliability Council of Texas
$\tilde{\varepsilon}$	Normally distributed residual variable
f	Function
fvd	Future value of a dollar
F	Forward price
γ	Volatility of volatility
Γ	Gamma risk
H	Hedge
HO	Heating oil

K	Option strike price
ξ	Volatility of long-term equilibrium price
λ	Cost of risk
L_t	Equilibrium price
LIBOR	London Inter-Bank Offering Rate
MAAC	Mid-Atlantic Area Council
MAIN	Mid-American Interconnected Network
MAPP	Mid-Continent Area Power Pool
MC	Mid-Columbia
MTM	Marked-to-market
M_1	First moment of a distribution
M_2	Second moment of a distribution
M_3	Third moment of a distribution
M_4	Fourth moment of a distribution
μ	Rate of return or drift rate
(N)	Normal distribution in some cases; in other cases the erf function
NG	Natural gas
NPCC	Northeast Power Coordinating Council
NYMEX	New York Mercantile Exchange
O	Option; option price or premium
$O(dt)$	Higher-order terms of dt
OTC	Over-the-counter
p	Probability of an upward move in a tree
$p(x)$	Probability of variable taking value x
P	Put price in some cases; in other cases asset price
Π	Portfolio
$\tilde{\Pi}$	Portfolio with stochastic behavior
q	Probability of a downward move in a tree
r	Risk-free rate
R^2	R-squared measure
$\rho_{1,2}$	Correlation between variables 1 and 2
S	Spot price
$\tilde{S}$	Spot price with stochastic behavior
S^{Und}	Underlying spot price (no seasonality)
SERC	Southeastern Electric Reliability Council
SPP	Southwest Power Pool
STD	Standard deviation
σ	Volatility
t	Time of observation
t_A	Annual seasonality centering parameter
t_{SA}	Semi-annual seasonality centering parameter
T	Time of contract expiration
τ	Time to expiration, T-t

Θ	Theta of an option or a portfolio
U	Option-underlying price
$U(R)$	Corporate utility function
V	Vega risk
Var	Variance
VAR	Value-at-risk
WSCC	Western Supply Coordinating Council
WTI	West Texas Intermediate (crude oil)
$\tilde{x}$	Stochastic variable
$\tilde{w}$	Stochastic variable
$\tilde{z}$	Stochastic variable
$Z[dx]$	The stochastic term in the change of variable x; the change in x with the expected change subtracted off
5×16	Weekly on-peak delivery hours of sixteen hours per business day
$5 \times 8, 2 \times 24$	Weekly off-peak delivery hours, 8 off-peak hours during the business days of the week and 2 full days during the weekend, holidays included

DEFINITIONS

American Option: An option that may be exercised early either for delivery or for cash. *See* European Option.

Annual Seasonality: In energy markets the occurrence of a single peak price period and a single low price period during the year.

Arbitrage: A trade with guaranteed profit, i.e. no risk gain opportunity. Pure arbitrage opportunities quickly disappear in an efficient market.

Arbitrage-Free: A modeling condition that requires a risk-free portfolio to earn the risk-free rate of return. States that there would be no arbitrage opportunity between two alternative strategies, where the beginning cash flow is the same and the end result is the same. For example, assumption applies to the user being indifferent between holding an asset vs. paying financing costs and entering into a properly priced forward contract on the asset.

Asian Option: A path-dependent option; common in energy markets. The option is exercised into an average of prices over a period of time, or into delivery over a period of time.

Ask: The price that sellers are asking for a product.

Asset: Something of value constituting the resources of a business.

Asset-driven Arbitrage: The use of the asset base of a business in order to capture market value, which can only be generated through the use of that asset base.

Assumption: Used in modeling; representation of the market or market variables.

At-the-Money: An option term used to say that the option-underlying price is equal to the option strike price.

Autocorrelation: The correlation of a variable with itself but with a time lag of one time step.

Average Price Contract: A contract which is conditional on an average of market prices rather than a single market price observed on a single day. Examples include monthly quotes for daily forwards and Asian options.

Back Office: A term used to denote the trading operation functions of processing the deals done by the trading operation and marking the trading books to market independently from the traders. Provides a basis for internal and external auditing of the trading businesses.

Backwardation: A forward price market where forward prices decrease as their expiration time increases.

Basis: The difference in prices between identical products but in two different markets.

Benchmark: A starting point in an analysis of a product, a market, or a business relative to which comparisons are made.

Beta: A statistical term defining the relationship between the changes in one variable in terms of changes in another variable and a residual term.

Bias: A consistent error in statistical measurements or pricing.

Bid: The price that a party is offering to purchase a particular contract.

Bid/Ask Spread: The differential between the price that buyers are willing to pay for a product and the price that sellers are asking for the same product.

Binomial Tree: A recombining valuation tree in which two outcomes follow each node.

Black-Scholes: The famous European option pricing methodology used widely in the financial world and across many markets. Based on the assumption of lognormal option-underlying price.

Black-Scholes Equivalent Volatility: Given a price for an option, the volatility implied from this price through the use of the Black-Scholes option pricing model. Same as the lognormal equivalent volatility.

Book: Another term for portfolio.

Bucket: A method of organizing contracts, contractual terms, risks, time, or other elements of a risk management portfolio.

Calibration: The process of determining model parameter values that best reflect a given data set.

Call (or Call Option):   An option which gives its purchaser the right—but not the obligation—to buy the option-underlying asset at some future point in time at the option's strike price.

Cap: A series of call options (with succeeding expirations but generally equivalent contractual terms) priced as a single contract.

Capacity Options: Options to purchase or sell additional capacity. The prices are not set until the actual purchase or sale of capacity.

Caplet: An individual option within the series of options contained in a cap or a floor. Same as a call in the case of a cap, and same as a put in the case of a floor.

Cash-Settled Contract: A contract in which counter-parties exchange money at settlement rather than delivering a commodity in exchange for cash. The money exchanged is based on the value of the underlying commodity.

Churn Ratio: The ratio of actual physical energy in a market to the notional value of derivative contracts based on that energy.

Close-of-day: The time at which trading stops at an exchange; the prices are settled at that time. Can also generally refer to the time of day when over-the-counter markets see routine slowing of activity.

Closed-Form Solution: The solution to a differential equation defining the arbitrage-free behavior of a financial product with boundary conditions being satisfied.

Commodities: Assets used for consumption.

Compound Options: An option on an option.

Contango: A forward price market where forward prices increase with their expirations.

Continuous Hedging: The process of constantly performing portfolio analysis to determine the optimum hedging strategies and immediately executing the necessary trades. While difficult to do in reality, continuous hedging is a common assumption in valuation and risk management analysis.

Convenience Yield: The net benefit minus the cost—with the exception of the financing cost—of holding the commodity in storage or entering into forward contracts for future delivery of the commodity. Can be either positive or negative.

Coordinating Area: An area within a reliability region; usually assigned to a large utility with the purpose of maintaining reliability. In trading markets, often used as a surrogate index.

Correlation: A statistical measure of the relationship between the behaviors of two price processes. Perfect positive correlation implies that the percentage change in the two prices is always the same. Perfect negative correlation implies that the percentage change in one of the prices is exactly equal to the negative percentage change in the other price. Zero correlation, or no correlation, results in the two price processes being entirely independent of each other.

Cost-Engineering Model: *See* Fundamental Analysis.

Cost of Risk: The cost associated with letting an asset price change unexpectedly over time in place of fixing its value with a forward price contract.

Counterparty Risk: The risk of one side of a party to a contract not fulfilling an obligation of a contract.

Credit Risk: *See* Counterparty Risk.

Cross-Gamma: The second-order risk representing the change in delta with respect to changes in forward prices.

Deal Capture: The process of recording a signed contract in the trading book.

Delivery: The delivery of a commodity to the purchaser.

Delta (Δ):   The first-order risk that represents the change in overall value given a one-unit change in portfolio-underlying price.

Derivative Contract: A financial contract that derives its value from some underlying asset.

Deterministic: Will happen with 100% certainty; carries no risk. Opposite of stochastic.

Deterministic Term: The element within a model that is assumed to exhibit deterministic or predictable behavior. Also known as the drift term or expected rate of return. "Opposite" of stochastic term.

Discrete: The smallest reasonable unit of measure. In forward pricing, discrete price usually means a daily price. Can also apply to appropriately defined time buckets.

Distribution: The range of possible prices with associated probabilities. Useful distributions include normal and lognormal.

Distribution Analysis: The statistical analysis of price levels over a period of time as represented by distributions. Used for benchmarking markets and judging models. Also used for understanding markets and testing models.

Distribution Moments: *See* Moments.

Drift: *See* Deterministic.

Driver: A market-based factor that affects the value of a spot or forward price.

Early Exercise: Indicates exercising the option prior to the expiration date. Limited to American type options.

Embedded Option: An optionality within a contract that is not specifically referred to as an option.

End User: Generally refers to buyers of derivatives contracts or risk management services who use the commodity for their own purposes.

Equilibrium: The state in which the supply and the demand are balanced.

Equilibrium Price: The price in the state of equilibrium. *See* Equilibrium.

European Option: An option that may not be exercised early, before expiration; predominant option form in energies. *See* American Option.

Events: Unusual or extreme economic crises such as extreme weather, technological failure, or wars that have a sudden and strong yet often rapidly dissipating effect on price behavior.

Exchange: A centralized trading operation offering standardized contracts and requiring the use of their clearing and margin account services.

Exercise: The act of executing the right conveyed by a contract. The process of exercising the option rights. Exercise rights are defined by the option contract.

Exotic contract: A contract with a new or complex structure. Opposite of vanilla.

Expiration (or Expiration Date):   The date on which a forward, futures or option contract expires.

Expiry: *See* Expiration.

Factor: A variable in a model that exhibits random behavior. A model that contains two factors is called a two-factor model.

Financial Markets: *See* Money Markets.

Firm Contract: A contract that requires delivery of energy — "no matter what."

First Order: A mathematical term for the dominant subset of building blocks used to express a change in the value of a deal or a portfolio. First order terms defining the change in the deal or portfolio value are calculated by taking the first order derivative.

First-Order Risk: A portfolio risk that represents the first-order sensitivity of the portfolio to changes in market variables or modeling parameters. Commonly known as a "Greek." (*See* Delta, Vega, and Theta.)

Floor: A series of put options.

Forward (or Forward Contract):   A contract for the delivery of a particular commodity or financial product in the future in exchange for a contract-specified price. May be discrete or averaging. In energy markets forwards include exchange-based futures and over-the-counter (OTC) forward contracts.

Forward Price Curve: A strip of daily forward prices starting with the spot price and ending with some point out in the future. The term structure of forward prices.

Front Office: A term used to denote the trading operation functions of marketing, trading, and managing the trading books. Provides the means of executing the company's trading strategies.

Full-Requirements Contract: A contract that allows the user to use as much energy as they desire; the quantity is sometimes banded by a maximum and minimum amount. The contract is an option contract since the user has the option to execute variable quantities. Also known as a swing contract or "flip the switch" service.

Fundamental Analysis: The family of analysis of markets which links the behavior of the markets to the fundamental drivers. Includes structural and cost-planning modeling.

Fundamental Drivers: The forces causing the market behavior to be what it is.

Future: A standardized forward contract offered by a central trading exchange (such as the New York Mercantile Exchange, or NYMEX). Characterized by typically greater liquidity and counterparty risk only with respect to the Exchange.

Future-Forward Bias: A pricing bias between futures and forward contracts due to the financial effects of margining accounts. Appears only when the futures prices are correlated with the interest rates used for cost-of-carry on the margining accounts.

Future Value of a Dollar: The value of a dollar at some point in the future, in present value terms.

Gamma: A second order risk defining how the delta will change if the underlying market price moves.

Greek: *See* "First- and Second-Order Risk."

Hedge (or Hedge Contract):   The financial product or asset used to offset risk.

Hedging: The process of entering into Hedge Contracts in order to minimize risks.

Higher Order Term: Mathematical term for the subset of building blocks used to express a change in the value of a deal or a portfolio. Not a first-order term. Typically assumed insignificant.

Historical Volatility: Volatility calculated using historical price data.

Illiquidity: Opposite of liquidity. *See* Liquidity.

Implied: A derived value based on other data. Synonyms include "calibrated" or "backed-out." (*See* Model Implied.)

Implied Volatility: The volatility implied from the market option price.

In-the-Money: An option term used to express the fact that option exercise would yield positive value.

Industrial Metals: Non-precious metals such as copper and steel.

Ito's Lemma: A mathematical relationship used for expressing the change in portfolio value over a very short time period in terms of changes in market variables and time. (*See* Equation 9–2.)

Kurtosis: Used in distribution analysis, describes how "fat" the tails are for a distribution. Indicates the probability of an event far away from the mean.

Leg: The period of time defined by the tenor of settlement or delivery within a swap or cap/floor contract. A one-year swap with a monthly tenor will have twelve legs; in this case each month would represent a leg.

Lemma: A preliminary or proposed theory. Demonstrated or accepted for immediate use.

Liquidity: The degree to which a particular contract is traded and reflects actual market pricing. The greater the liquidity, the greater one's confidence in the market price information, and the greater is the flow of deals in the marketplace.

Lognormal Distribution: A type of distribution often used in financial modeling. Lognormal prices are always positive.

Long: A trading term that generally refers to owning an asset, or having positive exposure to the price of an asset (the opposite of "short").

Margin Account: The account used by an exchange to continuously manage the position between counter-parties trading contracts through the exchange. *See* Margining.

Margining: The process of marking a position between two parties to market.

Mark-to-Cost: The valuation of a contract or portfolio based on an individual player's costs of producing the underlying asset. Different from mark-to-market.

Mark-to-Market: The valuation of a contract or portfolio that is consistent with all available and reasonable market information at the time of valuation. Values are based on aggregate market information as opposed to individual player's views.

Market Maker: A firm whose purpose is to buy and sell derivative contracts.

Market Variable: A variable used in a market pricing model that exhibits stochastic behavior.

Maturity: The time at which a contract expires.

Mean-Reversion: The process of reverting to some equilibrium level.

Mean-Squared Error: The average of squared errors. If the errors are unbiased, then the variance of model residuals.

Mid Quote: The average of bid and ask.

Middle Office: A term used to denote the trading operation functions of capturing the trading book's overall value at risk. Provides the basis for bridging the front and back office functions. Often also used as the approval body for models used by front and back offices.

Minimum Variance: A method of calculating the number of contracts within a portfolio which would result in the smallest change in the portfolio value given market moves.

Model Implied: The parameter implied by a model given a data set, or data implied by a model given the model parameters.

Model Parameter: A parameter used in a model that is assumed to have a known value, either fixed or changing in a deterministic fashion.

Moments: The mathematical characterizations of a distribution. The *n-th* moment of a distribution for a variable x is the expected value of the variable raised to the *n-th* power. The first moment, M_1, measures the center of a distribution and is equal to the mean. The second moment, M_2, measures the width and is related to the standard deviation. The third moment, M_3, measures symmetry and is related to skew. The fourth moment, M_4, measures the width of tails and is related to kurtosis.

Money Markets: Loosely defined as the non-commodity markets of interest rates, equities, foreign exchange, and other markets where the products are not contingent on physical assets used for consumption.

New York Mercantile Exchange (NYMEX):   An exchange offering energy futures and options contracts for the U.S. market.

Node: In valuation, refers to individual points between branches within a pricing tree. In physical and trading terms, refers to a point at which energy is delivered or valued.

Noise: Refers to information within a data set that is embedded in the measurements, but is not part of the price behavior being analyzed.

Non-Firm Contract: A contract that allows the seller to elect not to deliver the energy or buyer not to take delivery. Non-delivery conditions are specified by the contract. Should be priced as an option.

Normal Distribution: A type of distribution used often in financial markets, and the most basic statistical distribution. Normally distributed variables are symmetrically distributed around the mean.

Normalized: The conversion of a value expressed in one set of terms into another set of terms. Volatility is normalized to be expressed in annual terms.

Normally Distributed Random Variable: A random variable which—when observed many times—"creates" a normal distribution.

Notional: The dollar value of the underlying asset(s) upon which a derivative contract or portfolio is based.

NYMEX: *See* New York Mercantile Exchange.

Off-Peak: All the hours of the week not covered by the On-peak hours. *See* On-Peak.

On-Peak: Used in electricity to refer to the hours of the day corresponding to high-demand period. These hours are standardized for use in contracts for delivery of electricity and vary across regions of the United States.

Option Contract: A derivative contract in which the buyer purchases the right to buy or sell an underlying asset.

Option Premium: The price one pays for an option contract.

Option-Underlying: The asset on which an option contract settles.

Optionality: The economic value of being able to choose. Can be financially expressed in an option contract.

OTC: *See* Over-the-Counter.

Out-of-the-Money: Opposite of In-the-Money.

Over-the-Counter (OTC):   Refers to contracts that are not offered and settled through a central trading exchange. Often characterized by illiquidity and counterparty risk.

Paper Contract: A contract that allows the counterparties to cash-settle and not through delivery.

Paper Markets: Generally refers to money markets. Sometimes refers to energy markets in which delivery is not required.

Parity Value: The difference between the option underlying price and the option strike price.

Peak: A period of time during the day corresponding to greatest demand and highest prices.

Physical Contract: A contract that requires physical delivery.

Portfolio: A collection of assets and financial positions based on such assets.

Portfolio Analysis: The process of measuring and achieving a firm's desired balance of risk and return.

Precious Metals: Commodities such as gold, silver and platinum that exhibit price behaviors similar to both industrial metals and money markets.

Price Discovery: The process of determining the market value of a particular contract.

Prompt Month: The first month forward for which a contract is being traded. Also known as the first-nearby contract.

Put (or Put Option):   An option which gives its purchaser the right — but not the obligation — to sell the option-underlying asset at some future point in time at the option's strike price.

Q-Q Test: *See* Quantile-to-Quantile Test.

Quant: *See* Quantitative Analyst.

Quantile-to-Quantile Test: A statistical test to determine if residuals are of a particular distribution.

Quantitative Analysis: Financial analysis of market behavior and valuation of market contracts based on this behavior.

Quantitative Analyst: The team member responsible for performing quantitative analysis.

R-Square (R^2):   A statistical measure of fit. Tells how much of the process randomness is explained away by the model. If equal to one, then the model explains the process fully. If equal to zero, then the model has no explaining power.

Random: *See* Stochastic

Random variable: *See* Normally Distributed Random Variable

Random Walk: A "walk" in which each step taken is purely random and independent of the steps previously taken.

Reliability: The guarantee of delivery and service for a particular energy.

Reliability Council: One of nine areas in North America defined by the North American Electric Reliability Council in order to organize the continent to help ensure reliability. Currently used as surrogate trading areas in the U.S. over-the-counter trading market.

Residual: In the case of model-fitting the difference between actual and model predicted values. In the case of regression analysis, the random behavior in the dependent variable not explained by the independent variable. In the case of hedging, the remaining risk not covered by hedges.

Retail Market: A market defined by the sale of energy to individual customers. In the U.S. electricity and natural gas markets represent the residential markets.

Risk: An uncertainty; anything that cannot be predicted with 100% certainty is risky.

Risk-Adjusted: Adjusted for the cost of risk.

Risk-Free Rate: The market rate earned by risk-free assets.

Risk Management: The process and tools used for evaluating, measuring and managing the various risks within a company's portfolio of financial, commodity and other assets.

Rollover Date: The day after future contract expiration. The second future becomes the first, the third becomes the second, etc. Introduces time series analysis bias unless properly taken care of.

Seasonality: The sensitivity of prices to particular periods of the year. In seasonal energies, the prices are sensitive to weather effects.

Second-Order Risk: A portfolio risk that represents the sensitivity of the portfolio to changes in first-order risks. (*See* Gamma.)

Semi-Annual Seasonality: In energy markets the occurrence of two peak price periods and two low price periods during the year.

Settlement: The terms of contract expiration. In case of option settlement, the term for face value exchanged when the option is exercised. The counterparties can "settle" by exchanging cash and/or physically delivering the option-underlying commodity.

Short: The opposite of "long." Represents the position of one who has sold a contract.

Simulation: The process of generating random variable and their processes.

Skew: Used in distribution analysis. Describes the symmetry of a distribution and whether it is unbalanced or "skewed" to the left or right of the mean. Special case of the third moment, M_3, for a randomly distributed variable with a mean (first moment, M_1) of zero.

Soft Commodities: Non-energy and non-metal commodities including agricultural markets.

Spark-Spread Options: *See* Spread Option.

Speculation: A type of trading strategy. The first-order risks are taken in an attempt to capture value from predicting market moves.

Spot Price: The commodity's price for immediate or next day's delivery.

Spread Options: Options on spreads between prices of different types of energy.

Standard Deviation (STD): Used in distribution analysis, describes the width of a distribution. Indicates probability of a variable or price falling within a certain width or band around the mean. (A price will fall roughly within one standard deviation 66% of the time; two STD 95% of the time; and three 99% of the time. These approximations are exact in the case of a normally distributed variable.) Special case of the second moment, M_2, for a randomly distributed variable with a mean (first moment, M_1) of zero.

Statistical Arbitrage: Not pure arbitrage; a strategy for taking advantage of market mispricing by performing many trades and over time. Relies on superior modeling and model implementation, particularly in illiquid markets.

Stochastic: Random, unpredictable. "Opposite" of deterministic.

Stochastic Term: The term in a mathematical equation or model for a random variable which carries all the randomness. "Opposite" of the deterministic or drift term.

Straddle: An option position in which a call and a put are held simultaneously. If the call and the put are at-the-money, the straddle carries no delta risk, but the position does carry gamma risk. Hence, it is referred to as a "gamma play."

Strike (or Strike Price): The price at which option right is exercised.

Strike Bucket: A bucket or portion of the portfolio grouped or analyzed by a range of strike price values.

Strike Structure: The volatility curve resulting from implying the volatilities from market prices of options with identical expirations but of different strikes.

Strip: A series of contracts observed at the same time for the same underlying asset, but at different periods.

Structural Model: A model built upon a collection of fundamental price drivers and often implemented using assumptions about probabilities. Includes most traditional engineering or cost-planning models. Does not satisfy arbitrage-free or mark-to-market standards.

Swap: A series of forward contracts all valued at the swap price.

Swaption: An option on a swap.

Swing Option: An option which is stand-alone or embedded in a swap and which allows for an increase and/or decrease of the base quantity delivered. The optionality may be price-driven or demand-driven.

Tail: Characteristic of a distribution to the far left or right of the mean. Indicates probability of extreme price values (thus events). Measured by the fourth moment, M_4, or kurtosis.

Tail Effects: The effects the distribution tails have on option pricing.

Taylor Series (Expansion): A mathematical process of expressing the change in a value in terms of changes in variables as defined by functional dependencies of this value on the variables.

Tenor: Frequency of settlement (monthly tenor implies monthly settlement).

Term Structure: The structure of variable or model parameter across time. Most common term structures are for forward prices and volatilities.

Theta (Θ):   The first-order Greek that represents the change in overall value given a one-unit change in time.

Tick: A trading term for a one-unit change in price.

Time Bucket: Period of time across which the risks are spread; used in portfolio analysis.

Time Decay: The phenomenon of an option portfolio losing value with the passage of time.

Time Series Analysis: The analysis of daily price returns; used for parameter calibration of models.

Trees: An option pricing implementation technique which allows for price distribution representations (through the branches of a tree) while providing a pricing framework for various types of options.

Trinomial Tree: A recombining valuation tree which "splits" into three nodes.

Underlying Price: Depending on context, either the price on which a contract is contingent, or the price stripped of seasonality effects.

Univol: A two-dimensional volatility matrix methodology.

Utility Function: Defines the level of happiness a corporation has with a particular combination of portfolio risk and return.

Value-at-Risk Analysis: A type of portfolio analysis that provides a sense of possible profits and losses with probability measures attached to various scenarios.

Vanilla: Basic, simple.

VAR: *See* "Value-at-Risk Analysis."

Variable: A term for a value that exhibits stochastic behavior. A variable changes over time with uncertainty and risk.

Variance: The square of STD. In order to calculate STD we have to first calculate the variance.

View: An individual person or firm's opinion of future market behavior.

Volatility: Measures the magnitudes of percentage changes in prices over time, in annualized terms. Equals the price return's standard deviation normalized by time.

Volatility Matrix: An implementation technique for measuring and expressing discrete volatility term structure across forward prices and through time.

Volatility Smile: The phenomenon in which the market implied volatilities for options of the same expiration and settlement price appear to be different across different strikes. When graphed, for some market, it looks like a smile.

Volatility Term Structure: The volatility values across time.

Wholesale Market: A market defined by the sale of energy in bulk amounts primarily between producers, marketers and large end-users. In the case of the U.S. electricity market, represents the non-retail portion of sales and has experienced the first effects of deregulation.

Yield: The compound growth rate. Typically estimated from today out to some point in the future.

Yield Curve: The curve of compounded growth rates across different points in the future.

SELECT BIBLIOGRAPHY

Managing Energy Risk, a collection compiled by Financial Engineering Ltd., London, 1995.

The U.S. Power Market, a collection compiled by Financial Engineering Ltd. London, 1997. "Standard Deviations Implied in Option Prices as Predictors of Future Stock Price Variability," *Journal of Banking and Finance* 5 (September 1981).

Abramowitz, M., and I. Stegun. *Handbook of Mathematical Functions.* New York: Dover, 1965.

Akheizer, N.I. *The Calculus of Variations.* Waltham, Mass.: Blaisdell, 1962.

Arnott, Robert D. "Modeling Portfolios with Options: Risks and Returns." *Journal of Portfolio Management* 7 (Fall 1980).

Assay, Michael R. "A Note on the Design of Commodity Option Contracts." *Journal of Futures Markets* 2 (Spring 1982).

Bachelier, Louis. "Theorie de la Speculation." *Annales de l'Ecole Normale Superierure* 17 (1900). Translated in A. J. Bones, *The Random Character of Stock Market Prices,* edited by Paul H. Cotner. Cambridge, Mass: MIT Press, 1967.

Birkoff, G., and G. Rota. *Ordinary Differential Equations.* Waltham, Mass: Blaisdell, 1962.

Black, Fisher, and Myron Scholes. "The Pricing of Options and Corporate Liabilities." *Journal of Political Economy* (May–June, 1993).

Boness, A. James, Andrew H. Chen, and S. Jatusipitak. "Investigations of Nonstationarity in Prices." *Journal of Business* 47 (October 1974).

Bookstaber, Richard M., and Roger C. Clarke. "Options Can Alter Portfolio Return Distributions." *Journal of Portfolio Management* 7 (Spring 1981).

Boole, G. *A Treatise on the Calculus of Finite Differences.* New York: Dover, 1872.

Boyle, Phelim, and A. L. Ananthanarayanan. "The Impact of Variance Estimation in Option Valuation Models." *Journal of Financial Economics* 5 (December 1977).

Boyle, Phelim, and David Emmanuel. "Discretely Adjusted Option Hedges." *Journal of Financial Economics* 8 (September 1980).

Burkill, J. C. *The Theory of Ordinary Differential Equations.* New York: Wiley Interscience, 1956.

Chiras, Donald P., and Steven Manaster. "The Information Content of Option Prices and a Test of Market Efficiency." *Journal of Financial Economics* 6 (June–September, 1978).

Christie, Andrew A. "The Stochastic Behavior of Common Stock Variances." *Journal of Financial Economics* 10 (December 1982).

Cox, John C., Jonathan E. Ingersoll, Jr., and Stephen E. Ross. "A Theory of the Term Structure of Interest Rates." *Econometrica* 53 (March 1985).

Cox, John, and Stephen A. Ross. "The Valuation of Options for Alternative Stochastic Processes." *Journal of Financial Economics* 3 (January–March 1976).

Cox, John C., and Mark Rubinstein. *Options Markets.* Englewood Cliffs, N.J.: Prentice-Hall, Inc., 1985.

Cramer, H. *Mathematical Methods of Statistics.* Princeton: Princeton, N.J. University Press, 1966.

Dennery, P., and Krzywicki, A. *Mathematics for Physicists.* New York: Harper and Row, 1967.

Dwight, H. B. *Tables of Integrals and Other Mathematical Data.* New York: Macmillan, 1968.

Fielitz, Bruce D., and James Rozelle. "Stable Distributions and the Mixtures of Distributions Hypothesis for Common Stock Returns." *Journal of the American Statistical Association* 78 (March 1983).

Figlewski, Stephen, and M. Desmond Fitzgerald. "Options on Commodity Futures: Recent Experience in the London Market." In *Option Pricing,* edited by Menachem Brenner. Lexington, Mass.: D.C. Heath, 1983.

Finnerty, Joseph E. "The CBOE and Market Efficiency." *Journal of Financial and Quantitative Analysis* 13 (March 1978).

Gabillon, Jacques. "Analyzing the Forward Curve." In *Managing Energy Risk*, a collection compiled by Financial Engineering Ltd., London, 1995.

Garman, Mark B., and Michael J. Klass. "On the Estimation of Security Price Volatilities from Historical Data." *Journal of Business* 53 (January 1980).

Gastinearu, Gary, and Albert Madansky. "Why Simulations Are an Unreliable Test of Option Strategies." *Financial Analysts Journal* 35 (September–October 1979).

Geske, Robert. "Pricing of Options with Stochastic Dividend Yield." *Journal of Finance* 33 (May 1978).

Greene, Myron T., and Bruce Fielitz. "Long-Term Dependence in Common Stock Returns." *Journal of Financial Economics* 4 (May 1977).

Gultekin, N. Bulent, Richard J. Rogalski, and Seha M. Tinic. "Option Pricing Model Estimates: Some Empirical Results." *Financial Management* 12 (Spring 1982).

Hamming, R. W. *Numerical Methods for Scientists and Engineers.* New York: McGraw-Hill, 1962.

Harrison, J. Michael, and Stanley R. Pliska. "Martingales and Stochastic Integrals in the Theory of Continuous Trading." *Stochastic Processes and Their Applications* 11 (1981).

Hildebrand, F. B. *Methods of Applied Mathematics.* Englewood Cliffs, N.J.: Prentice-Hall, 1965.

Hoag, James W. "The Valuation of Commodity Options." In *Option Pricing*, edited by Menachem Brenner. Lexington Mass: D.C. Heath, 1983.

Hull, John C. *Options, Futures and Other Derivative Securities.* Englewood Cliffs, N.J.: Prentice-Hall, 1993.

Jarrow, Robert, and Andrew Rudd. "Approximate Option Valuation for Arbitrary Stochastic Processes." *Journal of Financial Economics* 10 (November 1982).

Jarrow, Robert, and Andrew Rudd. *Option Pricing.* Homewood, Ill.: Richard D. Irwin, Inc., 1983.

Jarrow, Robert, and Andrew Rudd. "Tests of an Approximation Option-Valuation Formula." In *Option Pricing*, edited by Menachem Brenner. Lexington, Mass.: D.C. Heath, 1993.

Kenna, A.G.Z., and A.C.F. Vorst. "A Pricing Method for Options Based on Average Asset Values." *Journal of Banking and Finance* 14 (March 1990).

Lee, Wayne Y., Ramesh K.S. Rao, and J.F.G. Auchmuty. "Option Pricing in a Lognormal Securities Market with Discrete Trading." *Journal of Financial Economics* 9 (March 1981).

Leong, Kenneth. "The Forward Curve in the Electricity Market." In *The U.S. Power Market,* a collection compiled by Financial Engineering, Ltd., London, 1997.

Manaster, Steven, and Richard J. Rendleman, Jr. "Option Prices as Predictors of Equilibrium Stock Prices." *Journal of Finance* 37 (September 1982).

Mathews, Jon, and R. L. Walker. *Mathematical Methods of Physics.* Menlo Park, Calif.: The Benjamin/Cummings Publishing Company, 1970.

McDonald, Robert, and Daniel Stiegel. "A Note on the Design of Commodity Option Contracts: A Comment." *Journal of Futures Markets* 3 (Spring 1983).

Merton, Robert, Myron Scholes, and Mathew Gladstein. "The Returns and Risks of Alternative Call Option Portfolio Investment Strategies." *Journal of Business* 51 (April 1978).

Moriarty, Eugene, Susan Phillips, and Paula Tosini. "A Comparison of Options and Futures in the Management of Portfolio Risk." *Financial Analysts Journal* 37 (January–February 1981).

Orear, J. *Notes on Statistics for Physics.* UCRL-8417. Berkeley, Calif.: University of California, 1958.

Parkinson, Michael. "The Extreme Value Method for Estimating the Variance of the Rate of Return." *Journal of Business* 53 (January 1980).

Pilipovic, Dragana. "Forward Roll." *Energy Risk* (August 1995).

Praetz, Peter D. "The Distribution of Share Price Changes." *Journal of Business* 45 (January 1972).

Press, S. James. "A Compound Events Model for Security Prices." *Journal of Business* 40 (July 1967).

Rubinstein, Mark, and Hayne E. Leland. "Replicating Options with Positions in Stock and Cash." *Financial Analysis Journal* 37 (July–August, 1981).

Sears, R. Stephen, and Gary Trennepohl. "Measuring Portfolio Risk in Options." *Journal of Financial and Quantitative Analysis* 17 (September 1982).

Spiegel, Murray R. *Mathematical Handbook of Formulas and Tables*. New York: McGraw-Hill Book Company, 1968.

Turnbull, Stuart M., and Lee Macdonald Wakeman. "A Quick Algorithm for Pricing European Average Options." *Journal of Financial and Quantitative Analysis* 26 (September 1991).

INDEX

American option, *See* Options
Annual seasonality centering parameter, *See* Seasonality
Annual seasonality, *See* Seasonality
Arbitrage
    arbitrage-free condition, 14, 35, 65, 85, 87, 141
    risk management strategy, 18, 200, 212
Asian option, *See* Option
Ask, *See* Bid/ask spread
Assumptions, 13–18, 21, 36, 112, 162
    bid/ask spread, 179
    continuous hedging, 178–179
    credit risk, 179
    fixed convenience yield, 93
    lognormality, *See* Black-Scholes
    non-negativity of prices, 63
    portfolio analysis, 178–179
    transmission rates, 179
    volatility, constant, *See* Black-Scholes
At-the-money, *See* Options
Autocorrelation, 48–49, 55
    autocorrelation test, 48
    negative, 63
    price returns, 73
Average price contracts
    seasonality, dampening effect on, 68
    volatility, dampening effect on, 69, 110

Back office, *See* Front/Middle/Back Office Paradigm
Backwardation, *See* Forward prices
Basis
    basis risk, 8
    basis-spread option, 155–157
    hedging, 186
Benchmarking, 11, 16, 41, 55
Beta, 156, 219
Bid, *See* Bid/ask spread
Bid/ask spread, 18
Binomial tree, *See* Trees
Black model, 154
Black-Scholes model, 13, 14, 15, 36, 56, 106, 113, 134, 162, 170
    equations, 143–144
    volatility, 14, 106, 111, 113, 121
Black, Derman, Toy model, 225
Bond price behavior, 34, 80, 223–235
Broker quotes, *See* Forward prices

Calibration, *See* Model parameter
California-Oregon Border (COB) futures contract, 59, 70, 75–78
Call option, *See* Option
Capacity, 161
Caplet, *See* Option
Caps, *See* Option
Cash-settled contract, 19, 20
Closed-form solution, *See* Options
Contango, *See* Forward prices
Continuous hedging, *See* Hedging
Contract terms, 18–20
    delivery, 19
    derivative contract, 18
    exercise, 127
    leg, 107
    settlement, 19
    strike, 56
    tenor, 107
    underlying price, 18
Convenience yield, 6, 23, 34, 85–87, 96
    dividends, equivalence with, 92–94
    fixed, 93
    forward prices, derivation of, 92
    long-term equilibrium price, 97
Corporate culture, 205
Corporate goals, *See* Risk management
Corporate utility function, 175, 194–195
Corrections, 43, 166
Correlations, 20, 74, 155
    between random variables, 219
    between short- and long-term forwards, 84, 113, 114, 118, 122
    between spot and equilibrium price, 115
    cross-market, 189, 193
    poor hedging, 185
    portfolio analysis, 183, 189
    volatility implications, 113, 114, 118, 122
Cost of financing, 141
Cost of risk, 23, 25, 88, 97
Cost-engineering models, 65–66
Counter-party risk, *See* Risk
Cox and Rubenstein, 140, 194
Cox, Ingersoll and Ross model, 224–225
Credit risk, *See* Risk
Cross-gamma, *See* Risk
Crude oil, *See* West Texas Intermediate